THE ANALYSIS OF OBJECTS
OR
THE FOUR PRINCIPAL CATEGORIES

*An Historico-Critical Analysis in the
Light of Scholastic Philosophy*

By

AUGUSTINE J. OSGNIACH, O.S.B., M.A., Ph.D.

*Professor of Philosophy, St. John's University,
Collegeville, Minn.*

WITH A FOREWORD BY THE
RT. REV. MSGR. FULTON J. SHEEN

NEW YORK CITY
JOSEPH F. WAGNER, Inc.

110
Os24

32651

ILLUSTRISSIMO AC REVERENDISSIMO

ABBATI ALCUINO DEUTSCH, O.S.B., PH.D.

ABBATIÆ S. JOANNIS BAPTISTÆ

PRÆSULI EGREGIO

ATQUE CONGREGATIONIS AMERICANO-CASSINENSIS

ORDINIS SANCTI BENEDICTI

PRÆSIDI DECORO

AUCTOR HOC OPUS

GRATO ANIMO

DEDICAT ATQUE DEVOVET

FOREWORD

The two most unpopular sciences to-day are Theology and Metaphysics. Descartes and Kant can both lay claim to the dark and dubious glory of creating the impression that both are "unscientific." During the Great Tradition of Common Sense the scientific was equalled with the *causal*, and hence to Aristotle, St. Thomas and their followers the wise man was he who knew the intelligible principles of the universe. In our day, on the contrary, the scientific is identified with the *factual*, and the wise man is he who counts and numbers. The great contrast then between the traditional concept and the modern is that the Scholastics were rich in principles, but poor in facts, while the modern is rich in facts and poor in principles. The idea is to be rich in both; but if one had to choose, it would be better to know the principles rather than facts, because principles can interpret facts. The solution of a fact problem—for example, the use of the optative mood in St. Optatus—has practically no reference-value to any other fact. Once the counting has been done in one field, one must start counting all over again in another problem. Such exclusive attention to details has produced minds who know the last word about everything and the first word about nothing; they know all about the X Y Z's and nothing about their ABC's. The Holy Father speaking to the writer on this subject remarked that "the world is full of educators who are capitalists as regards a knowledge of a few empirical facts, but are proletarians as regards a knowledge of first principles which would lead them to God."

Some years ago Professor Bradley defined Metaphysics as "the science of finding bad reasons for what we believe on instinct." This prejudice is repeated to-day by the practical man who asks: "How much do they pay a good metaphysician a week now?" The pathos of this view rests in the assumption that the only valuable knowledge is practical knowledge. There is need of a strong reaction against this view, and one which will restore in the natural order the primacy of Metaphysics. It must be re-asserted once again that action is only a means to contemplation, and that *thoughts* not *things* must ride in the saddle of true culture and civilization. The really great problems of life must be submitted to a test, and the test must not be only that of the laboratory, but primarily the consonance and harmony of facts with the fundamental laws of thought.

To this task of restoring metaphysical values Dr. Osgniach has dedicated himself in this book which treats the four fundamental categories: substance, quantity, quality, and relation. The exaltation of the empirical approach has made the consideration of these categories imperative. The idea of substance needs to be studied once again to correct the false impression that modern physics has invalidated substance by dissolving the concrete into electrical behavior. The idea of quantity needs to be presented once again to those who feel that the Quantum Theory has reduced individuation to a spineless indeterminism. The idea of quality needs to be studied by philosophers like Alexander who think God is a quality whose Body is space and whose Soul is time. Finally, the idea of relation needs consideration on the part of those who think the Theory of Relativity denies the Absolute even in the physical universe.

In giving such a detailed study of these important categories Dr. Osgniach has done his part in the important philosophical crusade to recover the Holy Land of Metaphysics. Modern philosophers, if they will but pursue it, will learn that Scholasticism grows, not by substitution of one theory for another, but by a deepening and fuller comprehension of fundamental principles. Metaphysics may once more have its day, and that day will mark the return of sanity and the unity of minds in common-sense elevated to the highest science to which human reason can attain.

RIGHT REV. MSGR. FULTON J. SHEEN.

AUTHOR'S PREFACE

Notwithstanding the great treasures of wisdom and truth contained in the volumes of the Schoolmen, the *philosophia perennis* of the golden age has been and still is very much ignored, misrepresented, and despised by modern thinkers. Such an unfortunate situation could no doubt be ascribed to many intrinsic and extrinsic factors.

We believe, however, that this attitude of aloofness is not one of indifference or aversion to truth. The modern mind is now more than ever desperately engaged in the pursuit of truth, and would eagerly accept and embrace it if Scholasticism were divested of its antiquated garments and exhibited under the attractiveness of a more modern garb. Unquestionably this is the crying need of the hour; hence, the task of modernizing Scholastic thought should be carried on by all its ardent defenders. Much has already been accomplished in this direction at home and abroad. The results are indeed gratifying, but much more remains to be done. Actuated by this laudable ideal, we have undertaken a detailed presentation of the four principal categories after the teaching of the Schoolmen.

The scope of this work, then, is an attempt to bring to light the genuine doctrine on these fundamental categories as taught by the great masters of the golden era of Scholasticism, especially by

Aquinas, while at the same time historically and critically estimating its high philosophical excellence.

The more important reasons advanced in justification of our task are the following. In the first place, it is well known that there is not a single English work dealing *ex professo* with this subject. Though a few excellent metaphysical treatises, such as those of Coffey and Rickaby, devote several chapters to the discussion of the predicaments, still they differ from our method of procedure; they are also, in our opinion, guilty of a serious mistake in not divorcing purely philosophical questions from revealed theology. We think that the persistent introduction of theological notions into the realm of Philosophy is not only needless, in so far as philosophy is concerned, but even very harmful, since it confirms rather than dissipates the inveterate prejudices of non-Scholastic thinkers who look upon Scholastic Philosophy with suspicion, regarding it rather as a humble "handmaid of Theology." Nor do we think that our attitude in this respect is anti-Thomistic, inasmuch as the Angelic Doctor himself assigned to each of these sciences a distinct sphere, a separate basis, and a different method of procedure. It would indeed be wise for the Neo-Scholastics to follow the example of their leader in this and other respects.

As to the vast number of Latin textbooks used in Catholic colleges, it suffices to say that the fundamental categories are treated rather inadequately and incompletely, to such an extent that no more than four or five pages are devoted to each category.

In the course of this work we propose to show that "being," which is divided into ten categories, is real, finite, contingent and actual. The addition of the term *actual* to the other characteristics of being sets us in opposition to some Scholastics, who would include potential being in the scheme.

The first two chapters treat of the genesis and objectivity of the categories, showing the contrast on this point between the Kantian and the Scholastic view; the third deals with the constitutive elements of the categories, a feature generally overlooked; the fourth and fifth chapters are devoted to the elucidation of the concept of substance. Here we adhere strictly to St. Thomas in placing the essence of this predicament in *inseity* rather than in permanence, a view defended by Balmes and a few other Scholastics. As the notion of substance constitutes the cornerstone of the Scholastic edifice, we think it necessary to consider it somewhat in detail and to give a critical outline of the principal systems which have either misunderstood or misrepresented its original meaning. For it is upon such supposition that this notion is relegated to utter neglect and oblivion.

Again, in showing the relation between substance and accident in the sixth chapter, we maintain the former to be inseparable from the latter, and vice versa—this in opposition to those whose tendency is to emphasize the separability of the two. The seventh chapter contains an historico-critical analysis of the concept of substance from John Duns Scotus to our own day. In the eighth chapter, concerning quantity, we have undertaken the defense of a view which is not commonly accepted by the Neo-Scholastics. Here we contend that the notion of quantity consists ontologically in divisibility and logically in measurability. In the last three chapters on relation and quality, a much more detailed account than is usually given has been based upon the works of Aquinas and Albert the Great.

Since categories are metaphysical concepts, a few remarks on the scientific value of Metaphysics will be appropriate as well as interesting. We contend that, if Metaphysics is not a real branch of knowledge, no other science can be real, since the latter must be based on the ontological principles of contradiction, of sufficient reason, and of causality. It is generally admitted that only concrete and particular objects exist in the order of reality; yet, it is not the knowledge of the particular but of the general and universal that constitutes science. All science is of its very nature selective. *"Experientia est particularium, scientia vero universalium."* The object of all metaphysical speculation being the universal nature, a philosophy which rejects all metempirical knowledge is vain and erroneous, because it not only cannot reach its object but also must mutilate many scientific values. Accordingly we are justified in maintaining that, if the general notions of Ontology are invalid, no notion of the particular and concrete can be valid, since the fate of the particular is indissolubly bound up with that of the general. Of course, it goes without saying that a sound theory of Ontology must have its foundation in the *unmutilated* facts of experience;

otherwise it would be like building castles in the air. It is natural, then, that we should expect real fruits from our metaphysical tree, and not a mere shadow from its luxuriant foliage. We may be anathematized as dogmatists and old-fashioned! But what of it? We shall not bear any resentment, knowing that the skeptics themselves are perhaps (without being aware of it) just as dogmatic and old-fashioned in their views as the most pronounced dogmatists. Furthermore, does not the very progress of sciences and their extreme diversity make Metaphysics more actual and necessary than ever? Natural sciences have expanded their domain prodigiously; and such unification, synthesis, and simplification obviously cannot be achieved without the aid of a higher science, namely, Metaphysics. Finally, do not the Positivists themselves in their classifications make use of ontological means, abstraction and systematic generalization? Indeed, the proper and formal object of Metaphysics is abstract, yet this object is simultaneously the most concrete of all; hence, Ontology must *de jure* and *de facto* be regarded as the science of the concrete and the real.

If, therefore, this labor of love for the truth shall have contributed even only a small part to the progress and welfare of humanity, as all true philosophy should, the author will feel amply rewarded. "Ut sit et fortes quod cupiant et infirmi non refugiant" (May the strong still have something to desire, and the weak not flee in dismay)!

St. John's University,   A. J. O.
Collegeville, Minnesota.

CONTENTS

xv

CONTENTS

Classification of Substance.—Aristotelian Definitions of Primary and Secondary Substance.—Explanation of the Two Concepts.—Justification of such a Division.—Formation of Such Concepts.—Contrast between the Predication of Secondary Substances and Accidents.—Various Modes of Predication.—Classification of Substance into Complete and Incomplete.—Fundamental Notions of Physical Dualism.—The Thomistic View of the Principle of Individuation.—Meaning of Subsistence, Nature, Supposit, Person.

Distinction between Logical and Ontological Accident.—Predicamental Accident Defined.—Its Nature.—Division of Accident into Intrinsic and Extrinsic.—Cartesian Attack on the Objectivity of Accident.—Defense of Scholastic Doctrine.—Presentation of some Modern Views.—Relation between Substance and Accident.

Quantity First of the Nine Genera of Accidents.—Controversy on This Point.—Essence of Quantity.—Critical Analysis of Various Views.—Divisibility the Ontological Essence of Quantity.—Measurability the Logical Essence of Quantity.—Elucidation and Proof of These Doctrines.—Division of Quantity into Discrete and Continuous.—This Division as Specific.—Fundamental Characteristics of Quantity.

THE ANALYSIS OF OBJECTS

CHAPTER I

CATEGORIES IN GENERAL

Meaning and Classification of the Categories.—St. Augustine's Exemplification.—Originality of the Aristotelian Scheme.—Early Controversies.—Exposition of the Kantian Theory.—Categories according to St. Hilaire, Cousin, Renouvier, Hegel, Gioberti.—Categories in Logic and Metaphysics.—Nominalistic Interpretation.—Objectivity of Categories.   ∴

FROM THE DAWN OF speculative thought philosophy sought to classify the world of real being, the self included, under certain generic concepts to which all other concepts are reduced. Logically, categories may be defined as the most generic classes of predicates applicable to an individual subject; ontologically, as the ultimate classes of real finite being. This task of discovering and defining categories has been attempted by every thinker worthy of note. Thus, Aristotle subsumes all objects of our thought under one or the other of the following ten concepts: substance, quantity, quality, relation, place, time, position, mode of being, activity, passivity. For a better understanding of these definitions, we quote St. Augustine's beautiful and appropriate exemplification of these concepts: "Wherefore, in speaking of this thing or that, we must not consider what the usage of our language either allows or does not allow, but what clearly appears to be the meaning of the things themselves. When we say he is a man, we denote substance. He, therefore, who says he is not a man, enunciates no other kind of predicament, but only denies that. As, therefore, I affirm according to substance in saying he is a man, so I deny according to substance in saying he is not a man. And, when the question is asked, how large is he? and I say he is quadrupedal, that is, four feet in measure, I affirm according to quantity; and he who says he is not quadrupedal, denies according to quantity. I say he is white; I affirm according to quality; if I say he is not white, I deny according to quality. I say he is near; I affirm something according to relation; if I say he is not near, I deny according to relation. I affirm according to position, when I say he lies down; I deny according to position, when I say he does not lie down. I speak according to condition (*habitus*), when I say he is armed; I deny according to condition when I say he is unarmed. I affirm according to time when I say he is of yesterday; I deny according to time when I say he is not of yesterday; and when I say he is at Rome, I affirm according to place, and I deny according to place when I say he is not at Rome. I affirm according to the predicament of action, when I say he smites; but if I say he does not smite, I deny according to action, so as to declare that he does not so act; and when I say he is smitten, I affirm according to the predicament of passion, and I deny according to the same when I say he is not smitten. And in a word there is no kind of predicament according to which we may please to affirm anything without being proved to deny according to the same predicament, if we prefix the negative particle." [1]

It is universally admitted that Aristotle, the prince among Greek philosophers, was the first one who completely classified and harmonized the categories in the first chapter of the *Organon*. There is no evidence that the Stagirite gathered data for his categories from Pythagoras, who discovered twenty ultimate groups of things, ten of which he called good and the opposite ten bad, or even from Plato who subsumed all things into the most universal ideas, being and non-being, like and unlike, unity and number, the straight and the crooked. This classification of Plato's highest kinds of Ideas is incomplete, and the attempt suggests the ten opposites of the Pythagoreans. There were not a few, influenced by the authority of Iamblicus and Simplicius, who have asserted that the originator of categories was Archytas of Tarentum, and that from him the Stagirite had derived his entire scheme.[2] This opinion, however, having been rejected by Themistius, Boëthius, and other ancient writers and exploded in the fifteenth century (especially by Lawrence Valla, a rigid censor of Aristotelian philosophy), has found no supporters among recent and contemporary authorities, who unanimously regard the fragments of Archytas as

---

[1] St. Augustine, *De Trin.*, lib. V, c. 7, in *Post-Nicene Fathers*, first series, III (English Translation), 90-91.

[2] Zeller's *Aristotle*, I, 147, note 5.

spurious and bearing too evident marks of Platonic influence.[3]

The contention that Aristotle was inspired by the Indian sage Kanâda, who compiled the *Vaisheshika philosophy* in the *Vaisheshika-Sûtras*, was called in question by Max Müller, who shows that this compilation dates from the sixth century of the Christian era.[4] It is certain, however, that the Vaisheshika philosophy was not unknown to Greek thought in the first century, B.C. According to Kanâda supreme happiness is to be attained by the knowledge of certain *padârthas*, or quasi-categories, namely: substance, quality, action, genus or community, species or particularity, co-inherence, and non-existence.

The Arabian and Christian philosophers of the Middle Ages did much work in interpreting the categories of the Stagirite and in settling the controversies arising from different interpretations. After the revival of letters, those philosophers who waged war on Aristotelian philosophy have attempted either to censure the categories or to reduce their number. Thus, in modern times Descartes and Leibniz make use of such categories as mind, matter, measure, shape, rest, motion, and position. Kant revived the age-old question of the categories, and the problem occupied again the minds of such eminent thinkers as Hegel, Gioberti, and others.

This problem of the existence and construction

---

[3] Turner, *History of Philosophy*, 39; Sir W. Hamilton, *Logic*, II, Lect. XI, 140.

[4] Turner, *op. cit.*, 24.

of the table of categories is of central importance in the *Critique of Pure Reason*. Hence, for a better understanding of the Kantian teaching on this topic it will not be out of place to give a summary of his "Transcendental Analytic."

Above the senses, which are *per se* receptive and passive, Kant places the faculty of judgment by means of which experience becomes organized and scientific. To the question of how we form the following judgment "All bodies are heavy," which is universal and necessary, Kant answers that as experience is always of the particular and contingent, no matter how often experience is repeated, it cannot furnish us with the higher notion of universality and necessity. It follows that universality and necessity must be derived from the subjective nature of the mind and attributed to *pure reason*. But reason must possess a special faculty in order to synthesize the data of intuition and to give unity to the manifold of experience.

Thus, the understanding according to its nature and in common with the sensitive faculties draws from its own mysterious depths the various modes of judgments whence follow the diverse concepts which give rise to the twelve categories. Judgments can thus be variously formed according to *quantity, quality, relation,* and *modality*. Needless to say, Kant bases the construction of his categories on the different kinds of relations that exist between subject and predicate.

According to *quantity*, judgments may be singular, particular, and universal. Consequently, the concept of quantity may express either *unity* or *plurality* or *totality*. This simply means that, where there is unity, a relation similar to that which reason places in attributing a predicate to a singular thing is verified in the perceived object; the same holds good of the remainder. According to *quality*, judgment may either affirm or deny or distinguish; hence, from quality emanate the concepts of reality, negation, and limitation. According to *relation*, judgments may be categorical as expressing the concepts of substance and accident; for accident is related to a substantial principle in the same way as the predicate is related to the subject in an absolute judgment. Again, the judgment may be hypothetical, expressing the concept of cause and effect and showing the dependence of the latter on the former in the same manner as the conditioned depends on a condition. Finally, the judgment may be disjunctive, and imply the concept of mutual dependence or reciprocity. According to *modality*, we have doubtful, assertoric, and apodictic judgments giving us the concepts of possibility (*i.e.*, of what is not but could be), of contingency (*i.e.*, of what is but could also not be), and of immutable necessity.

Such is the famous table of the new categories which in Kant's own estimate are by far superior to those of Aristotle. Aristotle, in Kant's words, did not realize that the right method to be pursued is not the *analysis of being* but the *analysis of thought*. The old categories are only ten in number without harmony and motive; the new ones possess symmetry and order, being arranged in threes under four groups of fundamental concepts. Moreover, they are constructed so that the first always expresses a condition, the second a conditioned, and the third both.

Obviously, the value of Kantian categories is purely subjective and derived from his inner experience. His categories, of course, have reference to objects, but these objects though purely phenomenal are necessary conditions of our knowledge. For no one can say *I think*, without apprehending an object distinct from the ego. In Kant's words, it is the unity of consciousness which alone constitutes the relation of cognitive representations to the thinking subject, and this establishes their objective value. Objectivity accordingly receives a new meaning in Kantianism. Since the concept must belong to one of the categories, he claims that the categories are real in so far as they are applied to perceived objects. This union of categories with the data of intuition renders thought possible.

In conclusion, a category in Kant's view is an *a priori* principle of the understanding, a principle without which science and experience of objects would be impossible. The function of the categories is to organize and interpret the manifold of sense material. Moreover, by means of these subjective forms reason constructs for itself the world of phenomena, since our knowledge is unable to reach a thing as it is in itself. Since Kant's time the term category has been used, without restriction to set groups, for any fundamental conception.

St. Hilaire advanced the opinion, which he attributes to Aristotle, that categories are but certain common terms that denote the highest predicates and represent diverse modes according to which the mind considers things not as related to the mind but as they are in themselves. His view was an attack on his contemporaries, whose aim was to exclude from Logic the treatment of categories. He contended that, in so far as categories are referred to things, they ought to be treated in Metaphysics; in so far as they are terms, in Logic.[5] Cousin and his followers held a conceptualistic view of the categories. In their opinion, whatever knowledge we have about things is apprehended under the aspect either of the absolute or of the relative. Renouvier's view was that all categories consist in relation.

According to Hegel, categories are both things and ideas, or *thing-ideas*; on which account they are nothing else than diverse determinations of the *idea-being*. As there is nothing outside the *idea-being* and its determinations, he confines the whole of Logic, which he identifies with Metaphysics, to the elucidation of categories. Gioberti agrees with Hegel that categories are both things and ideas, his divergent point being that Hegel was mistaken in separating them from the Creative Act and including them in a Pantheistic principle (*i.e.*, in the confusion of the real and the ideal). In Gioberti's estimation categories are things because God, who is the first category or proto-category, includes in Himself through the Creative Act a second category, namely,

[5] St. Hilaire, *Logique d'Aristote,* p. 71.

all contingent being. Categories are also concepts
or ideas because, in our intuition of God perennially
creating the world, we recognize God as the supreme
category and all created beings as coming under a
second category. Hence, Gioberti taught that the
intuition of God creating the world is the principle
and the foundation of all science.[6]

That categories have objective reference, surely
no one will deny, except those who accept the conceptualistic teaching of Kant. According to him,
human reason is incapable of knowing through the
categories the totality of things as they are in themselves, the mind being limited to such knowledge as
it construes and formulates by the subjective nature
of the categories. From these assumptions it would
follow that categories would not in any way depend
upon real objects, but merely exhibit the nature of
objects as they are conceived by reason. This postulate would force the conclusion that such categories cannot be anything but wholly subjective
forms. Philosophers such as Aquinas, however, who
hold that knowledge is not purely phenomenal but
that it also depends on extra-mental objects, wisely
insist that being which is divided into ten categories
is distinct from a mere figment of reason, on the
ground that some reality always corresponds to the
former and never to the latter. Nothing is ever
placed in any category that has not extra-mental
existence.[7] In another place [8] the Angelic Doctor

[6] Gioberti, *Protologia,* pp. 247, 664.
[7] *Quæst. Disp., De Potentia,* q. 7, a. 9.
[8] *In Lib.* I *Sent.,* Dist. 33, q. 1, a. 1, ad 3.

remarks that, although categories are formally in
the mind, there is always something extra-mental
corresponding to them. He also teaches that categories hold a middle place between notions referring
to a real existent (as, for instance, a man or a
stone), and notions having no corresponding objective reality (as, for instance, a chimera).

Since categories are generic notions to which
all other notions are reduced, they must also correspond to certain modes according to which things
exist in nature. Thus, categories, viewed as the highest classes of being, belong to Metaphysics, as notions do to Logic. Hence, in all treatises categories
ought to be considered as the most generic predicates, as elements of judgment, and as fundamental to the inferential order. But predication,
judgment, and inference are mental activities.
Therefore, categories ought to be considered as notions by the logician. Such being the case, it will
not be difficult to perceive the error of Hegel and
of those who with him regard categories simultaneously as things and concepts and treat them in this
light. Hegel maintained that being and idea are
one and the same; consequently, in categories which
he regarded as the determination of the *idea-being*
he could not discern a twofold aspect. On that account he insisted that, from the fact that they are
concepts, they must also be things and *vice versa*.
It is in consequence of this assumption that Hegel
confused Logic with Metaphysics, and confined the
treatment of categories to Logic.

Again, the diverse modes of predication cannot

be true unless they represent distinctly the various modes of existence; nor are concepts true unless they exhibit clearly the diverse modes of predication. It logically follows that categories which are discussed in different branches of philosophy should be absolutely the same; they should not differ except in certain diversity of aspects under which they are considered. But Metaphysics regards them as modes of being and principles of diversity of things; Logic views them as types of predication upon which all syllogistic inferences are based. Therefore, categories must be accepted as concepts in the field of Formal Logic and as a classification of existence in Metaphysics.

The whole treatment of categories according to Nominalism should be limited to the enumeration and explanation of the highest genera of terms to which all other categorematic names are to be reduced. Nominalism rests upon the theory that universality lies only in words. "Outside of the mind there exists nothing, they argue, but singular concrete objects; groups of these resemble each other in their qualities, and they ticket them by a common name." [9] This theory that universals do not exist in the mind, but that they are mere words, necessitates the consideration of categories as common names by which singular concrete objects are denoted, and categories must be treated as such in Logic. Against this view Scholastics rightly contend that categories, not as mere names but as concepts, are the proper and direct object of Logic;

[9] Maher, *Psychology,* p. 248.

for the purpose of Logic is to formulate universal laws, thereby aiding us in our progress from the known to the unknown. Now, categories are intimately connected with ratiocination and fulfill this end not as names but as concepts; for to elicit the unknown from the known, we must know the relations and order the concepts have to one another.

We may add that Nominalism as a consequence utterly destroys the nature of human language. It would mean that our words no longer express our ideas. All knowledge would be limited to sense perception and representation; the metempirical world would disappear altogether. The imagination, according to Nominalists, is the test of truth. What we can realize with our imagination, they say, is true; what cannot be pictured in this way is either false or non-existent. This alone shows that Nominalism is false in principle and fatal in its consequences. Our conclusion is that knowledge depends not on names or single designation of things, but rather on objective concepts expressed by words. In this acceptation categories retain their true meaning and scientific value.

CHAPTER II

DERIVATION AND NATURE OF THE CATEGORIES

Categories as Innate *a Priori* Forms.—Scholastic Doctrine.—Being as the Source of Categories.—Three Acceptations of the Term Being.—Diversity of Opinion.—Examination of Kant's Doctrine as to the Source of Categories.—Hegel and Gioberti.—Explanation of Thomistic Theory.—Actual Being as the Source of Categories.

∴

THE FACT BEING ESTABLISHED that categories are regarded as the most generic concepts in the domain of Logic and as the ultimate classes of real being in Metaphysics, it is imperative that two questions should be considered. First, whether reason discovers categories as innate in the mind, as Kant claimed; or whether it derives them from the concept of being, as many Peripatetics taught. Second, whether categories are derived from one single source, and if so, what the nature of this source is. It is quite evident that these two questions are so constituted that the solution of the first is contained in the solution of the second. Hence, these two questions may be reduced to a single one, of which the other is a mere corollary. In this connection a synopsis of the Aristotelian thought on the question must be brought to the fore, notwithstanding the fact that this view has been the subject of controversies among ancient and modern philosophers.

In the first place, however, we see that thinkers interested in the dispute really agree on two points, namely, that categories have but one source and that this source is being. It has been shown that categories by their nature are intrinsic to the act of predication; and since each predication exhibits some mode by which a property is predicated of some being, it follows that being must be the universal subject of predication. As a consequence, categories represent the diverse modes by which that common being is determined. The genesis of the categories, therefore, cannot be anything but being. Says Aristotle: "The first of all things which is predicated is being." [1] And indeed, whenever anything is predicated of a subject, it is meant that it inheres in the same, for it would be impossible that something should be found in the subject if it were not contained therein. Therefore, whatever is predicated of the subject must inhere in it. Hence logically proceed the highest genera of predication denoting diverse modes of being. And, if they denote the diverse modes of being, it is clear that categories exhibit being as determined by many diverse modes, and that being is the source from which they arise. This is, perhaps, better demonstrated by the following arguments.

Unquestionably our intellect cannot know the diverse modes by which concepts are predicated of things unless it has knowledge of the concepts, and

[1] *Met.*, VI, c. I.

it cannot possess that knowledge without reflecting upon itself.   Now, the intellect in considering the concepts it possesses must apprehend them according to the nature of its own power.   But the intellect first apprehends things under the confused notion of being, inasmuch as directing its attention to things it must first perceive that they are.   Therefore, in this act of reflection the intellect apprehends things under the general notion of being.   As being is the first perception of the intellect, it follows that the concept of being is also the source of the order of predication, consequently of the categories.   Since the term being admits of many significations, it has come to pass that philosophers have taken the term "being" as the source of the categories in very different senses.   It is necessary to investigate under what aspect being is the source of categories.

Aquinas has often noted that there are three distinct acceptations of this term.   At times, being denotes the logical truth expressed by the copulative verb in judgment—as, for instance, when we say: "Socrates is a philosopher."   Since the truth of judgment consists in the fact that the judgment declares that to be which is and that not to be which is not, it is inferred that being, in the sense which in judgment expresses the logical nexus, denotes logical or conceptual truth.   Again, being may denote the essence or quiddity of a thing, namely, that which makes a thing to be what it is and distinguishes it from all others by placing it in its proper species—as, for instance, humanity in Socrates, because through humanity Socrates is a man.   Finally, the term being may signify the actual existence of a thing, namely, that by which a thing is actually constituted in nature, and whatever is in nature is an actually complete existent.

It must be borne in mind, then, that the term "being" accepted in the third sense connotes a complete and concrete entity. Such a being obviously is more perfect than being connoting essence, since it embraces not only essence but also the realization of that essence; in other words, because it connotes an essence completed through existence. It is also more complete than the being expressive of the logical nexus, because the latter is also applicable to things deprived of essence (as, for instance, to blindness or any other privation).

If, then, being has several meanings, it will be quite natural to encounter different schemes of categories according as philosophers have attributed to them distinct characteristics and have accepted a distinct meaning of the term "being." And, if diversity of opinion among philosophers concerning the nature and properties of predicaments were emphasized, it would be manifest that this divergence has its source in the dissimilar acceptation of the term "being."

Immanuel Kant accepted categories according to the first view, that is, in so far as they denote logical value. Kant took Aristotle to task for deriving his categories from a single source, and consequently failing to draw up a scientific and complete table of the highest genera, because "that acute thinker" did not realize that the right method to be pursued is not the analysis of being but the analysis of thought. As we have pointed out in the previous chapter, categories according to Kant denote exclusively the diverse modes whereby the predicate in judgment is referred to the subject. But relation between subject and predicate is expressed by the copulative verb *is*, which performs the office of the logical nexus. Therefore, the source of the Kantian table of categories is "being" denoting logical values. In this light, categories originate from the universal forms of judgment as from a single source. Since judgment is a mental activity, it follows that categories are nothing but subjective laws according to which the human mind formulates judgments of things. This Kantian postulate was the fruitful source of Idealism; for if the laws by which reasoning is construed are purely subjective, they cannot give any knowledge of extra-mental objects. This was not denied by Kant, who insistently affirms that pure reason knows the world, not as it is in itself, but only as it is constructed by the mind, or to use his own words: "The understanding knows only the world of phenomena and not that of noumena."

Hegel, though attempting to avoid Subjective Idealism, identified being with idea, and from this *ideal-real* being he educed his categories. As we have previously noted, he taught that categories are but diverse modes whereby the Ideal Being—God or the Absolute—evolves, posits, and determines itself in eternal self-movement; proceeds from itself and becomes Nature; and then reverting to itself be-

comes self-conscious Spirit. Thus, Hegel sets up as
the source of his categories a being in which existence is not distinguished from essence. Moreover,
Hegel falls into Pantheism without avoiding Idealism, on the ground that, if all categories denote
naught but positing the Absolute, all that is must
be considered as Absolute.

Gioberti realized that the only way of avoiding
these consequences was to derive the categories, not
from the one source of the *idea-being*, but from the
complex source of the Being creating the world—
that is, from God and the world related to Him by
the act of creation. Since in the creative act God is
really distinct from the world, it follows that the
categories elicited therefrom, otherwise than in the
Kantian system, are objective; and do not, Gioberti
argues, like the Hegelian categories lead into Pantheism. Furthermore, from the fact that God is the
first term of the creative act, Gioberti inferred that
God is the first category containing all finite categories.[2]

At this point the doctrines of Aquinas and his
followers may be defended. According to them,
being which is divided into ten categories is neither
the one denoting the logical nexus in judgment nor
the one indicating essence or quiddity, but the one
signifying the actual existence of things. In defense of the Scholastic view we find in Aquinas, who
more than once refuted certain precursors of Kant
among the ancient philosophers, many arguments
of great weight. The "solitary of Koenigsberg"

[2] Gioberti, *Protologia*, p. 593.

always taught that categories are *a priori* forms of judgment denoting the various modes by means of which the understanding attains knowledge of objects of experience. His point of contention was that we do not know whether or not categories represent those modes of being as they actually exist in themselves. Although the being which in judgment expresses the logical nexus denotes, indeed, that something inheres in the subject, it does not by any means indicate what the nature of that inhering being is, whether it is substance or accident or quality or some other modification of being. For instance, in the proposition, "Socrates is a philosopher," the copulative verb *is* affirms that to be philosopher inheres in Socrates, but it does not indicate whether to be philosopher is the substance of Socrates or a quality inhering in substance. By categories, St. Thomas says, it is not asked primarily whether a thing is (*an sit res*), but what the nature and properties of the thing are. But, the being which expresses the logical nexus in a proposition does not answer the second question.

The same Doctor continues: "Being may be taken in two meanings. First, according as it denotes existence of a thing, inasmuch as it is divided into the ten categories and has objective reference. Being, taken in the second sense, is logical and consists in the propositional nexus expressed by the copulative verb *is*; being thus accepted answers the question *whether a thing is*, and it is neither converted into objective reality nor divided into the ten

predicaments." [3]   Furthermore, the use of logical
nexus demands that the knowledge of categories be
already possessed by the mind, for we cannot join
one thing to another unless we know the nature of
the object, and the qualities so joined. This we
cannot know unless the categories exist as already
formed in the mind, and this being the case it is
clear that the being which denotes the logical nexus
in judgment is not the one which is the principle or
source of categories.

We may add that this doctrine of Kant is not
only inconsistent, but if logically followed would
lead to Idealism. It is obvious that the being which
denotes the logical nexus in judgment exists only in
the mind, which considers the predicate in relation
to the subject; if this be the only significance of
being, Idealism must result. Even though whatever
exists in reality is under a certain respect manifold,
yet its attributes are united and joined to itself.
However, because of the limitations of our intellect,
we are prevented from obtaining perfect knowledge
of things unless we resolve those things into their
elements or constitutive parts, which being mentally
analyzed are again through a mental process synthesized. But this analysis and synthesis which
takes place in judgment does not exist in the objective world, but only in the mind. Now, analysis and
synthesis are those functions which involve being
as expressed by the logical nexus. Therefore, such
being exists only in the mind.

Again, being that denotes the logical nexus in

[3] *Sum. Theol.*, I, q. 48, a. 2, ad 2.

a proposition does not *per se* signify the inherence of the predicate in the subject; rather it denotes the composition of both formulated by the mind, the mind thus conforming itself to the object.   From this it follows that the mind synthesizes not only elements inhering in the subject, but sometimes also elements which are lacking in the subject.   Thus, in the following proposition, "Homer is blind," the verb *is* does not denote that blindness as a positive entity really inheres in Homer, for that which is not cannot inhere in another; it denotes, however, the composition of the predicate (blindness) with the subject (Homer), inasmuch as this composition is construed by the mind, and by means of this synthesis the mind perceives that Homer is deprived of the virtue or faculty of sight.   If, then, being expressed by the logical nexus does not exclusively signify the inherence of the predicate in the subject but the composition of both as construed by the synthetic mental process, the conclusion is that such being does not exist in the objective order but only in the mind.

Kant, therefore, erred in deriving his categories from *a priori* forms of judgment as from a single subjective source, because such forms depend on the being expressed by the logical nexus.   "It may be observed, in criticism of the Kantian system of categories, that an analysis of judgment is not an analysis of thought; for the ideas of which judgment is composed are themselves capable of analysis.   Indeed, while the analysis of judgment may be made the basis of a system of predicables, it is on an an-

alysis of ideas that a system of categories must be
based. Moreover, it is evident that in the Kantian
table of categories correctness of analysis is sacri-
ficed to the symmetry of arrangement." [4]

Neither does the being of Hegel and Gioberti
offer a genuine classification of categories. According to these two philosophers, God or the Absolute
is the highest category, and His determinations are
second categories. Here agreement ends, and disagreement begins. Hegel contends that second categories are but diverse modes whereby the first category posits and knows itself; Gioberti maintains
that God produced categories outside Himself
through the creative act, simultaneously manifesting them to created minds. It will be well to pause
for a moment and examine the implications of these
doctrines.

That God should be the first and all other categories should be contained in Him as species in the
genus, is repugnant to sound Logic. For, category
of whatever kind it be signifies a peculiar mode of
predication. According to Aristotle, the mode by
which something is predicated of an object denotes
the mode whereby something inheres in the same.
Consequently, any category, by the very fact that
it denotes a peculiar mode of predication, signifies
also a peculiar mode of objective existence. Scholastics have held that categories are applicable only
to finite contingent being wherein essence differs
from existence. Only of God can it be said that
existence is of His essence. God is an unconditioned

[4] Turner, *op. cit.,* p. 533.

and necessary existent; contingent beings are conditioned and dependent. No category, therefore, can, strictly speaking, include God in its scope. God is in no category; He is unique or *Sui generis*.

But if it is repugnant to include God under any category, it is even more so to regard Him as the subject of another category, as Hegel and Gioberti did. As a matter of fact, if finite categories were to be certain peculiar determinations under which the supreme category would manifest itself, two objections would naturally arise. First, the subject would determine itself, and secondly, the Absolute would be capable of being determined. But if the Absolute is *per se* a category and at the same time the subject in which other categories inhere, essence and existence both in a relative and absolute sense could simultaneously be predicated of it—absolutely, as far as it is of itself a category, and relatively, as far as it is the subject of other categories. Since the determinations of the Absolute are in a state of flux, these determinations cannot be understood in any other but a relative sense. This conclusion is inconsistent. For, if nothing can be predicated of the subject except that which is understood to inhere in it (as maintained in the above view), we would have to maintain that some relative being falls under the Absolute. This, however, seems to be altogether incompatible with the notion of the Absolute, on the ground that in the Absolute essence and existence are identical; and the essence whereby the Absolute is, cannot be any other than absolute; the perfect cannot include the imperfect.

According to the Hegelian system, however, contradictory notions can be simultaneously predicated of the Absolute. If such were the case, the support of all our knowledge, the principle of contradiction, would be without meaning and would have no real or possible application. Neither can it be said that the Absolute contains finite categories in the same manner as genus contains species, whether it be asserted that species are potentially or actually contained in the genus. Adopting the first alternative, it would follow that some being of the second categories would not be contained in the first. This is substantiated by the following: in the case that species were potentially and not actually contained in a genus, they could nowise result from the genus except through a difference added to genus thus determining it and forming a species. But every difference is some thing, since that which is not can neither determine a genus nor constitute a species. Therefore, if the highest category contained second categories potentially, the latter would result from the first only through some added determination. Nothing, however, can be added to the Absolute, for the simple reason that the Absolute includes all being. Hence the absurdity in maintaining that the Absolute potentially contains the species.

Accepting the second alternative, one would be compelled to affirm that the essence of contingent existents is really not distinct from the essence of

God.   For if finite categories were actually in God, the diverse modes of being denoted by the second categories would be the very essence of God, and hence identical with the supreme category which is God.   Gioberti, however, contends that second categories are really distinct from God.   Therefore, even if it be granted that the genus actually contains species, Gioberti is inconsistent in maintaining that categories are related to God in the same manner in which species are related to genus.

Furthermore, no matter in what sense genus be understood, it is always repugnant to regard the Absolute as a genus category; firstly, because the Absolute would then be confused with the Relative, inasmuch as a genus cannot be understood except in relation to its species; secondly, because the Absolute would then contain the nature of the contingent, inasmuch as species contains in a manner the determined essence of the genus.   But as the notions of the Absolute and Relative are mutually exclusive, it would obviously be absurd to suppose that the notion of the Absolute is identical with the notion of the Relative, or that the Absolute should contain the nature of the contingent.

Hegel's Idealism is manifestly pantheistic.   In reality, according to Hegel there exists only one being, the Absolute or Idea, which proceeding from itself becomes Matter, then receding within itself becomes Spirit.   Gioberti also, notwithstanding his earnest attempt to avoid Pantheism, fell a victim to the same error.   The Italian ontologist, in his interpretation of categories, confused the Absolute with the Relative; made God of the same nature as the world; failed to discriminate the being of God from the being of created things. Moreover, Gioberti seems practically to identify the human mind with the divine.

An additional argument may be advanced here to corroborate the Scholastic contention that the source of the categories is an actual existent. Whatever is apprehended by our mind is apprehended first under the general notion of being. For, before we know what a real existent is, we must know that it is. Passing from this stage of knowledge of mere acquaintance, the mind goes on to compare and enumerate the common modes by which being is determined; these common modes of predication are called categories. Thus, Scholastics have enumerated as many categories as there are modes of existence. Now, if this be the true origin of categories, it is obvious that the source of the categories is actual being.

The being which is determined by the predicaments, according to Aquinas, is neither the being of the logical nexus nor the being of abstract essences but the actual existent. The diversity of categories, then, arises from the various modes by which they represent actual being. Being in general, however, cannot be regarded as a genus with reference to the categories. "Being," St. Thomas remarks, "cannot be contracted to something determined in the manner that genus is contracted into species through the difference. For, since difference does not participate in the genus, it is outside the essence of being, which by way of addition to being constitutes the given species of being. For that which is outside being is nothing and cannot be the difference. Thus, in the third book the Philosopher proved that being cannot be genus." [5]

Again, if being should be regarded as genus, it would follow that the whole being or the whole definition of being would be contained both in the notion of substance and accident because the entire essence of a genus is found in each species. But neither to substance nor to accident is the complete notion of being applicable, for substance contains one part of the notion of being, and accident another. Therefore, although being is divided into substance and accident, it is, nevertheless, not their genus.

[5] *Met.*, V, 9.

CHAPTER III

ANALYSIS OF THE CATEGORIES

The Constitutive Elements of Categories.—Essence as the Material Element.—Existence as the Formal Element.—Distinction between *Perseity* and *Inaleity*.—Aristotle's Division of Being.

HAVING OBTAINED AND ESTABLISHED the source of the categories, it will not be difficult to discover their constitutive elements and also their number and distinction. Since the source of the categories is actual being, it is expedient that each category should denote a peculiar mode of actual being. If every category denotes a peculiar mode of actual being, every category must consist of the same elements of which actual being consists. As previously noted, two aspects must be distinguished in actual being, namely, essence and existence. These two are distinct in every contingent being. Such being the case, it logically follows that categories must consist of two elements, namely, essence and existence.

According to this view, essence in its widest acceptation is the *material* element; its existential mode is the *formal* element of the categories. Essences do not differ, absolutely considered, among themselves; for the notion of essence, considered in an absolute sense as something undetermined and capable of assuming existence, is simple and one. Therefore, essences cannot differ in any other way than according to the diverse mode of existence whereby the mind perceives them to be determined. Since the material element of any being is that which it has in common with other things, and the formal element is that which distinguishes it from others, we may conclude that essence in its widest meaning constitutes the matter and existence the form of the categories.

To make this point clear, it will be helpful to use the example of substance and accident into which categorical being is divided. Essence is the material element both in the category of substance and in the category of accident, because it is intrinsic to both to have essence. Existence, however, is the formal element because the essence of substance is determined through the mode of existence which is not in another, and because the essence of accident is determined through the mode of existence which is in another. Hence it appears, first, that in categories there is a twofold element, namely, essence and existence; secondly, that categories do not differ according to their essences absolutely considered, but according to their essences determined by diverse modes of existence. But if every ontological category has thus an internal duality, it may be said of logical categories that they are apprehended from two points of view, namely, from the point of view of their essence and from the point of view of their existence.

How does one category differ from another?

We have already seen that each category is composed of essence and existence. Now, an existent is distinguished from another existent through the formal element which places it into its proper species. But this formal element is existence, because the essence through its actualization in reality is constituted into a special category. Therefore, categories are distinguished from each other in so far as their modes of existence differ. Since the diversity of categories results from the diverse modes of existence, it follows that the being which is predicated of them cannot be predicated univocally but only analogically; otherwise they would differ and agree under the same respect of being. Therefore, the concept of being is not predicated of substance and accident in exactly the same sense; the same may be said of the remaining categories into which accident is divided.

From what has been said, it clearly appears that being is not determined by the categories in the sense that each adds something to being which is over and above its essence, but in the sense that each determines being according to a peculiar mode of existence. Here Harper pointedly remarks: "The objective concept of being and the objective concept of substance, for instance, are not in one and the same objective distinct realities, but it is the same reality in both, with the sole difference, that in the former concept it is objected to the mind in its simplest, most confused and indeterminate form; whereas in the latter it is contracted and determined by the distinguishing mode of *perseity*. Accordingly, both concepts are equally simple. It is utterly impossible to resolve substance into being and *perseity*, as two distinct components of one composite, because *perseity* is a determination of being, and therefore, being. Consequently, it determines being and thereby contracts it; but it cannot really differentiate it." [1]

If being is not predicated univocally of the categories, for stronger reasons it cannot be said to be predicated univocally with reference to God and the categories. For, if being were applied to God and to the categories in exactly the same sense, the two would be in some way identical. This, however, involves contradiction, because there is no proportion of nature between the finite and the infinite, between *aseity* and *inaleity;* moreover, essence and existence in God would not be identical. "Being, as regards God and creatures, is not universal, nor entirely equivocal, but midway between the one and the other, *i.e.*, analogous. This point is of no little moment, because the admission that with respect to God and creatures being is univocal, ultimately leads to Pantheism. Univocal predication is predication *secundum eandem rationem*. Now, being *secundum rationem* in which it is proper to God, is totally in God. Therefore, it cannot in the same sense be extended to other things, unless the Divine Being Himself extends Himself to them." [2] In consequence, we conclude that being cannot be predicated alike of God and categories.

---

[1] *Metaphysics of the School,* Vol. I, p. 64.
[2] Liberatore, *On Universals,* p. 30.

The following questions here present themselves: "How is being divided into the ten categories? What is the ultimate ground of this division?" The Scholastic doctrine on this point may be summarized in this manner. The one idea that underlies all others is the idea of being. Whatever we think of, we think of as having some sort of being; else we could not think of it. The notion of being is the first and most universal object, of thought; it is at the basis of all our thinking. Hence, our ultimate or primary principle will be that which exhibits the primary relation of being. But such a relation cannot exist without something to be related to it. Even logical relation involves two distinct terms. Therefore, the first relation of being must be something distinct from being. But that which is different from being must necessarily be not-being; consequently, our ultimate and primary principle must pronounce the relation between being and not-being. What is this relation? Obviously, it is one of exclusion or contradiction between things, as stated in the law of things: "Nothing can at the same time possess being and not-being." Or, as in the law of thought: "We must not affirm and deny simultaneously."

Thus, the intellect before proceeding to any division of being must know that simultaneous affirmation and negation concerning it is impossible. In this principle it finds the first division of being, that is, into being and not-being. As every division is made through its opposites, so also every opposition proceeds through affirmation and negation. In order to make clear the nature of this division, it should be noted that opposites must proceed in this way. Since that which is divided into the categories is being, it is manifest that the opposite of any category must also have in view a certain mode of being so that one part of the division should posit a mode of being which the other denies. And as the idea of being is absolutely simple, no other opposition can take place within it except between the modes of being.

But the principal modes of being are substance and accident, the former denoting that mode of existence which is not in another as in a subject, and the latter denoting that mode of existence which is in another as in its subject. "The intellect not only understands things, but also perceives that they receive their being from another, on the basis that since things, whatever they are, cannot have their being *ex se*, they must necessarily receive it from another. If all things receive their being from another, the intellect perceives also that things have their being either *in se* or in another; hence, the first division of being into substance and accident. This is arrived at through a contemplation of nature, for whatever there is *in rerum natura* exists either in itself, *e.g.*, man, or in another, *e.g.*, white." [3] Since accident has being not in itself but in the substance, it follows that accidental being depends on substantial being. Our conclusion is that there are contingent substances which in their own order are

[3] St. Augustine, *De Trin.*, lib. V, c. 4, 6.

ultimate subjects and do not inhere in other subjects in so far as they exist *per se*.

"Aristotle divided being not only into substance and accident but also taught nine genera of accidents. Of the completeness of this framework Aristotle is convinced, but he nowhere tells us how he came to set out only these categories and no others; and among the categories themselves there is little indication of any fixed principle for their evolution."[4]

[4] Zeller's *Aristotle*, Vol. I, pp. 279–280.

CHAPTER IV

THE CATEGORY OF SUBSTANCE

Notion of Substance Grounded on Universal Experience.—Thomistic Definition of Substance.—Impossibility of a Logical Definition of Substance.—Substance as Distinguished from Accident.—The Essential Characteristics of Substance.—Scholastic Doctrine of Objectivity of Substance.

∴

THE NOTION OF SUBSTANCE according to St. Thomas is grounded on universal experience. Experience manifests to us a world of many individuals which, although related to other beings, are complete in themselves in the sense that we can think of them as independent of other individuals. Right order demands that we should arrive at the metaphysical concept of substance from the objects of experience; otherwise Metaphysics would indeed be nothing but intellectual "moonshine," a guesswork, a dream. The most ordinary observation upon the objects of our experience shows that they may be classified into two great categories, that is, substance and accident. Some objects (as a horse, tree, or man) we perceive as existing by themselves; others (as color, size, figure, hardness, volitions, cogitations) we apprehend as existing in something else. In other words, experience clearly shows that there are no such things as color or size or figure existing in themselves or independently; such entities, therefore, require a more profound reality which is their subject of inhesion. It follows logically that accidents or attributes must depend on substantial being. Substance, then, is being in the strict sense of the word; whereas accidents are called *entia entium* (*i.e.*, beings dependent on substance).

How is our knowledge of substance acquired? St. Thomas answers that this knowledge is immediate, though vague. First we apprehend substance as something existing in itself, undivided in itself, and distinct from other things. In this initial stage, however, accidents are not formally distinguished from substance, and the latter is not known in the proper light of substantiality in as far as it is opposed to accidents; so far it is only an object of intuition or a *sensile per accidens*. Upon further analysis of this cosmic reality intuitively perceived, we are led to distinguish those characteristics which are basic and absolute from features which are relative and dependent. From such an analysis arises the notion of substance and the distinction between substance and accident.

It is important to note that, according to Aquinas, substance cannot be included in a logical definition consisting of proximate genus and specific difference. Should substance be regarded in this light, substance and accident could be referred to being as species to their genus. But being as being cannot be taken as a genus, for every genus has differences distinct from its generic essence. Now, no difference can exist distinct from being, for non-being cannot be a difference. On this account St. Thomas rightly says: "Being does not contain the conditions of a genus."

Substance, then, may be described as that which exists in itself; *inseity* being the most complete and perfect realization of an essence. However, the term *inseity* must be understood as denoting merely non-inherence in another subject, and this does not in any way exclude the notion of efficient causality distinct from the entity of the substance itself. This clarifies the Thomistic description of substance "as an essence or thing to the nature of which it is due that it should not exist in another." [1]

From the above it might appear that the nature of substance is essentially negative. But that this is not really so is shown as follows. That which essentially denied of substance is inherence or *in-aleity*, namely, to be in another as in the subject of inhesion. But the notion of inherence is itself negative; for that which inheres in another as in its subject has its being, not in itself, but through the subject of inhesion; the notion of inhesion implies negation of substance or existence *in se*. Consequently, what is essentially denied in the description of substance is negation. Now, negation of negation, to use Scholastic phraseology, is affirmation; for instance, if one denies that an animal is irrational, he simultaneously affirms it to be a rational animal. Therefore, the notion of substance as a matter of fact is positive and not negative.

As substance is composed of two elements,

[1] *Quodlib.*, IX, q. 3, a. 5, ad 2.

namely, of essence and a mode of existence, it will be worth while for the elucidation of its notion that we should consider it in relation both to its essence and to its existence. If we consider substance related to essence, its chief characteristic consists in *inseity*, in not having its being in another as in its subject. Through this characteristic it is contracted or determined to that sort of being which is not in another. On the other hand, if we consider substance in relation to existential condition, its essential characteristic will consist in being the subject of accidents.

And, indeed, when the essence is determined to the being to whose nature it belongs *to be not in another*, it becomes opposed to the essence to whose nature it belongs *to be in another*. But this other cannot be anything but substance. For, if this other were not substance, then it would be accident, since between substance and accident there is no medium, and since any accident requires ultimately a substance in which it inheres; otherwise we would have to admit an infinite series, which is absurd. Aquinas ascribes these two characteristics to substance, namely, *inseity* or *perseity* and the fact that it is the subject of accidents.

As to the first of these characteristics, the essence, inasmuch as it is determined through its being not in another, is less in extension than essence from the absolute point of view; or, as Scholastics would say, it is referred to essence in general as the lower is related to the higher. But the lower in the series of those things which are predicated stands under the higher. The essence which is determined through its not being in another is precisely what we mean by substance.

As to the second characteristic, the essence to whose nature it belongs *to be not in another* is the subject of accidents because it receives these into its own being. But the essence in which the accidents inhere is understood to be *under* the accidents or the subject of accidents. Therefore, the essence which is determined by its being not in another and also from the fact that it is the subject of accidents, vindicates to itself the name substance. Hence, the essence to whose nature it belongs to be not in another is called substance, both because it is a special determination of the essence absolutely taken and also because it is the subject of accidents. Essence, considered in the first sense, is also called subsistence from the fact that it has its being *in se* and not in another.

"Substance," says Aquinas, "has two characteristics. The first consists in the fact that it has no need of extrinsic foundation in which it is sustained, but is sustained in itself as if it were existing *per se* and not in another. The other consists in the fact that it is the *fundamentum* of accidents sustaining them, and so far is said to exist." [2]

Although the characteristic of substance as a special category is due to the fact not only that it has being not in another but also that it is the subject of accidents, the notion of substance consists essentially in the fact that it is an essence to

[2] *Qq. Dispp., De Potentia,* q. 9, art. 1, c.

whose nature it belongs to be not in another. This can be corroborated by the following argument. The notion of being or a thing should properly be placed in that which makes the thing to be what it is; yet substance, as we have explained above, is constituted not because it is the subject of accidents but because its being is not in another. Moreover, the notion of substance undoubtedly consists in that which differentiates it from the accident, inasmuch as it is opposed to the accident through the first division of being. Now, the differentiation of substance from the accident results from the fact, not that it is the subject of accidents, but that it has its being *in se* and not in another.

However, there are a number amongst both ancient and modern philosophers who maintain that substance is but a permanent subject of changes, or something which amid all variations continues unchanged. In order to harmonize the varieties and continuous changes perceived in the world of sense with the unity of being or the Absolute, Pantheists identified the world of sense with the universal substance or the Absolute. They regarded the Absolute as substance, and all the various changes by which the Absolute is manifested in the world as accidents. These considerations led them to define substance as that which persists unchanged amid various changes, and the accidents as that which changes.

Recent Atomists, following in the foosteps of Democritus and Leucippus, maintained in harmony with the above principles that all the changes and variations to which the atoms are subjected arise from various modes, dispositions, and configurations of the atoms themselves. They came to the conclusion that there is in every being something which undergoes change and something which remains, calling the former accident and the latter substance. Descartes fell into the same error; for although at first he defined substance "as a being that so exists as to require nothing for its existence," [3] yet, influenced by the mechanistic view of the universe, he modified this definition by regarding substance as that which is permanent amid the constant appearances and disappearances of qualities, regarding these as accidents or modifications.[4]

It may be noted that, although many recent philosophers differ from the pantheistic conception of substance, they nevertheless accept the logical notion of substance proposed by the Pantheists. For instance, Wolff of the Leibnizian school considered substance as a permanent and modifiable subject.[5] Such notions of substance and accidents are far from being true, for it has been explained that the two notions denote the first two modes whereby being is determined in the natural order. The characteristics of permanence and mutability are not the first two modes of determinations of contingent entity. As a matter of fact, we cannot understand the permanence or stability of a being without first understanding the *inseity* of such a being. On the

[3] *Principia Philosophiæ*, pars I, sect. 51, p. 24.

[4] *Op. cit.*, pars I, sect. 73, p. 37.

[5] *Ontologiæ*, pars II, sect. 11, c. 2.

other hand, the changeableness and variability of a being cannot be understood without first understanding its characteristics of *inaleity*. Therefore, even if permanence and mutability were the modes into which being is divided by means of categories, these two modes would still not be substance and accident, inasmuch as the two modes into which being, the principle of categories, is contracted are rather *inseity* and *inaleity*.

Furthermore, permanence and mutability are not the modes of being denoted by the term category, because predicaments are those modes of being whereby contingent entity is determined. But mutability and variability do not denote the peculiar modes of such determination, since they of their own nature require a being already constituted and determined. It follows that permanence and mutability are so far from being the first two categories that they cannot even be included in their number. Finally, it is beyond doubt that the notions of substance and accident consist exactly in those notes by which they are differentiated. But substance is not distinguished from accident because accident is subject to change, nor is the accident distinguished from substance because the latter is permanent and invariable. As a matter of fact, some accidents, especially those which flow from the essence of a thing, may also possess such characteristics. In conclusion, we repeat once more that the nature of substance consists in *inseity*, not in permanence under successive changes. "Permanence," Rickaby observes, "is not of the essence of substance any more than non-permanence or succession of accidents is of their own essence. Kant, therefore, and Green are wrong in the leading position which they assign to permanence. A substance would have been a substance, though its duration has been but for a moment." [6]

In addition to what has been said concerning the objectivity of substance, the following arguments are apropos. First, whatever exists objectively exists either in itself or in something else; there is no alternative between these two, since they are contradictorily opposed. But if the thing exists *in se* (in itself), the reality of substance is already admitted. If it inheres in something else, this something else is either a being *in se* (and consequently a substance) or finally is reducible to a being *in se*; otherwise we would be under the tyranny of an infinite regress. Therefore, conceding a congeries of qualities or any reality, we must also concede the reality of substance. Again, external experience manifests to us a series of mutations in things which always remain the same as subjects of these changes. But substance considered relatively is the permanent subject of changes. Internal experience convinces us that there are things existing *in se* which remain the same under diverse modifications, that there are subjects in which all vital operations are received. Finally, a congeries of qualities or modifications which modify nothing is absurd. To the objection that induction gives us no knowledge other than the phenomenal, we answer that we know at least this of the specific substance, that it is the subject of

[6] *General Metaphysics,* p. 259.

certain observed modifications and the cause of certain observed effects.

Another point that is interesting in this connection is the unfortunate attribution of inertia to substance. Such an idea is traceable to the Cartesian philosophy. On the other hand, Scholasticism does not regard either the soul or a material atom as inert except by a mental abstraction which is practised upon the idea of nature to reach the simple conception of "that which is capable of existing in itself." A substance without activity would be altogether unknowable, meaningless, and unthinkable. Finally, to "argue with Spencer [7] that we can never know the unmodified substance of the mind is correct, but substantialists never made such a claim. According to them, what is known is the modified substance of the mind. The concrete reality of the mind is therefore a substance plus its modifications, the two being indissolubly united both in reality and in our knowledge of them, yet being distinct." [8]

Therefore, the negation of the reality of substance logically leads to the negation of all reality and to pure philosophical Nihilism or Solipsism. If we do away with the reality of substance, we must at the same time do away with the reality of accidents, consequently with the reality itself. Wherefore it may be rightly stated that the notion of substance is not less objective and real than the very notion of being. Hence, "no accidents without substance." From this it results that the division of

[7] *Principles of Psychology*, p. 859.
[8] Dubray, *Introductory Philosophy*, pp. 461–462.

being into substance and accidents is adequate, for
no intermediary can be conceived between being *in
se* and being *in alio*. It is indeed gratifying that
many modern thinkers have come very close to accepting the Scholastic and common sense doctrine.
Thus Dr. McCosh says: "Now I give up the idea of
an unknown substratum behind the qualities. I
stand up only for what I know. In consciousness
we know of self, and in sense—perception—we
know the external objects as existing things, exercising qualities. In this is involved what we reckon
the true idea of substance. *We can as little know
the qualities apart from an object exercising them,
as we can find an object apart from qualities.* We
know both in one concrete act, and we have the same
evidence of the one as of the other." [9] McDougall
states: "Whenever we refer to a fact of experience,
we simply imply *some one* thinking of *something*." [10]
Professor Spearman writing on this matter says:
"Any psychology of cognition that fails to account
for this universal apprehending of an *ego*, must be
disfigured by a gap so wide and so deep as to render
it impotent to explain thoroughly the simplest event
in either ordinary life or experimental procedure.
The simplest way to account for such a notion of
an underlying *ego* is to derive it from our first
principle, taking it to become known by direct apprehension in experience." [11] "Consciousness does
not occur impersonally. Consciousness, on the con-

[9] *Agnosticism of Hume and Huxley*, p. 19.
[10] *Outline of Psychology*, p. 40.
[11] *The Nature of Intelligence*, p. 54.

trary, always is a somebody—being—conscious. There is never perception without a somebody who perceives, and there never is thinking unless some one thinks." [12]

In conclusion, we can do no better than to quote the significant dilemma of Johnson directed against his opponents on this point: "In one breath, they shelve the physical continuant by supposing that the percipient is observing a continuity in the qualitative changes of the object perceived; and while in this way rejecting any physical continuant, they have recourse to a psychical continuant—namely, the percipient. Here I submit that the perception by an individual of certain processes offers no explanation whatever of what in objective reality determines the stability of any given nexus. Then again, on the other hand, when it is urged that the upholders of this view are all along assuming a psychical continuant—*viz.*, the percipient—which from their standpoint must be repudiated, they, in effect, retort that it is quite unnecessary to postulate any psychical continuant, inasmuch as the nervous system itself will take the place of the ordinary conception of an Ego. Here they only eliminate the psychical continuant by reinstating the physical continuant." [13]

[12] Calkins, M. W., *A First Book in Psychology*, p. 1.
[13] *Logic*, Part III, p. 101.

CHAPTER V

DIVISION OF SUBSTANCE

Classification of Substance.—Aristotelian Definitions
of Primary and Secondary Substance.—Explanation of the
Two Concepts.—Justification of Such a Division.—Formation of Such Concepts.—Contrast between the Predication
of Secondary Substances and Accidents.—Various Modes
of Predication.—Classification of Substance into Complete
and Incomplete.—Fundamental Notions of Physical Dualism.—The Thomistic View of the Principle of Individuation.—Meaning of Subsistence, Nature, Supposit, Person.

∴

THE TRUE NATURE AND objectivity of substance having been established against the attacks of Phenomenalism, the logical order of events presents to us
another question which has long been debated in the
schools, namely, whether the division of substance
into primary and secondary can be justified.
"Primary substance," according to Aristotle, "is not
that which is predicable of a subject or present in a
subject, but rather that which denotes a concrete
individual, for instance, the individual man or
horse." [1] Secondary substances are *species* or *genera*
within which the primary substances are included as
parts in a logical whole, as, for instance, rationality
and animality are found in every individual man.

[1] *Cat.,* III, pp. 2, 29 ff.

Primary substances are called substances in the truest and strictest sense of the word (*maxime proprie, et primum et maxime dicta*), inasmuch as the concrete individual thing is the subject of all others. We must bear in mind that only *species* and *genera* are secondary substances; and species are more truly substances than the genera because the former come more closely to and denote better the nature of primary substance than the latter. In explaining the meaning of the term *man*, for instance, one would give a more explicit and complete notion of the term by denoting the *species* to which man belongs than by pointing out its proximate *genus*.

This doctrine of the Stagirite will become clearer if we call to mind that the essence related to an individual can be understood in a twofold manner. This essence may be regarded, in the first place, as that which is determined through the existence of this or that individual thing. For instance, humanity, in so far as it is realized in Peter and Paul, becomes Peter and Paul. In the second place, essence may be considered as that which constitutes the individual in a certain *species* or *genus*, because by the essence of a thing is meant the principle whereby a thing belongs to a certain *species* or to a certain *genus*. Thus, humanity, by the very fact that it is realized in Peter and Paul, places Peter and Paul in the species man. Hence, essence considered from both points of view is substance.

But it is also apparent that the name substance is applied to essence in various manners according to the diversity of modes from which it is considered.

And indeed it is applied to the individual primarily because, as in the case of humanity, it is realized in the individual and becomes the subject of accidents, since the individual alone is the ultimate subject of accidents. To illustrate, humanity has no subsistence apart from Peter or Paul or some other individual, and hence is incapable of being the receptive subject of accidents; it becomes receptive of accidents only in so far as it is realized in Peter and Paul.

Although essence cannot have its being except in the individual, it is only in virtue of such an essence that an individual is what it is and belongs to a definite species or a certain genus. Humanity really has no existence separate from the individual Peter or Paul; each individual, however, receives through humanity the perseity which is the proper characteristic of man. From these considerations it will be easily seen that the notion of substance is not found perfectly in the genera and species, but only in the individual. To obtain the notion of perfect substance, three conditions are required which are fulfilled as was shown only in the individual: first, that substance should have its existence not only in the mind but also in the natural order, since what is reified or has extra-mental existence is of a higher order than mere mental existence; secondly, that its being should have the note of inseity which is the basis of all other being, that is, that it should have a determination or a unity of its own; and, thirdly, that it should be the subject of accidents. Genera and species exist formally only in the mind, but have objective reference.

Although genera and species do not possess perfectly the notion of substance, still they are included in this class and justly so, because these two constitute the essence of the individual to which the term substance most properly applies. The notion of inseity belongs to the individual, because the essential property of the individual is to exist as the subject of accidents. Hence it follows that the essence which species and genera have in the individual must likewise exhibit the characteristics of inseity.

Such a classification of substances into primary and secondary shows also the remarkable wisdom of Aristotle both in synthesizing and also in following the proper method of knowledge. For as our knowledge begins with sense experience, we first perceive in the individual the two elements entering into the notion of substance, and then through the abstractive process of the mind we apply it also to genera and species. This clearly shows the empirical procedure of cognition, which starts from the individual and then passes to the general according to the axiom: *Nihil est in intellectu quin prius fuerit in sensu* (There is nothing in the intellect which was not previously in the senses). Incidentally, this serves to show the ignorance which is so widespread even nowadays on the part of those who regard the Scholastic theory of knowledge as an *a priori* theory devoid of all basis in experience.

Moreover, Aristotle taught that primary substances denote the individual on the ground that only an individual as such has its matter determined and specified by individuating notes, and becomes thus subjected to spatio-temporal conditions. He even prefers to call it *hoc aliquid* rather than the individual. In view of the fact that, since logical categories denote the supreme genera of things, primary substance is not any specified individual but the individual in general—that is, a *vague* individual, to use the words of Trendelenburg.[2] Secondary substances, on the other hand, denote qualities, not indeed, as Haureau remarked, the accidental ones (namely, those that belong to the category of quality), but the essential qualities either potentially as genus or actually as species.

From what has been said we may draw the following conclusions. First, substance cannot be univocally predicated of the individual and of species and genera, but only analogically, since the term substance does not apply to them in exactly the same sense; secondly, that substance which is the first category and the foundation of the others is the individual; and, thirdly, species and genera do not form special categories but are reducible to that of substance.

After the explanation of these points we proceed to the elucidation of the most obvious characteristics of substance. As we have stated at the beginning of this chapter, Aristotle described primary substance as that which is neither in a subject nor moreover can be predicated of a subject, and secondary substance as that which does not require a subject of

2 In lib. 2 *De Anima*, c. 1, 92, 325.

inhesion but is predicated of a subject. In the first place, the common characteristic of every substance is that it should not inhere in a subject. As substance and accident are mutually opposed in virtue of the fact that the former is capable of existing in itself whereas the latter must exist in another as in its subject, it follows that the essential property of accident cannot belong to any substance. Indeed, primary substance, inasmuch as it denotes an individual, cannot possibly inhere in a subject, since the individual itself is a concrete and an ultimate subject.

On the other hand, although secondary substances do not inhere in the first as accidents in a subject, they are in the primary substance in some such way as a higher genus is in a lower; since species and genera constitute the individual, they must be in the individual as the higher is in the lower. On this account, secondary substances can be predicated of the primary. Such a predication must obviously be different from that of the accidents which constitute the other nine categories. Indeed, secondary substance is predicated of the primary not only nominally but also according to definition, inasmuch as the essence of the former belongs to the essence of the latter. Thus, not only its term but also its essence contained in the definition belongs to primary substance. But an accident is attributed only nominally to the subject in which it inheres, because the accident does not belong to the essence of the subject, which is the cause only of the existence and not of the essence of the accident. Thus, we predicate of Peter, not only the term man, but also that whereby

Peter is man; although Peter is called white due to the whiteness which is in him, whiteness does not belong to him inasmuch as he is man, for whiteness is not a constitutive note of his essence.

When something is predicated of something else both nominally and essentially, such predication is called univocal; when only nominally, it is called denominative. Hence, secondary substance being univocally predicated of primary is distinct from accidents, which admit of denominative predication alone. We conclude, first, that substance can be predicated in no way of the subject as in the case of primary substance, or that it admits of univocal predication as in the instance of secondary substances, but never of denominative predication in the manner that accidents are predicated of a subject in which they inhere; secondly, that primary substance is substance in the strict and proper sense of the word, because it cannot possibly be predicated of a subject. Hence, St. Augustine wisely observed that substance or person cannot be predicated, "as we apply the predicate man which is common to all men, but only inasmuch as we denote such a man as Abraham or Isaac." [3]

Before we pass to further considerations, it is well to answer an objection which might be advanced in some such terms as these: A category, as was stated, denotes that which is predicated of another; therefore, it is repugnant that the first category should be something which cannot possibly be predicated of the subject.

[3] *De Trin.*, lib. 2, c. 13.

This objection upon closer examination will not disclose great difficulties. Aristotle maintained that primary substance denotes the individual, but by the term individual he did not intend to signify this or that individual (*e.g.*, Peter or Paul). His aim was rather to denote that which constitutes its essence or nature, or individual in general. As St. Thomas says: "The vague individual thing, as *some man*, signifies the common nature with the determinate mode of existence of singular things, that is, something self-subsisting as distinct from others. But the name of a designated singular thing signifies that which distinguishes the determinate thing, as the name Socrates signifies this flesh and this bone." [4]

But what constitutes the essence or nature of the individual is not this or that individual, but a mental concept which is common to all the individuals of a class; such a concept obviously represents a vague individual. Therefore, substance as a category can be predicated of each concrete substance, not indeed in the manner in which accidents are predicated of each concrete subject or in the manner in which secondary substances are predicated of the primary, but in as far as substance denotes a mental concept common to all individuals. For a clearer understanding of this point we must note with St. Thomas that things considered in themselves or absolutely are neither universal nor particular nor singular, due to the fact that their universality, particularity, and singularity are notions or, as the Schoolmen would say, second intentions of the human mind. When we intellectually

[4] *Sum. Theol.*, I, q. 30, a. 4, c.

perceive in a thing that which is common to all members of a species or genus, our mind forms a universal notion. But when we apprehend certain characteristics in reality common to all but *hic et nunc* limited to some members of the same species and genus, we form a particular notion. Finally, if we consider the same common feature in as far as it is absolutely determined, we obtain the notion of singularity.[5]

It is apparent that, although real things are indeed singular and individual, yet the notion of singularity as such is not in things but in the mind. It follows that such a notion must be common to every singular entity, and not a peculiar property of this or that singular thing. Consequently, the notion of singularity does not denote a determined principle in virtue of which a thing is particularized or individualized, but a mode by which the common nature is determined in all the individuals. Aquinas wisely remarks that in every individual substance there is not only a common nature (as, for instance, humanity which is realized in all individual substances), but that there is also a mode of existence whereby the common nature is individualized. However, there is no determined principle in virtue of which a common nature becomes this rather than that individual (for instance, Peter and not Paul). For although there is but one identical principle through which the common nature (*e. g.*, of man) is individualized in Peter and Paul, which principle is quantified matter, the quantified matter whereby the common nature of man is individualized in Peter is other than the matter

[5] *In Lib. I Sent.*, Dist. 19, a. 1, c.

which is individualized in Paul. Although the mode of existence whereby common nature becomes a primary substance or an individual is common to all individuals, yet the concept of primary substance is a concept which embraces all individual substances. Consequently, primary substance, as a category, is capable of fulfilling the functions of predication.

A third mark of substance is that it has no contrary. Aristotle puts this point admirably as follows: "What could be contrary of any primary substance, such as the individual man or animal? It has none. Nor can the species or the genus have a contrary. Yet, this characteristic is not peculiar to substance, but is true of many other things, such as quantity." [6]

Substance, again, does not appear to admit of variations of degree. This serves to discriminate substance from certain qualities such as heat which possess different degrees of intensity. Nothing, however, can be added to or subtracted from that which is the same. Although substance is said to increase and diminish according as it undergoes quantitative changes, yet substance regarded exclusively from the viewpoint of substantiality is indivisible and consequently unchangeable. St. Thomas elucidates this point as follows: "When we say that substance does not admit of more or less, we do not mean that one species of substance is not more perfect than another; but that one and the same individual does not participate in its specific nature at one time more than at another; nor do we mean that a species of substance

[6] *Cat.*, III b, 25–29.

is shared among different individuals according to what is more or less." [7]

Finally, "the most distinctive characteristic of primary substance appears to be that, while remaining numerically one and the same, it is capable of admitting contrary qualities," [8] "the modifications taking place through a change of the subject itself." [9] The reason of this is that primary substance, as we have previously remarked, is the ultimate subject or basis of accidents. To illustrate, a line may be either straight or crooked, a surface black or white.

Substances are also divided into complete and incomplete. Complete forms are perfect in themselves; they have every necessary perfection for the integrity or complement of substance; they are in their nature free from all need of union with something else. Incomplete substances are imperfect and, although not inhering in another, still require union with something else to be substantially perfect. In the instance of these latter, the perfect substance is constituted by the union of the two, not in the form alone; and in that union each part gives and takes. [10] This Scholastic doctrine is derived from and exemplified in the theory of physical dualism or hylomorphism of bodily substances.

This brings us to the discussion of primary matter and substantial form; our task on this point

[7] *Sum. Theol.*, I, q. 93, a. 3, ad 3.
[8] *Cat.*, IV.
[9] *Ibid.*, IV b.
[10] Harper, *Metaphysics of the School*, p. 270.

shall be simply that of exposition of the teaching of
the School.

According to St. Thomas, the ultimate and intrinsic principles which constitute the essence of
bodies are primary matter and substantial form. It
is well known that the Ionians and Atomists en-
deavored to explain material natures by matter
alone, that is, by some sensible and extended principle; on the other hand, the Pythagoreans had recourse to a certain suprasensible and unextended
principle called form. Plato in his system comprised both principles—namely, matter, which is the
principle of sensibility and extension, and form or
Idea. This form, however, in Plato's view is not immanent in but transcends matter, although it is in
some way participated in by matter. Aristotle cor-
rected this opinion by including forms in the things
themselves. From the dualism found in living
nature, he argued by analogy to a similar dualism
in inorganic nature. Hence, he did not separate the
formal organizing phase of nature from its material,
atomic, quantitative aspect. Aristotle was followed
by St. Augustine and all the Scholastics, who, while
differing on secondary questions, agreed in teaching
that every natural unit of both the organic and inorganic world consists of a twofold principle, matter
and form.

Generally, prime matter is conceived as an incomplete and absolutely indeterminate principle common to all bodies, which extends their substance into
parts outside parts, and which is capable of receiving successively different determinations. Aristotle

described it negatively as follows: it is not anything complete in itself, it is not quantity, nor is it quality, nor is it any of those things which determine the nature of a being, of itself it is nothing, can do nothing; it has no essence, no existence, no independence. Primary matter must not be confused with the simple chemical elements, because the simple elements themselves are composed of matter and form in the same way as all other bodies are.

From the above definition we may infer some characteristics of primary matter. (1) Prime matter being identical in all material substances is not subject to change, for what undergoes substantial change ceases to exist; but since primary matter is the common element to the old state of being and to the new, it consequently persists. (2) It is simple, because the resulting compound consists of matter and form. (3) It has an aptitude to receive form. Scholastics recognize in matter an innate tendency to the reception of essential forms. "Prime matter," says De Wulf, "contains potentially, or in promise, the series of forms with which it will be invested in the course of evolution." [11] (4) Primary matter is homogeneous in all bodies, for the characteristics common to all bodies (e. g., quantity, extension, passivity, gravity, inertia, etc.) are founded in matter; therefore, it must be said that matter itself in virtue of which these properties inhere in bodies is common to them all. (5) It is not something capable of existing alone. In other words, primary matter must be united to some sort of substantial form in the

[11] *Medieval Philosophy*, p. 72.

same way as secondary matter, or what is called body in the popular sense, cannot exist without an accidental form (*e. g.*, extension, figure, or shape). From the above characteristics we may infer that all the diversities manifested by bodies must be attributed to the diversity of forms.

Substantial form may be described as an incomplete principle or element whereby primary matter, of itself indeterminate, is determined into diverse species of corporeal substances. In other words, substantial form specifies and determines the potential element (*i. e.*, primary matter). For instance, in an atom of iron we distinguish a certain element of itself indeterminate, called prime matter, and the substantial form of iron whereby the indeterminate matter is determined to the specific essence of iron. Matter and form compenetrate each other like roundness in a round thing. The two co-exist; they are the co-principles of being, and together make up a complete or individual substance which is the source of operation. Primary matter bears to substantial form the same relation that potentiality bears to actuality, passivity to activity.

Here it is important to distinguish subsistent from non-subsistent forms, which latter are also called physical. Their nature is such that they cannot exist independently of matter, as, for instance, the forms of minerals, of plants and animals. Through corruption or disintegration of the body such forms return into the potentiality of matter. Hence, these non-subsistent forms depend on matter both for existence and the exercise of their activity;

that is, they emerge or are educed from primary matter in virtue of the aptitude of matter to receive them. For instance, the moulder forming clay gives it an artificial or accidental form; likewise by their generative powers animals give already existent matter new substantial form. Thus, there is the disappearance of the old and the emergence of the new.

To avoid confusion, it is also necessary to distinguish between accidental and substantial forms. A piece of wax, for instance, may by skillful artifice pass in succession from a spherical to a cubical form. By this process it will change its figure, its shape, without however undergoing a substantial alteration; it will be the same wax as before. This is called accidental form, since it determines the subject to exist under such a shape. A substantial form, on the other hand, is the principle of specification; it determines its subject to be such a substance. It is in virtue of the substantial form that man is a man, a lion a lion, or a chemical unit such a unit. Says Aquinas: "The substantial form differs from the accidental form in this, that the accidental form does not simply make a thing exist but only makes it hot. Therefore, a thing is not said to be made or generated by accidental forms, but is said to be made such and such, or to be given a new relation; and in like manner, when an accidental form is removed, a thing is said to be changed only relatively. Now, the substantial form gives simple existence; therefore, a thing is simply said to be born by the oncoming form, and to be destroyed by the disappearance of the old form. For this reason the old natural philosophers

who held that primary matter was some actual being—for instance, fire or air or something of that
sort—maintained that nothing is generated simply
or corrupted simply, and stated that every generation is nothing but an alteration as we read in
Phys. 1." [12]

We may now proceed to the explanation of the
most important characteristics of substantial form.
(1) Form is the fundamental or ultimate source of
operations, for that which gives existence to a thing
gives it also its activities. Activity follows being;
therefore, it must ultimately flow from the form. A
source of activity may be of two kinds, one being
identical with the agent which acts, the other being
merely that by which the action takes place. Thus,
in reasoning man is the agent which acts; the rational
soul is that by which reasoning takes place. But
because the soul in reasoning employs the understanding, a faculty distinct from itself and immediately connected with the act, the soul is called
the fundamental source, and the faculty is called the
proximate source of operation. (2) Form is simple
both as to essence, because it does not consist of matter and form, and as to quantity, because it is not
the principle of extension and division, being essentially simple. In itself it is simple, and only becomes
compound when intrinsically united to matter.
(3) A more perfect form contains virtually whatever
belongs to the inferior forms; that is, a superior
form gives all the perfections given by the inferior
forms to bodies. For instance, "the same essential

12 *Sum. Theol.*, I, q. 76, a. 4.

form makes man an actual being, a body, living, an animal, and man." [13]   (4) Forms are an outcome of the potentiality of matter, or "forms are extracted from the resources of matter." This shows the almost "nothingness" of matter and the "everything-ness" of the form. It is doubtful whether these statements may be taken as favoring the doctrine of evolution. Forms presuppose in matter a capacity to receive them, and are produced because that capacity exists. Primary matter, being so imperfect itself, is also a source and origin of imperfection in things, not in the sense that it can exert an active influence over them (for it is without energy), but in that it is the source of inertia in things. Since there are certain developments which are grounded upon matter and which cannot exist without it, these follow lines and partake of the imperfections which are inherent in matter. (5) Finally, "in all corruptions, whether substantial or accidental, the desinence of the previous specific form arises out of the incompatibility of the two forms; that is to say, out of the natural impossibility that the form of the corrupted substance and that of the newly generated substance should co-exist in the same body. To illustrate: it is impossible that the substantial form of a clover and the substantial form of a sheep should exist together in the same subject; the presence of the new form postulates, as an essential condition, the cessation of the old form. Accordingly, the latter is said to be expelled by the former. The matter ceases to

[13] *Sum. Theol.*, I, q. 76.

belong to the clover, because it is now under the substantial form of the sheep." [14]

The Scholastic theory of physical dualism is simply an application to the material universe of the more general theory of actuality and potency which is the cornerstone of the Aristotelico-Thomistic Metaphysics. We shall base our first argument on the above concepts as follows. It is, we believe, universally admitted that every cosmic substance is an actual existing thing. But whatever exists must have either in itself or in another the reason of its peculiar type of existence. Obviously, a body is not a pure actuality possessing self-existence, because it receives existence and becomes what it is in virtue of its act or form. All this, however, implies two things: first, the idea of a potency capable of assuming this or that particular existence or actuality—a potency which in the order to existence cannot be anything else than the simple and indeterminate prime matter; and secondly, an actuality known as substantial form which actualizes, determines, and specifies matter to such and such an existence. The conclusion to be drawn is that the ultimate constitutive principles of physical substance are prime matter and substantial form.

The following examples may serve to illustrate this important point in greater detail. The human individual is a complete substantial unit consisting of body and soul. Considered in relation to the soul, the body has a tendency or rather an *exigentia* or need for the reception of an act, life, being, existence.

[14] Harper, *op. cit.*, Vol. II, p. 384.

The soul, on the other hand, is the element which contributes this act, this life, this being, this existence. It is in virtue of the soul that whatever is called body can be truly called a *human* body. If the soul is the organizing principle that contributes such a form and such modality to the body, it must be admitted that it is the intrinsic cause which gives a certain determination to a being that was formerly indeterminate and indifferent to become a human body. Here, the body plays the rôle of matter, and the soul the rôle of substantial form. In all living beings, whether animals or plants, the case is the same. As universal experience confirms, living units vegetate, grow, move, feel, and reproduce themselves. Shall we conceive of this group of activities as of so many automatic evolutions? Whatever evidence we have points to the contrary. Consequently, we are justified in attributing to all living things an organizing and unifying principle, that is, the substantial form which specifies, integrates, and determines them.

The soundness of the Scholastic theory may also be defended by the following considerations. Biological sciences recognize the essential difference between living and inorganic substances. Professor E. B. Wilson, dean of contemporary cytologists, concludes his book on the cell with the statement that "the study of the cell has, on the whole, seemed to widen rather than to narrow the enormous gap that separates even the lowest forms of life from the inorganic world." [15] This obviously implies the

[15] *The Cell.*

reality of substantial changes of bodies, for inorganic substances, as universal experience teaches, are being constantly changed by the processes of generation and nutrition into living units. Likewise living units are being resolved into non-living. It follows that bodies are composed of matter and form as of two really distinct elements. In every substantial change the old substantial determination or form disappears and a new form or determination takes its place, and that which remains unchanged is called primary matter. As the biological and sentient activities cannot be explained in terms of brute matter, we are forced to ascribe such activities to some unique substantial form which, although dependent on matter, is still distinct from it. Hence, in living things there is a mode of operation radically distinct from the mode of operation of brute matter, which must be explained by a special type of substantial form which, though distinct from matter, is nevertheless dependent on it. From the dualism found in plants, animals and man, Scholastics generally argue to a similar dualism in inorganic nature, claiming that chemical changes imply a real change of nature recognizable by an entirely different set of properties which follow upon the disappearance of the previous determinations. In consequence, they conclude that, if bodies are made up of atoms and electrons, these atomic and electronic units themselves are composed of matter and form.

To show that the Scholastic theory of physical dualism is not in disagreement with the scientific views of the day, we will quote the following expression of the views of Dr. Nys: "As to the application of this scientific theory of electrons to cosmology, here in a few words is my opinion:

"(1) The electronic theory is a generally successful attempt at synthesis, but as yet it raises serious difficulties. Hence, it is premature, to wish to base upon it a cosmological conception of matter, or to employ it as a conclusive argument against an adverse philosophical system or theory.

"(2) Anyway, this scientific synthesis can easily be reconciled with the Scholastic theory. In effect, it results in a real and inevitable dualism, a plurality of primordial substances. Physicists admit, as primordial elements of the chemical atom, a positive nucleus and negative electrons, both linked to the central nucleus. Thus, there are constituents, two electrical elements described by the same name (electricity), but mutually irreducible. Now, it is just as easy for a Thomist to conceive the formation of the world starting from a simple primitive dualism as to do so in terms of eighty or a hundred simple bodies actually admitted by chemists.

"(3) Even if the two kinds of electricity were reduced to one, the diversity of the chemical species, in the Scholastic sense of the word, could still be maintained; allotropy and polymerisation show us that the same matter, subjected to different influences, can be transformed into different species.

"(4) Finally, as is admitted by numerous writers, it is by no means established that the theory of electrons completely excludes the existence of extended matter in the ordinary meaning of the word." [16]

In conclusion, we wish to say that modern philosophy in rejecting the Aristotelico-Thomistic system not only has gained no advantage, but has not even succeeded in escaping the confusion and chaos that confronted the ancient sages. The views advocated by modern atomists such as Descartes, Newton, Secchi, and Tongiorgi are essentially but repetitions of the opinions of Thales, Democritus, and Anaxagoras, just as the doctrines supported by such thinkers as Leibniz, Wolff, Boschovich, Kant, Eddington, and Jeans are but a reiteration of the Eleatic and Pythagorian tenets. It is at once evident that neither Atomism nor Dynamism can account for the diversity of substances and substantial changes. Furthermore, refusing to emerge from the domain of the sensible phenomena, Atomism fails to explain many well-established facts of experience, such as the conscious and vital processes in animals, the chemical laws of cohesion and affinity, and the law of gravitation. It cannot, in fact, explain even the unity of extension itself. In the same manner Dynamism fails to account for the real extension; and while emphasizing the dynamic aspect of nature and its manifold energies and activities, it remains silent as to the sources and underlying realities which exhibit these various energies and activities. Both reason and experience tell us that there cannot be motion, rotation, vibration, etc., without *something* that moves, ro-

[16] Mercier, *A Manual of Modern Scholastic Philosophy*, Vol. II, p. 550.

tates, vibrates, etc. Again, there is no justification
whatsoever for attributing thought and perception
to the monads created by Leibniz, nor is it possible
for the simple force-centers of Boschovich to constitute the real extension of bodies. If these considerations are valid (and an unbiased mind must confess that they are), Scholastic hylomorphism seems
to be the only possible theory about inner constitution of the sensible universe. From the above considerations it is apparent that Atomism and Dynamism fail miserably to solve the metaphysical problem
chiefly because they misunderstand the question at
issue. In the attempt to explain the essence of physical substances, they have recourse to certain basic
properties of matter such as extension, force, or energy, as if substance could be accounted for in terms
of "its accidental attributes and modifications." According to St. Thomas, substance as such, whether
spiritual or material, is not a datum either of sense
or intellectual intuition, but a conclusion arrived at
by argument. Consequently, neither extension nor
energy which are objects of sense perception can be
regarded as the constitutive principle of matter.
And because prime matter and substantial form are
derivative concepts, it does not follow that they are
pure mental figments: they have an objective foundation, although, like all other abstractions, they
exist formally only in the mind. Thus, the scientific
monument erected by the Stagirite and perfected by
the Scholastic art and acumen seems to be the only
system capable of solving this problem in consonance
with reason and the verified conclusions of science.

After these remarks on physical dualism we can approach the problem of individuation in the light of Thomistic doctrine. According to this view, the principle of individuation (namely, that by which one individual is distinguished from others of the same species) is *materia signata quantitate* or quantified matter. For a clear understanding of the thesis, the following remarks should be borne in mind.

(1) An individual is a being which is undivided in itself and at the same time separated from other individuals of the same species. It implies, therefore, the characteristics of unity and separateness or distinctness. Individuality in general may be described as the aggregation of properties in virtue of which any given individual possesses a certain unity, and is separated from other beings.

(2) The principle of individuation is twofold, namely, formal and material. The formal principle is that by which a being is intrinsically undivided in itself, and distinct from other individuals of the same species. The material principle of individuation in every being is the complete entity of the thing, inasmuch as it has a unity of its own, is numerically distinct from another, and is conceived by us as a numerical difference. For a being is such a being in virtue of its form, and is numerically distinct from others by its complete entity. The ultimate principle of individuation is the cause of numerical difference. We may ask, then, what is the ultimate source of numerical difference.

In defense of the Thomistic teaching we advance

the following arguments. The principle of individuation of a material substance requires, first, that it
be something substantial. Although individuals are
recognized by their accidental qualities, yet the individuation of substances implies something substantial, for between individual substances there is a substantial difference. With regard to accidents which
inhere in substances, it is clear that they suppose a
substance already individuated; hence, it is more
appropriate to say that the accidents themselves are
individuated by substance rather than substance by
accidents. The second requirement is that the principle of individuation should multiply and constitute
this and that substance without multiplying and
changing the species; rather it requires that it should
preserve one and the same species in various individuals. But only quantified matter (*i.e.*, matter
conditioned by quantity) is something substantial
which multiplies substance without change of species.
The basic principles of material substances are matter, form, and existence. Now, existence cannot be
the individuating principle, since it supposes an essence already individualized; nor can the form perform this office, for it is the principle of specification
only—that is, the form being changed the species is
also changed. Moreover, the principle of individuation cannot be primary matter, for primary matter
is undetermined and common to all things; therefore,
it can only be matter in so far as it is determined
and becomes this or that through quantity. Moreover, an individual implies incommunicability; hence,
the source of incommunicability must be also the

source of individuation. But the source of incommunicability is matter determined by quantity.

For a better understanding of this argument it must be noted that there is a twofold incommunicability, namely, physical and metaphysical. Now, metaphysical incommunicability is based on the physical incommunicability. Hence, species or metaphysical form is communicable to many owing to the fact that physical form can have existence in many subjects. It follows, then, that species is divided numerically into each individual of the same species, and that purely numerical difference is rightly called material. Again, matter is the principle of multiplicity, because both the plurality of integral parts in the same substance and the multiplicity of individuals in the same species arises from matter. Matter is also the principle of limitation; thus, the form through its reception in matter becomes subject to spatio-temporal conditions.

Accidental forms are individualized by the subject in which they inhere, and such forms stand in the same relation to their subject as substantial forms to primary matter. Quantity, however, has a twofold mode of individuation, one from the subject as every other accident, one from itself inasmuch as it has position. Matter determined by quantity does not denote a compound resulting from matter and quantity, for in such a case the source of individuation would be something accidental. Moreover, in order that quantity should actually modify the subject it presupposes that the subject is already individuated. Therefore, matter determined by quantity is matter displaying as source of this quantity rather than another.[17]

The notions of subsistence, nature, supposit, and persons are intimately related with and inseparable from the topics discussed in the last two chapters. It is, then, necessary and desirable to explain the Scholastic significance of these concepts. *Subsistence* denotes that manner of existence whereby a substance in virtue of its inseity becomes absolutely incommunicable. This applies to all substantial entities. *Nature* signifies the essence as the principle of activity. *Supposit* indicates a complete individual nature existing and acting in every way distinct and incommunicable to any other being, so that it exists and acts in its own right autonomously (*e.g.*, a tree, a horse, etc.). In other words a supposite or hypostasis must be something complete in itself as a nature, and self-possessed—that is, not actually a part of the physical whole nor destined by nature to be such a part. Finally, the term *person* in its ontological connotation signifies a complete individual substance endowed with intellect and will.

With his usual clearness of expression St. Thomas thus defines the above terms, for we cannot do better than to quote his own words: "Substance is also called by three names signifying a reality— that is, a thing of nature, subsistence, and hypostasis, according to a threefold consideration of the substance thus named. For, as it exists in itself and not in another, it is called subsistence; as we say that those things subsist which exist in themselves and

[17] Cajetan, *Commentaria de Ente et Essentia*, c. II, q. 5, 37.

not in another. As it underlies some common nature, it is called a thing of nature; as for instance, this particular man in a human natural thing. As it underlies the accidents, it is called hypostasis, or supposit." [18]

The principal axiom that flows logically from the notion of the supposit and person is the following: actions and passions (or reactions) are proper to the supposita (*i.e.*, to the wholes as such and not to parts or powers). Thus, strictly speaking, it is not correct to say that the hand strikes, that the eye sees, that the ear hears, that the intellect thinks, etc., because in the last analysis it is a complete substance, a *man* or a person, who is really the agent, who elicits these actions, and to whom all these activities are ultimately attributed. From the above premise it follows also that actions participate in the dignity of the person.

[18] *Sum. Theol.*, I, q. 29, a. 2.

CHAPTER VI

ACCIDENT IN GENERAL

Distinction between Logical and Ontological Accident.
—Predicamental Accident Defined.—Its Nature.—Division
of Accident into Intrinsic and Extrinsic.—Cartesian Attack
on the Objectivity of Accident.—Defense of Scholastic Doctrine.—Presentation of some Modern Views.—Relation between Substance and Accident.

∴

THE ANALYSIS OF THE concept *substance* logically
entails the discussion of the concept *accident*. Substance is the first category and the source of other
categories. If a thing is not substance, it is called
accident (*i.e.*, something added to a substance).
Here accident is not taken in the same meaning in
which it occurs in Logic. The logical accident is distinguished into genus, species, difference, and attribute; the metaphysical accident now spoken of is a
mere negation of that special manner of existence
which belongs to substance. Accident does not constitute a genus of which the nine classes of accidents
(*i.e.*, the nine remaining categories) would be the
species, because "being" which is predicated of each
accident is not taken univocally. For example, qualities, relations, time, place, etc., are accidents of substance, but are so different from one another that
they have nothing strictly in common which is not

identical with that which is peculiar to each; and the mere negation of substantiality cannot constitute a genus. Still, accident may be called a *quasi-genus*.

Predicamental or categorical accident may be defined as "a thing to the nature of which it is due that it should exist in a subject of inhesion." [1] For a clearer understanding of this definition and of the nature of accident, the following observations will not be out of place. The proper difference between accident and substance is this, that accident in contrast to substance is *ens in alio*—that is, a being inherent in another and having existence distinct from the nature of substance.

The first characteristic of any accident consists in the fact that it inheres in and presupposes a subject; consequently, accident does not inhere in the subject as a constitutive part, but inheres in it in such a manner that independently it could not naturally continue in existence. This inhesion is immediate, if the accident affects the substance itself (*e.g.*, quantity modifying a bodily substance), and mediate, if it inheres in another accident (*e.g.*, figure affecting quantity). It is not of the essence of accident that it should actually inhere in the subject, but only that it should have an aptitude or exigence for inherence. Accident, though distinct from substance, cannot properly be called *id quod existit* (that which is), but rather *id quo aliquid existit* (that whereby the substance is modified).

"There is no such thing as walking or sitting or health existing independently. The accidents are

[1] *Quodlib.* 9, 3, a. 5, ad 2.

said to be, not because they possess existence themselves, but because the concrete subject is walking and is healthy. Hence, as Aristotle says, they are called 'things,' because in their respective ways they determine that which is a thing in the sense of being a substance." [2]

An accident cannot migrate from subject to subject; for being by its very nature dependent on the subject in which it inheres, it can indeed cease to exist, but it cannot be said to migrate, except by an improper use of the term. For instance, an accident of one subject may somehow produce in another an accident equal to itself while in the act of production it ceases to exist, a phenomenon usually observed in local motion.

The nature of accident follows the nature of substance. This axiom militates against the materialistic tenet which regards knowledge as an accidental quality resulting from inert matter. It frequently happens that accidents do modify matter, that is, modify and perfect its nature; however, they can never produce an activity which is not connatural to substance. Since to operate or to act (*agere*) is the characteristic of substance and not of accident, it follows that the latter cannot be regarded as the agent (*suppositum*), although it is that whereby the substance performs its activities, according to the Scholastic maxim: *actiones sunt suppositorum* (actions are proper to the supposit).

Scholastics are accustomed to divide accidents into intrinsic and extrinsic. The former expression

2 Joyce, *Logic*, p. 139.

denotes the form which intrinsically modifies the subject as to quality and quantity, and to which the name of accident is applied in a special manner, for intrinsic accidents are really inherent in the subject and are consequently called physical accidents. The expression extrinsic accidents denotes the form which denominates a substance in respect to external things, for instance, in respect to time or place.

After these preliminary observations our next task will be to defend the Scholastic doctrine of accident. The question concerning the nature of categorical accident gave rise to a great controversy among the ancients. Those who taught that there is nothing in nature besides matter (as Democritus and the followers of Epicurus) attributed all the diversities of substance to the various positions, configurations, and constellations of material parts and to the local motion of atoms. On this account they called accidents only those phenomena which affect matter extrinsically. The Peripatetics, on the other hand, were of the opinion that many accidents are determinations and forms inhering in substances; they considered them as certain entities destined by nature to inhere in substance.[3] As we perceive some trees to have enough strength to sustain themselves (*e.g.*, an oak), others on the contrary to be in need of support (*e.g.*, ivy), so they distinguished beings subsisting in themselves (namely, substances) from other entities of a more infirm nature (namely, accidents). This comparison is feeble, but it helps to illustrate the point in question. Descartes and his

3 *Sum. Theol.*, III, q. 77, a. 2.

followers, relying on their fundamental principle that all forms both accidental and substantial are nothing else than vain verbal expressions of the Scholastics, deny the existence of realities distinct from substance. All those entities that in popular parlance are called accidents are according to them finally reduced to the modes of the soul (as thought, volition, etc.), or to purely local motion and its privations (as rest), or to the figure and position of the material parts, or to the various relations whereby the body unmoved in itself begins to exhibit various characteristics or properties.

All of these characteristics suppose the accidents to be the substances themselves variously modified and determined, and not new realities superadded to substance. Against these objections we advance the following arguments. Both internal and external experience clearly shows that real changes continually take place, and that these are by no means substantial; thus, the soul thinking, willing, feeling, etc., and the body decaying, growing, moving, etc., undergo many alterations without undergoing any substantial change in their being. But such changes are inconceivable and unintelligible except inasmuch as substances acquire or lose a certain reality which does not belong to their essence; for that which does not lose or receive anything does not change in any way. It logically follows that realities distinct from substance—that is, accidents—must be admitted. To this it might be objected that in order to explain mutations in things it could be said that substance is merely modified in various ways. But such an objection seems to be merely a play on words. For what do we mean when we say that a substance is modified, if not that it receives a new modification? This new modification is either something or nothing. In the latter case it is falsely said that substance is really changed, for that which neither acquires nor loses anything does not really change. If, on the other hand, that modification is anything, it is an entity, since being and something are mutually convertible terms. This being, however, is such that it is not in itself but inheres in the subject which it modifies.

This being inhering in another is plainly an accident. Therefore, from the very fact that substance is diversely modified, it must be admitted that there are realities (*i.e.*, accidents) really distinct from substances. Again, the notion of efficiency demands that through its power something new and real should be produced (an efficient cause causing no effect cannot be thought of). But very frequently the things upon which this efficiency is exercised actually exist according to their whole substantial being.

The obvious conclusion is that besides the substantial being other accidental realities must be admitted. "The modern views of accident, so far as they accord to it any objectivity, are based on the physical theory that all, at least material, phenomena (light, color, heat, sound, etc.) are simply varying forms of motion. In fact, this kinetic element in such phenomena was known to Aristotle and the

Scholastics; [4] but it is only in recent times that physical experimentation has thrown light on the correlation of material phenomena as conditioned by degrees of motion. While all Neo-Scholastic philosophers maintain that motion alone will not explain the objectivity of extension, some (*e.g.*, Gutberlet) admit that it accounts for the sensible qualities (color, sound, etc.). Haan (*Philos. Nat.*) frees the theory of motion from an extreme idealism, but holds that the theory of the real, formal objectivity of those qualities affords a more satisfactory explanation of sense perception. The majority of Neo-Scholastic writers favor this latter view (Pesch, *Phil. Nat.*)." [5]

The presentation of the Scholastic doctrine on this topic would not be complete without some remarks concerning the relation existing between substance and various accidents. This consideration is important because it touches on the problem of the unity of a substantial composite. In the first place, Scholastics claim that substance is the cause of accidents—by the term *cause* they generally denote that which by its positive influence produces the existence of something else. It seems that the subject is both the final cause and, in a way, the active cause of its proper accidents. It is also the material cause, as it were, inasmuch as it is receptive of the accidents. "The emanation of proper accidents from their subject is not by way of transmutation but by a certain natural resultance; thus, one thing results naturally

[4] Cf. St. Thomas, *De Anima*, 3, lect. 2.
[5] Siegfried, F. P., in *Cath. Enc.*, Vol. I, p. 79.

from another, as color from light." [6]   It must be noted that, while substance exercises the function of receiving and sustaining with regard to every accident, it does not exercise the power of efficiency with reference to all accidents but only to its proper accidents.   In the second place, St. Thomas teaches that accidents have an existence really distinct from that of substance.   He illustrates this as follows: "Now, it must be borne in mind that there is a formal nature which does not pertain to the personal being of the subsisting hypostasis; this being is not said to belong to the person simply, but relatively; for example, to be white is the being of Socrates, not as he is Socrates, but inasmuch as he is white, and there is no reason why this being should not be multiplied in one hypostasis or person; for the being whereby Socrates is white is distinct from the being whereby he is a musician.   But the being which belongs to the very hypostasis or person in itself cannot be multiplied in one hypostasis or person, since it is impossible that there should not be one being for one thing." [7]

Another important corollary is that substance cannot exist apart from its modifications or accidents, and this because of the necessary connection existing between the subject and the proper modifications flowing from that subject.   This is exemplified by Aquinas.   "Although," he says, "the faculties of the soul, namely intellect and will, are qualities distinct from their substance, nevertheless, it

6 *Sum. Theol.*, III, q. 77, a. 6, ad 3.
7 *Sum. Theol.*, III, q. 17, a. 2, c.

cannot be understood how the soul could exist without them, as they emanate from the soul with which they are necessarily joined." [8] In other words, whilst it is possible for the mind to *conceive* (not imagine) substance without attributes, inasmuch as it is contradictorily opposed to them, yet, when there is a question of real substances, it is absolutely impossible to know them without their properties and accidents from which they are inseparable, in view of the fact that these properties constitute and determine substances in their concrete reality. It follows that the concrete being has but one existence, which is its substantial existence. But how can this unity in plurality, or rather the plurality of accidents and the unity of substance, be explained? This synthesis is explained by St. Thomas by the fact that "unity does not exclude multitude, but division which logically precedes oneness or multitude. Multitude does not remove unity, but division from each of the individuals which compose the multitude." [9]

These conclusions further show that the antinomies which Empiricism believes to have discovered in the notion of substance cannot arise save from a physical conception of reality. It is from such a conception that the paradoxical and unintelligible claim of a *substratum*, inert, undetermined, and divested of accidents, originates. If substance should be such a thing, St. Thomas would be more of an idealist than Locke (who is not but should be), Hume, or Kant. As a matter of fact, the anti-

---

[8] *De. spir. creat.*, a. 11.
[9] *Sum. Theol.*, I, q. 30, a. 3, ad 3.

nomies of the pure speculative reason are nothing but antinomies of the imagination, because they arise from the intrusion of an imagination essentially atomistic in the domain of Metaphysics. There is no greater sin in philosophy, according to St. Thomas, than to mistake forms for things.

We may conclude with the significant words of Professor Perrier: "There is no doubt that we can no more imagine a substance without attributes than attributes without a substance, so that a substance without attributes would mean a substance without elements, or, in other words, a thing would be equal to nothing. But the self-existence of a substance does not and cannot mean that it exists without attributes. It means that it exists by itself, while the attributes do not; and herein lies the essential difference between them." [10]

[10] *Revival of Scholastic Philosophy*, p. 61.

CHAPTER VII

HISTORICO-CRITICAL ANALYSIS OF THE CONCEPT OF SUBSTANCE

Critical Analysis of Substance: From John Duns Scotus to Descartes.—From Descartes to Immanuel Kant. —From Kant to Our Own Day.

∴

A. From John Duns Scotus to Descartes

Scotus, as is well known, opposes the Thomistic theory of individuation and knowledge. The individuation of concrete existing things, according to the Subtle Doctor, does not come from quantified matter but from an ultimate formal difference called *thisness* (*hæcceitas*) ; and the proper function of the intellect does not consist in the knowledge of abstract entities or essences, as Thomas claimed, but rather in the knowledge of the concrete existing object which is the ultimate reality. These views seem to pave the way in the direction of Nominalism, and, as we shall see, Occam and his disciples appeal to them in favor of their terministic doctrines. However, by means of the *formal distinction a parte rei* Scotus succeeds in reconciling the above views with two others which give expression to an extreme type of Realism. For him the specific concepts and the concept of being itself are univocal; he also claims that logical notions and distinctions are not mere mental acts, but have a reality corresponding to them.   Scotus argues as follows: if the universal be purely and simply a mental product without a foundation in reality, our knowledge of things would have no objective value.   As a matter of fact, the universal and the particular, far from opposing one another, correspond with each other; in other words, the individual essences, even before the operation of the mind, entail a whole hierarchy of forms or metaphysical degrees down to the individual difference by which singularity is obtained.   Thus, Peter is constituted by those generic formalities which are substantiality, corporeity, vitality, sensibility, and Petreity.   It follows that these diverse forms denote for Scotus something real in the particular object. Moreover, he places among them a formal distinction *a parte rei*—an intermediate distinction between the logical and real.   It is not difficult to perceive the consequences of this doctrine: in the first place, the realities to which Thomism denies a distinct existence are raised to some sort of absolute existence, and, in the second place, the unity of the substantial being is disrupted.

According to St. Thomas, material substance is composed of a double principle: one essentially passive (pure potentiality), namely, primary matter; and the other active and determined, namely, substantial form.   Both are not being but *the principles of being*—the essential elements that constitute and determine substantial being.   If the forms which constitute real being have each an objective and distinct existence, primary matter will have to be conceived as an actualized being, a positive entity existing in itself and by itself. The *principles* of the Thomistic doctrine would thus become *things*; for, if matter is by itself an act or an existent, it could be logically considered as an immovable substratum of material substances. This, of course, is not the teaching of Scotus, but his principles would lead to such a conclusion.

At this point we may ask: what becomes of substance in the light of this doctrine? It ceases *ipso facto* to be one being, *unum per se*, and becomes a sort of an aggregate, or what St. Thomas would call *unum per accidens*—a mere combination of beings. From the fact that a certain degree of entity in the particular object corresponds to each universal notion, it follows that each universal notion must have a unity of its own. This unity in the Scotist theory is not the numerical unity constitutive of singularity, but is a real unity though somewhat inferior to the numerical one. Since the mind intuitively perceives such entities thus affected by unity, the Subtle Doctor is forced to consider them as real data in the concrete object. Accordingly, he has left to his successors a momentous task, namely, the task of reconciling the unity of the individual with the multiplicity of its constitutive forms of which each enjoys a unity of its own. Does not this imply an irreconcilable antinomy?

Having reached the terminus of the so-called ancient ways of thinking, we must now direct our footsteps along the modern path of Occam and his

followers.   According to the Venerabilis Inceptor,
particulars alone exist.   These are known through
intuition only, and apart from intuitional cognition
there is no certainty, no objective knowledge.   This
intuition through which we apprehend the real in its
concrete status is not sense intuition, for sense knowledge leaves us only on the surface of things.   Only
intellectual intuition enables us to know contingent
facts, internal and external, which are the proper
object of science.   However, we must not exaggerate
its power, Occam reminds us, as this intellectual intuition does not and cannot reach the core of reality.
The object of individual intuition is not the metaphysical individuality, but only the external and internal facts of concrete experience.   Since for Occam
universal concepts are divested of all objective value,
he rejects as vain and useless all metaphysical speculation, in one word, whatever is not an object of experience.   Substance then, conceived as identical with
essence, will be inaccessible to experience; consequently, it will have no meaning unless identified
with the accidents apprehended in intuition.   Particulars in his view are but more or less stable aggregates of qualities or phenomena in time and space.
This being the case, the unity of being becomes
weakened and the great effort for the unification of
the real set to naught.   Such is the logic of Occam-
ism—the spatial and temporal dispersion of the individual, the dissolution of the one into pure multiplicity.   True it is that Occam rejects these consequences, but other philosophers soon to appear on the
scene will unhesitatingly accept them.   At any rate,

despite the fact that Occam apprehends individuality in intuition as an empirical fact based on irresistible evidence, he is incapable of advancing a single reason for this fact. It is a datum, of course, but an unintelligible one.

We come now to Nicholas of Autrecourt who applies the empirical principles of Epistemology to the discussion of the notions of causality and substance. The principle of causality, he states, consists in inferring that from the fact that a thing is (the effect) another must also be (the cause). However, such reasoning is fallacious, because the thing whose existence we infer is other than the thing given in experience; consequently, the principle of causality cannot be reduced to the principle of contradiction, which necessarily requires that the antecedent and consequent (predicate and subject) of a given proposition should be identical. From this it follows that the principle of causality is devoid of value; and as it enters into a vast number of our metaphysical affirmations, it will deprive these affirmations of all objective value. Hence, we cannot clearly demonstrate that the external world exists, or that the soul possesses faculties distinct from its essence. On the same grounds, Nicholas continues, we must reject as inconclusive the reasoning process by which we pass from accidents to substance. The mind cannot pass from the knowledge of one thing to that of another, for, if the latter is really another, it is not capable of being identified with the first, and the judgment attributing a predicate to a subject from which it differs would not admit of a reduction to the principle of contradiction.

Moreover, as only experience furnishes us with accidents, we cannot obtain definite knowledge of substances except of those which are apprehended by intuition. With the exception of the human soul, which Nicholas maintains is known intuitively, no certain affirmation can be made of the existence of any material substance. It is also vain, he asserts, to distinguish between substance and accidents; these two being identical, it is impossible to prove that what is termed substance is something different from the accidents, and vice versa. In conclusion, he declares that all abstract systems erected upon natural appearances are vanities; they are the *virtutes occultæ* of dialecticians intoxicated with metaphysical abstractions. Only particulars exist; only facts are real; any attempt to explain sensible phenomena by an appeal to entities invisible or inaccessible to experience must be a waste of time and energy.

At this critical time Suarez appears on the scene. His ambitious aim is to devise an extremely ingenious compromise between the doctrines of the Middle Ages, that is, between the moderate Realism of St. Thomas, the exaggerated Realism of the Scotists, and the terministic Nominalism of Occam. His scheme revolves around the question of (a) the unity of substantial composite, (b) the relation of matter and form, and (c) the relation between substance and accidents.

From a general point of view, the problem of the relation of matter and form in the substantial

composite depends on the conception one has formed
of primary matter; it is a question of finding out
whether primary matter is in itself such a pure potentiality that it is devoid of any formal or entitative
act. Scholastics distinguish two kinds of act: the
formal act, which is the form in so far as it is united
to matter for the production of the composite; the
entitative act, which is existence by which a thing is
placed outside its causes and is directly opposed to
nothing. Granting that primary matter is not by
itself a being in actuality, must we say that it is so
because it lacks simultaneously a *formal* and *entitative* act, or simply because it lacks a *formal* act?
The first opinion is espoused by St. Thomas, the
second by Suarez. The latter's view is the logical
consequence of his rejection of the real distinction
between essence and existence. Since, according to
Suarez, matter has its proper essence, it must by that
very fact have its proper existence; otherwise it
would be nothing, because once existence is destroyed
the whole reality vanishes, is reduced to a simple
objective potentiality, to a pure non-entity. It is
easy to see where the difficulty lies. For the Thomists primary matter is ordained for existence not
immediately, but only through the mediation of
form which it receives *before* existence ("before"
having reference here to priority of nature and not
of time); matter is pure potentiality both in the essential and existential order. For Suarez primary
matter is not pure potentiality except in the logical
order; in the existential order it necessarily possesses
a certain entitative act of its own by which it is

placed outside its causes, so that through the absolute power of God it could subsist without form.

Are we justified in holding with Suarez that prime matter is immediately and by itself susceptible of existence? The following exposition by Aquinas is worthy of note. In every composite there can be only one substantial existence, by which both matter and form enjoy oneness of existence. Matter alone is not ordained to exist by itself, but is ordained by nature to be united to some form; it receives existence only in receiving form. Since matter is only in pure potentiality with reference to form, it can only be in pure potentiality with reference to existence. And, whatever is in actuality must be so either as an act or as a potentiality participating in an actuality. But matter is not an act; it is repugnant to the concept of matter to consider it an act. It is never an act except by participation in an act; but the only act capable of being participated in by matter is its form. Therefore, to say that matter is an act is equivalent to saying that it has received a form.

This argument, however, fails to convince Suarez. From the fact that matter is deprived of its natural existence which results from the form, Suarez argues it does not follow that matter is deprived of its own complete entity. Primary matter must have some sort of real entity prior in the order of nature to its actuation by the form, and *a fortiori* prior to its entire composite. For how can that which has no real entity, no actuality of being, be truly capable of receiving anything? Herein is to be found the Gordian knot of the whole discussion. Out of solicitude to safeguard the unity of the composite, St. Thomas refuses to attribute to matter an actuality of its own. On the other hand, if matter is in a certain manner a being by itself, as Suarez claims, material substances will have to be conceived as possessing two distinct beings, and their unity will no longer be essential but only accidental. It logically follows that the problem of accounting for the unity of the material composite becomes extremely difficult in the doctrine of Suarez.

The Suarezian position is plainly distinct from the Scotist position. Duns Scotus ascribes to primary matter a proper form, namely, the form of corporeity which is common to every material being. Suarez rejects this form of corporeity on the ground that, if matter be an act of corporeity, it would not be able to constitute with the subsequent form a being *in* and *by* itself. He agrees with Scotus, but on entirely different grounds, namely, in attributing to primary matter some sort of existence independent of form. If this primary matter, Suarez says, cannot have the form of corporeity conceived by the Subtle Doctor, it must nevertheless possess an entitative form. Thus, itself united to the form, primary matter preserves its real substantial entity distinct from formal entity; it has in itself and by itself an actuality of existence distinct from the existence of the form, yet depending upon the form. It is not a mere nonentity in isolation, much less in the composite; consequently, in substantial changes primary matter persists under its successive forms. If this be not true, Suarez concludes, substantial change will no longer be a generation or a corruption but a sort of transubstantiation, because then there would be a total annihilation of one substance and an absolute beginning of another. In fact, there would be more than a transubstantiation, since succession would affect not only the whole substance but the totality of accidents as well.

In the light of Suarezian teaching, it seems obvious that the union of matter and form engenders a *tertium quid*, that is, the composite which must always be a thing other than the sum of its constituents. Such a conclusion is meaningless in the Thomistic system, where matter and form are not conceived as entities having a positive existence by themselves. According to St. Thomas, the complete material essence is not distinct from its metaphysical parts; it is the selfsame reality of the metaphysical parts united with each other. Suarez endeavors by many arguments to show the substantial union of his matter and form. Were we to admit that this union is realized by something extrinsic to the constituents, we could not admit this to be a substantial union; such a union could not be other than accidental.

In the Suarezian discussion of the relation between substance and accidents we encounter the same difficulties. The real accidents, according to Suarez, are those which have a proper entity and a reality distinct both from substance and other accidents; in other words, he accords to accidents some sort of autonomy. Suarez claims that the distinction between substance and accident is due to the fact that the former is being *simply* and *absolutely*, whereas accident has being in a less degree and by reference to substance. If this be the only difference, being could be attributed to accident in an absolute sense and without restriction. If accidents enjoy this sort of autonomy, how can this theory account for the unity of the concrete substance? The first consequence of the Suarezian theory is this: substance thus separated in a certain way from its accidents will have to be considered as a *substratum*, since its essential characteristic will be no longer *perseity* but rather an aptitude to support its accidents. On the other hand, the unity of the composite of substance and accidents will consist in a mere unity of aggregation, that is, an *unum per accidens*.

As Suarez refuses to admit the thesis of individuation of the form by matter, so also he rejects the Thomistic theory of the individuation of accident by the subject. According to Suarez, the accident individualizes itself. From what has been said it is clear that the tendency of Suarez is to disrupt the unity of the substantial composite and to make of it an aggregate of distinct entities. He seems to be influenced by Terminism, and because of a pronounced taste for individuality he conceives as things and entities what Thomism considers merely as principles. Divided between two tendencies which he attempts to conciliate, Suarez fails to find the equilibrium which characterizes the doctrine of the Angelic Doctor, and constantly wavers between Terminism, moderate and exaggerated Realism, and Nominalism.

B. From Descartes to Immanuel Kant

We now come to an analysis and criticism of the Cartesian and Spinozan notion of substance, the Leibnizian view, the Empiricism of Locke and Hume, the Immaterialism of Malebranche and Berkeley, and the Transcendentalism of Kant. It is not without reason that Kant considers Descartes as the most outspoken modern representative of that philosophic Realism which upholds the existence of true substances accessible to human reason. In fact, the Cartesian *"Cogito, ergo sum"* (I think, therefore I am) predominates in all subsequent speculation; it is the first act and the fundamental affirmation of the realism of thought and of substantial being. The question which immediately presents itself at this point is: "What sort of entity is this object apprehended by the *cogito?"* Descartes' answer determines the course of all his teaching. "Mais qu'est-ce donc que je suis? Une chose qui pense, c'est à dire une chose qui doute, qui entend, qui conçoit, qui affirme, qui nie, qui veut, qui ne veut pas, qui imagine aussi et qui sent." (But what then am I? A thinking thing, that is to say, a thing that doubts, understands, conceives, affirms, denies, wills, refuses, imagines also, and perceives.)[1] Obviously, in the thinking subject Descartes includes all conscious processes. Moreover, the knower is a substance, as is shown from numerous passages of the Second Meditation, from the *Discourse on Method*, where he states without hesitation: "Je connus que j'étais une substance" (I

[1] *2° Medit.*, IX, 21.

thence concluded that I was a substance).[2] The
same is also corroborated by Descartes' answer to
the objections of Hobbes. Thus, the being which he
intuitively perceives in the *cogito* is a substantial
being. It may be asked: "Is this *cogito* an act of intuition or an act of inference?" The *cogito ergo
sum* is not an inference. It is, he tells us, the for-
mulation of intuition: "I myself the thinking, doubt-
ing subject exist." How is this sudden transition
from the subjective to the objective world accomplished? Descartes answers that the existence of a
substance can be manifested only by an act; for, if
one be deprived of all activity, one cannot know one-
self as a substance. Hence, it is this act of intuition
which reveals an objective reality, and in the same
act this reality becomes the object of true experience.
With the *cogito* we find ourselves in the firm abode
of Realism.

By means of this thinking process (or the
cogito) consciousness apprehends being. The notion
of being in general, according to Descartes, preëxists
vaguely to the intuition of the concrete individual,
which is myself the thinking subject. The very moment he apprehends himself in the *cogito* as a thinking substance, he knows by a "natural light" that
in order to think one must exist, since qualities cannot exist without a subject. Consequently in the
cogito, that is, in the very exercise of thought apprehending the being of the thinking substance, Descartes finds implied the general principles of knowledge: the principle of contradiction, of intelligibility,

[2] *Discourse 4ᵉ*, Part VI, 33.

of causality, and of substantiality.   It is here that
we come to realize the profound meaning of Cartesian
Realism.   After the enumeration of these principles
he proceeds to prove their objectivity.   The validity
of knowledge, he claims, depends on the rational or-
ganization of experience.   Antecedently to the establishing of the fundamental principle, "I think, therefore I am," Descartes tries to discover in this
principle the conditions which every judgment must
possess in order to be true and certain.   What is the
general criterion of truth and motive of certitude?
It is this: things which we conceive very clearly and
very distinctly are all true.   We have already seen
that Descartes discovers the universal principle of
knowledge in the incipient exercise of thought; the
cogito is not a syllogism but a form of intuition implying the common notion that in order to think one
must exist, and that qualities must have a subject of
inhesion.   The primary objects of thought are not
the principles but the objective reality apprehended
in the concrete being which is I, the thinking subject.
This thinking subject can neither be thought of nor
affirmed without simultaneously thinking of and
affirming the general principles of knowledge; it is
in the intuition of this concrete being, the thinking
subject, that the mind apprehends the general laws
of being.   The justification of these criteria consists in their immediate evidence.

We may define the Cartesian intuition as an
intellectual vision endowed with the privilege of in-
fallibility.   It has for its object simple not complex
natures, for that which is seen must necessarily be

seen whole and entire.   Among these simple natures
intuitively perceived Descartes includes expressly the
principles which are the bonds of cognition.   These
principles enjoy immediate evidence; they are im-
pressed on the mind, which by "a natural light" perceives them as evidently true.   Upon such and similar
grounds Descartes bases his philosophical Realism.

Descartes' thinking subject is a substance.
What does this mean, and what precise sense must
we attribute to the idea of substance?   The constitutive elements of the idea of substance, which Descartes received from the Scholastic teaching of La
Flèche, are the same as those of Suarez, divested only
of the subtleties of the Spanish Jesuit.   The Suarezian elements are contained in the Cartesian doctrine,
though the latter presents them in a rather ambiguous form.   In *Principles of Philosophy*, he defines
substance as follows: "By substance we can mean
nothing else than a thing which so exists that it needs
no other thing in order to exist."   Accordingly, substance in the absolute sense can be applied only to
God; on the other hand, minds and material things,
since they need coöperation of God, may be called relative or created substances.   This definition modifies
profoundly the notion of substance elaborated by the
Schoolmen.   In effect, substance in the Cartesian acceptation implies an absolute independence of being,
whereas the only independence which belongs to substance is that of an ultimate subject of inhesion.
Substance, because of the implication of the Cartesian definition, cannot be conceived as a thing which
exists in itself (*in se*) and which is opposed to acci-

dent, to whose nature it belongs to exist in something else.

In the Cartesian system Physics is joined in perennial wedlock with Mechanics. By means of extension, which constitutes the essence of bodily substances, he explains figure and movement. All the phenomena of the external world are modifications or modes of extension; all variation of matter depends on motion. From such principles it logically follows that all real distinction between substance and accident is obliterated. The attribute, as conceived by Descartes, is an inseparable quality of substance, manifesting it in its proper nature. Each substance possesses a fundamental attribute constituting its essence, whence all other properties flow so that between substance and its essential attribute there is only a logical distinction. In consequence, the whole substance of the soul consists in thought or the power of thinking, and the essence of the body consists in extension. According to this extreme dualism, mind is diametrically opposed to body, since the latter is essentially passive whereas the former is essentially active. Obviously, in the light of this doctrine the profound unity of substantial being becomes unintelligible. If the soul and body are two things mutually exclusive, how can they constitute one sole substance? Yet, in face of all difficulties Descartes inconsistently maintains the substantial union of soul and body to be an incontestable fact,[3] one of those "primitive notions" which can never be dispelled. Thus, Cartesianism, like Terminism, fails

[3] Cf. *6ᵉ Medit.*, IX, 64.

miserably to reunite things it has set apart; for in order to explain the union perceived in experience it is forced to have recourse to a multiplicity of miracles.

The negation of the real distinction between substance and accident gives rise to additional difficulties. This negation applied to spiritual substance results in nothing less than in rendering all progress impossible. In effect, according to Descartes, substantial being is determined by its specific perfections; hence, without a substantial change a spiritual substance becomes incapable of receiving an increment; walled in its own essence, it is fixed by a definite immobility. Experience, however, imposes upon us the fact of change: "Une chose qui pense est une chose qui doute, qui entend, qui conçoit, qui affirme, qui nie, qui veut, qui ne veut pas, qui imagine aussi et qui sent." (A thinking subject is a thing that doubts, understands, conceives, affirms, denies, wills, refuses, imagines also, and perceives).[4] This change cannot be explained by the modifications in the various parts of the substance, as Descartes is here concerned with a purely spiritual substance. Opposed to the permanence of the thinking subject (which is also a fact, since it is always the subject that doubts, understands, and desires), change becomes unintelligible, for permanence renders change inexplicable. In the Cartesian doctrine of a simple being devoid of parts, in which the accidents are not really distinct from substance, permanence and mutation are incom-

[4] *2° Medit.*, IX, 21.

patible; one of the two terms must necessarily be eliminated.

Moreover, the Cartesian system includes several of the contradictions resulting from subsequent speculation. In some of its theses there are germs of Idealism and at the same time germs of exaggerated Realism. For Descartes the substance of body is extension, as the substance of the soul is thought. It is an easy task to show that extension of its very nature lacks the unity which the notion of substance requires. Lachelier makes the following brilliant observation: "It is of the essence of extension to have parts outside parts; and, if it exists by itself, it cannot be anything but an aggregation or sum of its proper parts. We can, no doubt, conceive an extended thing as a unique whole by prescinding from the multiplicity of its parts, but this unity of extension is only a mental aspect having no corresponding extra-mental reality." [5] This demonstration is logically conclusive; extension is pure multiplicity. In reality, however, organic bodies, though extended, are one. If such is the case, as experience forces us to admit, this oneness of the organic body cannot be explained except by a principle distinct from extension; consequently, extension cannot be identified with the substance of a body. Similarly, thought cannot be the substance of the soul, because it is not continuous; thought also requires a unifying principle distinct from itself—a substance which is its source and cause. Rejection of this conclusion does not escape Substantialism; rather in substan-

[5] *Psychologie et Metaphysique*, pp. 128–29.

tializing accidents, such as thought and extension, it substitutes an exaggerated for a moderate Realism. It is in this extreme view that Cartesian Nominalism ends. Conceiving thought and extension as really distinct, Descartes' theory of distinctions renders them real subsistences and terminates by placing before the mind an unintelligible reality full of contradictions.

Descartes also introduces in his concept of substance another contradiction no less apparent. In the Second Meditation he endeavors to show that the substance of wax can be apprehended by the intellect only. "But what is that piece of wax which cannot be perceived except by the mind? Assuredly it is the same that I see, that I touch, that I imagine, and finally the same I have always believed it to be. Now, what should be taken into consideration here is the fact that such apperception is neither a phase of vision nor of touch nor of imagination—but only an intuition of the mind, which may be imperfect and vague, or clear and distinct." [6] This is rather a peculiar conception pretending to know the wax, or better still "this piece of wax," before it had been divested of all its properties. If, according to Descartes, bodily substance consists in extension and its accidents are not real (since they are only the mechanical modifications of matter), how can we attribute to mind alone the power of perceiving substance? If extension and all other things fall "under taste, smell, touch and hearing," [7] they should, ob-

[6] *Op. cit.,* IX, 24.
[7] *2° Medit.,* IX, 24.

viously, be known immediately by the sense. The following dilemma may be to the point: either material substance consists in extension and is wholly accessible to the senses, or it can be known only by the intellect. Accepting the latter alternative, we shall have to admit that extension, figure, and motion are properties really distinct from material substances. Descartes oscillates between these views, and the inconsistent tendencies of his thought plainly indicate that his notion of substance is opposed both to reason and experience.

The motives which prompted Descartes to identify substance with the accidents, and in consequence forced him either to relegate substance to the inanity of metaphysical entities or to substantialize phenomena, must be sought in the idea of intelligibility implied in his theory of distinctions. He divests substance of all its contingent and proper accidents, and avers that nothing remains for the mind to grasp. In this acceptation substance appears not to possess a reality of its own. In order to render it intelligible, that is, clearly and distinctly conceivable, he endeavors to make it a thing subsisting by itself or something capable of subsisting in isolation from all properties. Substance becomes thus a *substratum*, or a thing underlying other things. In this struggle Intellectualism succumbs to Empiricism. Considered in his spiritual offspring, Descartes is simultaneously the most pronounced metaphysician and the most bitter enemy of Metaphysics; erecting upon the *cogito* an edifice of Realism, he makes the same Realism untenable by his theory of substance.

Pantheism implied in Spinoza's *Ethics* is entirely a logical deduction from his definition of substance. Spinoza adopts the Cartesian definition, omitting however the restriction by which the latter distinguishes infinite from finite substance. "By substance I understand that which is in itself and is conceived through itself; in other words, that, the conception of which does not need the conception of another thing from which it must be formed." [8] Resting upon this definition, Spinoza maintains that in nature there could not be two or more substances of the same nature or attribute, "for each substance must be in itself and must be conceived through itself; that is to say, the conception of one does not involve the conception of the other." [9] Hence, he deduced that one substance cannot be produced by another substance, for if two things have nothing in common with each other, one cannot be the cause of the other. From these and other postulates he concludes that there must be but one infinite substance, namely, God. Again, God is a being absolutely infinite of whom no attribute can be denied which expresses the essence of substance; [10] and since He necessarily exists, [11] it follows that, if there were any substance besides God, it would have to be explained by some attribute, which is absolutely absurd; [12]

[8] *Ethics*, Part I, Def. III, p. 1.
[9] *Op. cit.*, p. 3.
[10] Def. 6.
[11] Prop. 11.
[12] Prop. 5.

therefore, there cannot be any substance except God. Consequently, no other substance can be conceived, for if any other could be conceived it would necessarily be conceived as existing, and this (by the first part of this demonstration) is absurd. Therefore, besides God no substance can be nor can be conceived: Q. E. D.[13] This, however, is but one aspect of Spinozism. Historically, the notion of substance developed in his *Ethics* presents itself, not as a postulate, but as a consequence of the doctrine devised for the solution of psycho-physical parallelism. We have already seen that the antithetical relation of extension to thought in the system of Descartes engenders a problem which the Cartesian principles cannot solve. Spinoza undertakes the solution of the problem. In the energetic affirmations of the substantial union of soul and body by Descartes he perceives a deplorable concession to the theory of the School, while the same doctrine becomes a puzzling enigma in the Cartesian system. In effect, the substantial conception of thought and extension renders the parallelism of soul and body absolutely incomprehensible.

Substance being self-sufficient and a closed system, it is impossible to conceive how two substances can be substantially united, especially when they are diametrically opposed as thought and extension. If thought and extension co-exist, Spinoza argues, they must be attributes of one unique substance.[14] Considered in this light, far from being mutually

13 *Op. cit.*, p. 13.
14 *Ibid.*, l. 1, Theor. X, Scholion.

exclusive, thought and extension are merely two partial aspects of the universe. Thus, the unity vainly sought by Descartes is established, and the infinite and necessary substance becomes the adequate reason of the universe. The admission of a plurality of substances, Spinoza claims, will render the science of the universe impossible, because it destroys all continuity both in the physical and psychical domain.

If, however, the modes necessarily emanate from the divine attributes, they will include the totality of the divine nature in which all is accord, harmony, and order. Thus, we shall be enabled to understand the empirical coincidence of the world of bodies and of the world of the mind. A perfect parallelism exists among the various modes of this unique substance; to each mode of an attribute corresponds a mode of the other attribute. *"Ordo rerum idem est atque ordo idearum."* True, Spinoza establishes the unity of the universe, but only by throwing overboard the veracity of experience. Notwithstanding this, we are convinced that geometry could never have been born from the simple consideration of pure space unless particular figures had been offered to sensible intuition. In the same manner it would not have been possible to deduce the whole universe from the notion of substance, unless experience had previously furnished us with particular objects. As experience is the point of departure in our knowledge, it must be included, explained, and justified in the final conclusions; experience must be the supreme arbiter of every system of thought. Among the empirical data one of the most certain and invincible is the consciousness of personality. Since particulars in the Spinozian system are nothing but modes or phenomena of the divine substance, it logically follows that the consciousness of self, the belief in our own personality and liberty, are all illusory. Obviously, here as elsewhere, Spinoza fails to render an account of our most intimate experiences.

The universe of Spinoza is the most abstract of theorems. His Divinity is a sort of metaphysical space of infinite dimensions, the modes of which compose the finite world of particulars. As from the nature of space we can deduce *a priori* all geometrical figures and all relations defining their properties, in the same manner from the divine essence we may deduce all divine attributes. This one universal and all-inclusive substance in which all qualifications are reduced to unity acts, not in pursuance of a purpose, but according to the necessity of its nature. Unquestionably in the Spinozian view a substance is nothing more than the abstract form of substantiality; the universe is neither a being nor the manifestation of being, but simply a system of algebraic symbols, a logic, and a mathematical equation. Thus, the Spinozian universe evaporates into pure Schematism; it cannot account for the facts of experience, and it is utterly incompetent to give a rational answer to the problem of personality and liberty.

The system of Spinoza abounds also in numerous paralogisms. From the notion of substance he illogically infers its necessary existence. From the fact that substance is conceived as that which exists in itself and is conceived by itself, he has no right to conclude that it must necessarily *exist*, but only that it must be *conceived* as necessarily existing. As in the ontological argument, we have here a *saltus mortalis*, namely, a transition from the logical to the real order, from essence to existence.

Again, assuming the existence of substance, Spinoza infers that this substance must be necessarily infinite because it exists *per se*. Dissenting from Spinoza also on this point, we categorically assert that there is not and cannot be any contradiction between the two concepts, "existence *per se*" and "a finite substance." A being may exist absolutely *per se* with reference to its entire intrinsic cause, although it could not exist absolutely with reference to its extrinsic cause. In other words, there is no inconsistency in maintaining that substance is simultaneously absolute and relative—absolute in so far as it exists in itself or *per se*, and relative in so far as it is a being by participation or *ab alio*. Absolute and relative are not affirmed of substance under the same respect.

Spinoza also assumed the possibility of a logical definition of substance. We maintain that the notion of substance cannot be comprehended in a logical definition, since being in general (*i.e.*, being as being) cannot be taken as a *genus*, because there is no difference outside being to divide it. Spinoza confuses substance with the Absolute. From the definition of substance he deduced that only God is substance consisting of infinite attributes. In criticism of this, we maintain that the Absolute cannot be

logically defined, since according to Spinoza himself
the Absolute is simple, and it would therefore be impossible to distinguish what constitutes the genus in
it and what constitutes the difference.

The doctrine of Spinoza here taken to task not
only arises from a false definition of substance, but
it is also inconsistent. For in the *genus* of substance
there is a highest *genus* and also other intermediate
genera, as illustrated by the Porphyrean tree. God
cannot be said to be in the genus of substance either
as the highest or as any subaltern *genus*. As to the
first point, since the highest genus is found according to its whole essence in all the *genera* down to the
lowest, it would follow that the whole essence of God
would be found in all substances and could be predicated of them. As to the second alternative, since
an intermediate *genus* adds something to the highest
or to a superior *genus* (as, for instance, the genus
"animal" adds sensation to the genus of living
things), God could not be devoid of all composition,
inasmuch as He would consist of a twofold element,
one of which would be indetermined.

It is interesting to know that St. Thomas even
anticipates and answers Spinoza's objection that God
would be necessarily limited by being defined. He
puts the objection: "What is here and not there, is
finite as to place. Therefore, what is this and not
that, is finite as to substance. But, God is this and
not that, for He is neither wood nor stone; and,
therefore, He is not infinite as to substance." He
replies: "The fact that the Being of God subsists in
itself and not in any subject, shows that His infinity

is different from all other infinities." "If whiteness
subsisted by itself, it would by that fact alone be distinct from all whitenesses existing in the subject." [15]
By His purity, the Being of God is distinct from all
other being; the individualization of the First Cause,
which is absolute Being, is by the purity of His goodness. Nor can we say that the world is outside and
by the side of God, since these expressions refer only
to conditions of space and not to dynamic relations,
for the world is in God and is upheld by Him and
filled with His presence.

Scholastics maintain that God cannot be substance in so far as substance is a category, for it
is certain that no category can belong to God. St.
Augustine sincerely repents his error in having applied categories to God. "What did all this profit
me, seeing it even hindered me, when imagining that
whatever existed was comprehended in those ten
categories, I tried so to understand, O my God, Thy
wonderful and unchangeable unity as if Thou also
had been subjected to Thine own greatness or
beauty, so that they should exist in Thee as their
subject, like as in bodies, whereas Thou Thyself are
Thy greatness and beauty?" [16]

Again, St. Augustine emphasizes the fact that
God can be called substance only abusively. "If,
however, it is fitting that God should be said to subsist. For this word is rightly applied to those
things, in which as subjects those things are, which
are said to be in a subject, as color or shape in

---

[15] *Sum. Theol.*, I, q. 7, a. 1. Cf. *de Ente et Essentia*, c. VII.
[16] *Confess.*, lib. IV, c. 16, n. 29.

body. For body subsists and so is their subject, and
they are not substances but are in a substance; and
so, if that color or shape ceases to be, it does not
deprive the body of being a body, because it is not
of the being of body that it should retain this or
that shape or color; therefore, neither changeable
nor simple things are properly called substances.
If, I say, God subsists so that He can be properly
called a substance, then there is something in Him
as it were in a subject, and He is not simple, that is,
such that to Him to be is the same as is anything
else that is said concerning Him in respect to Himself; as for instance, great, omnipotent, good, and
whatever of this kind is not unfitly said of God.
But it is an impiety to say that God subsists and
is a subject in relation to His own goodness, and
that this goodness is not a substance, or rather essence, and that God Himself is not His own goodness, but that it is in Him as is a subject; and hence
it is clear that God is improperly called substance
in order that He may be understood to be, by the
more usual name essence, which He is truly and
properly called, so that perhaps it is right that God
alone should be called essence." [17]

Substance, however, taken in an absolute sense
as denoting perfection, is applied to God. "It will
give us the key to a host of difficulties of substance.
According to it, we see that God is a substance,
though He has no accidents and does not present
within Himself the double fact of a permanent essence, modified by perpetual changes of state.

[17] *De Trin.*, lib. 7, c. 5.

Etymologically, indeed, substance suggests *substare accidentibus*, but many a word when applied to God has to give up its etymological meaning, which even as applied to creatures often presents a superficial aspect, rather than an essential nature." [18]   Of this we find beautiful illustrations in St. Augustine. "For it is the same thing with God to be (*esse*) as to subsist (*subsistere*)." [19]   "He is, however, without doubt a substance, or, if it be better so to call it, an essence.   For, as wisdom is so called from the being wise, and knowledge from knowing; so from being (*esse*) comes that which we call essence.[20]   For, as from being, He is called essence, so from subsisting we speak of substances.   But it is absurd that substance should be spoken of relatively, for everything subsists in respect to itself; how much more God!" [21]

According to Leibniz, substance must be considered from the point of view of activity, for a substance without activity would be altogether unknown, meaningless, and unthinkable.   Extension cannot be the primary quality of matter, because it is synonymous with passivity and inertia, while everything in nature is action and motion.   The essence of body must, therefore, consist in something different from extension, and this for Leibniz is impenetrability or the power of resistance.   Extension itself, being but a continuation of resistance, is a product of this force.   Accordingly, he defines substance as *an active force*.   Leibniz tells us that

[18] Rickaby, *Gen. Meta.*, p. 259.
[19] *Op. cit.*, lib. 7, c. 4.
[20] *Op. cit.*, lib. 5, c. 2.
[21] *Op. cit.*, lib. 7, c. 4.

we obtain this notion of substance by passing through the following five stages. We conceive successively (a) an *entelechy* or primitive force, or soul. Descartes' mistake, he tells us, consists exactly in the elimination of this notion so necessary for the understanding of nature. Without this notion it is impossible to explain the inertia of bodies, and we would be compelled to say that a body is in the state of rest, which is contradictory. This entelechy, however, though resembling the substantial form of the ancients, must not be identified with it on the ground that the substantial form being conceived by the Schoolmen as an act would *ipso facto* exclude all possibility of change and all contingency. An entelechy is something intermediary between action and the power of acting; it is a force which of its very nature tends to operation provided the obstacles are removed. We next conceive the (b) *first matter*, or a primitive passive power or a principle of resistance which consists not in extension but in the exigency for extension. Primary matter as a pure privation cannot subsist by itself; but being united with an entelechy, it gives rise to (c) a *monad*, which is a simple and indivisible substance, a metaphysical point. Monads are infinite in number. Since matter is pure multiplicity, it cannot be real, save by a principle of unity; and since without this unity it is only a phenomenon divisible *ad infinitum*, it must be constituted in reality by an infinite number of immaterial unities. These unities, however, must not be conceived after the atomistic fashion, which is incapable of explaining finality and order in the uni-

verse.   For the Atomist each concrete element in
the universe is isolated from all others by a vacuum;
hence, his theory cannot explain the unity of bodies
and the reality of substance.   Substance, therefore,
does not consist of pure mathematical points, which
are only abstractions of metaphysical points, that
is, of something real and active.   This monad which
is the substance of things consists in the power of
activity and passivity.   (d) *Mass* is secondary or
organic matter, which is made up of innumerable
subordinated monads.   Mass is a phenomenon because the composite is something altogether exterior
to and cannot affect the substance as such.   At the
same time this phenomenon has a foundation in the
monad, which though not constituting real extension nevertheless engenders continuity of resistance
or, what is the same, the exigency for extension.
Finally, we conceive the (e) *animal* or corporeal
substance which constitutes the unity of the monad
and dominates the machine or the mass.

By this doctrine Leibniz succeeds, indeed, in
obviating the Cartesian and atomistic difficulties, but
not without substituting new and additional ones.
In the first place, he cannot account for the reality
of extension.   For how can an indefinite series of
simple substances, such as monads, constitute a true
whole, that is, a being by itself or *per se*?   On the
other hand, if monads are but metaphysical points,
how can they engender mass?   In this situation not
only mass but the body itself would be reduced to a
phenomenon, for the obvious reason that body cannot arise from the union of inextended and simple

metaphysical points.   Finally, the element of unity appears to be lacking in this theory.

To explain the reality of the substantial composite, Leibniz gracefully introduced the new notion of a substantial nexus or *vinculum substantiale*. Were we to deny that which is superadded to monads (*i.e.*, the *vinculum substantiale*), in order to effect a substantial union, the body itself, he contends, would cease to be a substance, since it would be a mere aggregation of monads.   The result of this would be Phenomenalism.   Therefore, to explain the unity of the substantial composite we must necessarily admit the existence of a substantial or metaphysical tie inaccessible to the senses.   The Leibnizian teachings of the *vinculum substantiale* is as follows: this nexus is not a simple modification of monads, because monads are substances without it and are not changed by it; it is not the sum of modifications, since these modifications result from the primitive active and passive power of the monad; it is not the sum of the component parts, for this would be only an aggregate and not a being *per se*. Again, it must not be confused with the dominating monad (*monade dominatrice*), with which it is only logically related.   The *vinculum* consists in the primitive active and passive powers of the composite, which have been called the substantial form and matter.   Still, it is not an ideal but a real bond whereby the modifications of the composite become also its own modifications.   In its proper acceptation, the *vinculum substantiale* is therefore the substance of the composite.   It is an absolute being, because every absolute being is a substance, and every substance is an absolute being. It has a natural, though not an essential, exigency for monads, since preternaturally a monad could exist without it and vice versa. It is the common subject of the monads, thus securing for them the bond of the predicate and modifications.

Leibniz contends that his doctrine of the substantial composite is essentially the same as that of the Scholastics, except that the latter failed to recognize the monads. The addition of this new element, he reminds us, is in no way detrimental to the Scholastic system. However, in spite of these asseverations we cannot accept his views. For Aristotle and St. Thomas, substance is the "*esse in se et non in alio tamquam in subjecto,*" whereas for Leibniz substance is being endowed with activity. Leibniz obviously confuses substance with nature. His substance would be, according to the Scholastics, only a property of substance and not its formal constitutive. Again, his active force denotes only an immanent power of knowing and willing, while Schoolmen attribute to substance true action as well as reciprocal reactions. Finally, the introduction of the monads upsets the whole theory by giving rise to a new problem unknown to the ancients, the problem, namely, of the unity of the composite.

This is the principal problem confronting the Leibnizian doctrine of substance. Does his *vinculum substantiale* solve it? It seems to us that it does not, for it is impossible to conceive that the material composite could result from the association of simple parts, and the composition of substance implies relations external to its parts, such relations being inadmissible in the Leibnizian scheme. Furthermore, no addition of simple parts will ever actually constitute a continuous being.

If we regard both the monads and the *vinculum substantiale* as true substances, and this is precisely what Leibniz does, we shall have two kinds of substances, the relation and union of which require an explanation. Shall we postulate a new *vinculum*? If we do, we shall be under the tyranny of an infinite regress. Leibniz has no answer to these difficulties. Yet, in spite of these deficiencies Leibniz shows in an admirable manner that a theory of substance must transcend the order of phenomena, and must consequently be established upon metaphysical grounds. He shows also, though he failed in his other endeavors, that the unity of the composite must be sought, not in the series of phenomena accessible to the senses, but in something more real and more profound, something accessible only to the intellect. Finally, the theory of monads and the *vincula* contains under a form, ambiguous though it be, the truth of the double aspect of substance—namely, the *essence* conceived abstractedly in so far as it excludes all accidents proper to a contingent being, and the *ens in se* in so far as the individuated essence becomes realized in the world of contingency.

Bound by an uninterrupted tradition to medieval Terminism, Locke and Hume undertake a criticism of the notion of substance, which fundamentally is but an amplified echo of the doctrines of Occam and Nicholas of Autrecourt. Their principles and conclusions are practically identical, with this difference that the former systematize and push their principles to their ultimate consequences.

Locke and Hume base their system on the empirical postulate that knowledge is limited to the data of phenomenal experience. Our soul, according to Locke, is originally a clean tablet. How is knowledge attained? The answer is simple. By a double rôle of experience, that is, by sensation or experience of external sensible objects and by reflexion or internal experience. Herein we have the source of all our ideas. By induction, he says, we can prove that there is no idea in the mind that is not either of one or the other kind. From such and similar arguments Locke concludes rightly that all knowledge begins with experience, but he goes far beyond his premises in deducing that all certain cognition is strictly limited to phenomenal experience.

The same principles are embodied in Hume's *Enquiry*. There is considerable difference, he remarks, between a sensation and the memory of the same. Memory and imagination can copy sensible perceptions, but they never attain the force and vivacity of the original sensations except in illness and insanity. The most lively thought is always inferior to the most feeble sensation. Thus, by the criteria of vivacity we can distinguish two kinds of perceptions, namely, thoughts and ideas which are less and impressions which are more lively and more forcible. Hence, all knowledge begins with and is limited to sensible experience.

Locke divides ideas into simple and complex. Simple ideas are those which are furnished to the mind by internal and external sensation; complex ideas are those which result from the combination of simple ideas. In other words, the mind *receives* the former, and it *makes* the latter. Among the primary complex ideas are the ideas of substance of modes and relation. Locke's doctrine of substance is contained in the following extracts from his *Essay Concerning Human Understanding:* "Because as I said, not imagining how these simple Ideas can subsist by themselves, we accustom ourselves to suppose some Substratum, wherein they do subsist, from which they do result; which, therefore, we call Substances. The Idea then we have, to which we give the general name Substance, being nothing but the supposed, but unknown support of those qualities we find existing, which we imagine cannot subsist, *sine re substante*, without something to support them, we call that support *Substantia*." [22] With reference to soul substance he says: "The same thing happens concerning the operation of the mind, *viz.*, thinking, reasoning, fearing, etc., which we concluding not to subsist in themselves, nor apprehending how they can belong to body, or be produced by it, we are apt to think these the actions of some other substance, which we call spirit supposed (with a like ignorance of what it is) to be the substratum to those operations we experiment in ourselves within." [23] This scepticism about a doctrine which seems to be at the

[22] *Sect.* I, 2.
[23] *Ibid.*, 13, 15, 19–32.

basis of all philosophy is carried to the very limit
by David Hume in his criticism of ancient philosophy.   As Berkeley before him had done away
with the bodily substance, he does away with the
soul substance itself.   But, fortunately for us, Hume
is attacking a philosophy of which he is altogether
ignorant.   "The whole system," says he, "is entirely incomprehensible." [24]   Had Hume approached
the Peripatetic system from a less dogmatic and
prejudiced point of view, he might have discovered
in it such wonderful order, clearness, and precision
that has never been equalled or surpassed by any
subsequent system.

The Hume notion of substance is practically
the same as that of Locke, since for both substance
is primarily a kind of substratum, something unknown and invisible, which continues the same amid
all variations.   "We have, therefore, no idea of substance, distinct from that of a collection of particular
qualities, nor have we any other meaning when we
either talk or reason concerning it.   The idea of a
substance, as well as that of a mode, is nothing but
a collection of simple ideas that are united by the
imagination and have a particular name assigned to
them, by which we are able to recall, either to ourselves or to others, that collection." [25]   Again he
says: "The notion of accidents is an unavoidable
consequence of this method of thinking with regard
to substances and substantial forms.   Every quality
being a distinct thing from another, may be con-

[24] *A Treatise of Human Nature*, p. 222.
[25] *Ibid.*, p. 1, Sect. VI.

ceived to exist apart, and may exist apart, not from every other quality, but from that unintelligible chimera of a substance." [26]   The idea of substance is therefore a product of *psychological association devoid of all objective value*. Hume also resolves mind into a series of mental states or an aggregate of perceptions. "Mind," he states, "is nothing but a heap or collection of different perceptions united together by certain relations and supposed, though falsely, to be endowed with simplicity and identity." [27] It is evident that here we have preceptions without a mind.

This rather brief exposition of the empirical doctrine clearly shows that the source of difficulties engendered by the notion of substance is due to the essentially atomistic conception of an inert unchangeable *substratum*, wherein qualities or accidents are in some way glued together, as garments which adhere to the body or as a picture which covers the surface of an object. Such conception of substance has been and is still falsely attributed to the Schoolmen. Naturally, this view leads to the rejection of substance itself, for everything that is distinct, according to Hume and Locke, may be conceived as being capable of separate existence, but we have no distinct idea of a *substratum* without qualities.

Obviously the Scholastic definition of substance as *ens in se et per se* does not of itself and in its abstract form imply the notion of activity, but this

[26] *Ibid.*, Part IV, Sect. III.
[27] *Ibid.*, p. 207.

static order is that of the concept and not of the
concrete substance.   Concrete substance is active, inasmuch as it is never apprehended without accidents.
In other words, we mentally distinguish between substance, nature, and essence.   In the real order every
substance is simultaneously essence and nature, that
is to say, affected by a proper individual and specific
dynamism.   "The terms substance, essence, nature,
severally denote the same object, but connote more
especially different features.   Substance points to
the general fact of existence *per se;* essence points
to the reality of which the being is constituted;
nature signifies the essence as principle of activity." [28]

On the other hand, *permanence* is not of the
essence of substance any more than *succession* or
non-permanence of accidents is of their nature.   According to Hume, we cannot think of a succession
of phenomena except under the form of persistence
of an object in time; hence, he infers that permanence of the constituted object is the only formal
basis of substance.   Such an erroneous conception
may be traced to naïve Realism,[29] of which Empiricism is but a consequence.   Though we readily
ascribe to substance a *relative* stability, in the sense
that it can survive the disappearance of one or more
accidents, still duration is not essential to its definition; whereas the accident, being an *ens entis*, must

[28] Maher, *Psych.*, p. 559.
[29] According to naïve Realism, the world is reflected in
consciousness as in a mirror.   Our minds faithfully and ac-
curately reflect things just as they are outside of us, in a
merely passive way.

necessarily cease to exist with the cessation of the substance it modifies. A substance would have been a substance though its duration had been but for an instant.

To conceive substance as a thing which subsists without accidents, is to render it unintelligible. In nature only individual substantial beings endowed with divers properties and activities exist. Isolated from these modifications, substance would be reduced to the mere concept of essence, for that which is conceivable without accidents is not substance but essence or a pure abstraction. Still, this abstraction is founded in reality, of which it expresses an aspect. Only concrete substantial being has real existence. Though accidents and properties do not enter into the abstract definition of substance, they must nevertheless form part of its concrete existence and description. A substantial composite, in so far as it denotes an individuated essence, is by nature inseparable from its accidents; therefore, it can neither be conceived nor *a fortiori* imagined without them. There is, however, a real distinction between them. But this distinction implies simply that the concrete individual, remaining essentially what it is, is capable of receiving new modifications; it is not the concrete reality but the essence or abstract substance which is immune from change. Hence, the opposition between permanence and non-permanence which Empiricism and atomistic philosophy are unable to solve is simply fictitious. There is nothing immutable in contingent substance; whenever accidents undergo change (and change is perennial), it is the

whole substance together with the accidents that undergoes mutation within the boundaries of the essence by which it is circumscribed. Of course, we
may speak of the *permanence of substance*, provided
we have reference not to concrete substance but to
the essence which defines it.

If this were not so, if change concealed an absolutely permanent *substratum*, generation and corruption would be impossible and unexplainable, because from a mere phenomenal change nothing warrants us to infer a substantial change. In conclusion, there is nothing more repugnant to the genuine
notion of substance than to conceive it as the permanent *substratum* isolated from its phenomenal manifestations. In the investigation of the nature of
reality experience must be our guide. But every
man experiences the consciousness of his own substantial reality and of his personal identity. Consciousness clearly testifies that we are the *subjects*
of our acts; it also manifests that all these acts converge to and emanate from the same principle,
namely, the soul which becomes actually conscious of
itself in its operations and activities.

It might furthermore be stated that Hume in
many places surreptitiously introduces *in fact* what
he denies *in words*—a mind substance, or something
which is supposed to fulfill its functions. In the
Treatise of Human Nature he says: "It will always
be impossible to decide with certainty, whether they
—the impressions—arise immediately from the object, or are produced by the creative power of the
mind, or are derived from the author of our

being." [30] "Upon the whole, necessity is something
that exists in the mind, not in the objects." [31] "Impressions are naturally the most vivid perceptions
of the mind." [32] "The mind falls so easily from the
one perception to the other that it scarce perceives
the change." [33] "We may pronounce any quality of
the mind virtuous which causes love or pride." [34]
"It being almost impossible for the mind to change
its character in any considerable article, etc. . . ." [35]
Pondering over such statements as these, one might
ask: "What right has Hume to speak of bodies and
of mind, of states of mind if there are no bodies,
if mind does not exist, if we can have perceptions
without mind?" Simultaneously we might ask the
vast number of modern psychologists and philosophers who have blindly accepted the basic tenets of
Hume in rejecting the notion of substance, why do
they make use of such antediluvian terms as "I,"
"we," "us," etc., if perceptions alone are and we
are not.

The logical order of events brings us now to
the Immaterialism of Malebranche and Berkeley.
The former begins with the problem of the communication of substances, which was left unsolved
by Descartes. If matter and mind are diametrically
opposed, substantial union, Malebranche says, is
simply incomprehensible; ideas cannot produce mo-

[30] P. 208.
[31] P. 165.
[32] P. 208.
[33] P. 208.
[34] P. 575.
[35] P. 608.

tion, nor can motion produce ideas. It is, therefore, a contradiction in terms to admit the blending of such irreducible substances as soul and body. He endeavors to solve the problem by supposing that the modifications of soul and body are reciprocal in consequence of a general law established by God. Accordingly, "soul and body proceed together like two independent clocks that keep the same time because, whenever the hands of one move, God moves the hands of the other correspondingly. On the occasion of some organic process, God produces in the mind the corresponding conscious process, and on occasion of some volition God produces in the organism the corresponding change." [36]

Assuming the principle that the exercise of efficiency is the exclusive prerogative of the Deity, Malebranche denies all activity to matter and goes near to making the soul inactive. To the question, "Whence come our ideas?" he answers that it is God Himself who produces them. In Him we see all things, and the things we see are ideas, not the extended material objects themselves. Obviously, in this theory the material world becomes a *terra incognita*. If the idea of extension exists only in God, it cannot prove the existence of the corporeal world. However, Malebranche believes in such a world because revelation establishes its existence.

Berkeley takes for his starting point the Lockian notion of substance which has been reduced to geometrical extension or to a permanent *substratum* of changeable phenomena. Secondary

[36] Dubray, *Introductory Philosophy*, p. 483.

qualities (such as odor, color, sound, etc.) are, according to Locke, purely mental phenomena devoid of objective existence; whereas primary qualities (such as extension, figure, movement, etc.), which constitute material substance, exist objectively without the mind.   Berkeley rejects this notion of substance.   It is illogical, he says, to distinguish between primary and secondary qualities so far as their objective value is concerned, since it is impossible to conceive extension and motion of a body without all other sensible qualities.   The so-called primary qualities are no more objective than secondary qualities. I get the ideas of extension and solidity through the sense of touch; hence, they are sensations of my mind also.   Thus, all the qualities of matter, primary as well as secondary, resolve themselves into mind-dependent phenomena.   *Esse est percipi.*   "It is said," Berkeley continues, "extension is a mode or accident of Matter, and that Matter is the *substratum* that supports it.   Now, I desire that you would explain to me what is meant by Matter's *supporting* extension.   Say you: 'I have no idea of Matter and therefore cannot explain it.'   I answer, though you have no positive, yet, you must be supposed to know what relation it bears to accidents, and what is meant by supporting them.   It is evident *support* cannot be taken in its usual or literal sense. . . .   In what sense, therefore, must it be taken?" [37]   Thus, matter being unimaginable and unthinkable becomes a veritable locus of contradictions.   We are limited so far as matter is concerned

[37] *Principles*, 1, 16.

to the states of consciousness; we cannot compare
our ideas with these material substances; we do not
know that they are, nor do we know what they are.
The consequences of the Berkeleyan postulates are
clear and logical. There are no material substances,
and even if they existed we would be absolutely incapable of knowing them. Everything having been
reduced to a system of ideas becomes mind-dependent, for an idea can be like nothing but an idea.
Nevertheless, the world is real, "and the things perceived by sense may be termed *external* with regard
to their origin, in that they are not generated from
within by the mind itself, but imprinted by a Spirit
distinct from that which perceives them. Sensible
objects may likewise be said to be 'without the mind'
in another sense, namely, when they exist in some
other mind. . . ." [38]

Berkeley's criticism, based as it is entirely on
the empirical conception of substance, does not in
any way affect the Scholastic doctrine of substance;
his attacks are misdirected. On the other hand, it
is a severe blow to the Cartesian theory. And indeed if geometrical extension is identified with matter, it must pervade the entire phenomenal order;
but there is nothing in the nature of extension that
would make it a being *in se*. If matter subsisted
by itself, Berkeley contends, it would be absolutely
unthinkable and unknowable, for the mind could
not apprehend a reality of an entirely different
nature. Only the mental, the spiritual, or what is
analogous to it, is accessible to the mind. But mat-

[38] *Principles*, I, 91.

ter or pure multiplicity is intrinsically contrary to
the nature of the mind; to apprehend matter, mind
would have to be transformed into some sort of multiplicity and be diffused into spatial externality, which
is contradictory.   Thus, by a strange paradox
Idealism is engendered by an exaggerated Realism.

As for Locke and Hume, the basic problem for
Kant is that of the possibility and value of metaphysical knowledge.   The solutions of this problem
are widely different.   On the one hand, Locke brings
us into the very vestibule of Idealism.   Hume, on
the other, drives the mind to Scepticism, and finally
Kant proposes a *via media* between these two extremes.   Both Hume and Locke end in denying the
objective value of the idea of substance, because they
try to derive it from experience.   Kant, on the other
hand, reëstablishes this idea by assigning to it a
place among his categories of the understanding.
The notion of substance, he says, cannot be derived
through the perception of a bundle of qualities.   For
a bundle of qualities is not substance.   And since we
cannot think of anything without this notion, we
conceive of a cluster of qualities apprehended in intuition to be substances.   As experience, however,
furnishes us only aggregations of qualities, it logically follows that the idea of substance cannot have
an objective but only a logical value for us.   Hence,
substance is for the understanding only a pure form
whereby we rationally organize the manifold of our
experience.   The noumenon or the thing in itself,
he claims, is unknown and unknowable.

Kant accordingly makes a desperate attempt to

prove the truth of his contentions from the fact that the metaphysical concepts of the self, of the world, and of God imply all sorts of contradictions or antinomies.

Rational Psychology, Kant says, is the science of the soul. It is based on the following dialectics: the soul conceived as an ultimate subject of all psychic activities is regarded as *substance; this substance*, taken simply as an object of the internal sense, gives us the concept of *immateriality;* its simplicity implies the idea of *incorruptibility;* the perception of its *numerical identity* gives us the concept of *personality.* Hence the following conclusion: an immaterial, incorruptible, and personal substance is a spiritual substance and consequently immortal.

The above line of reasoning is, according to Kant, vitiated by four paralogisms. The arguments which consider the soul as substance are the causes of the remaining three. Kant endeavors to show that this paralogism is contained in the following argument: "That the representation of which is the absolute subject of our judgments, and cannot be used therefore as the determination of any other thing, is the *substance.* I, as a thinking being, am the absolute subject of all my possible judgments, and this representation of myself can never be used as the predicate of any other thing. Therefore I, as a thinking being (soul), am *substance.*" [39] This reasoning, Kant observes, is evidently fallacious, as the word substance is taken in two different mean-

[39] *Critique of Pure Reason,* p. 284.

ings. In the major, "the concept of substance is a purely intellectual concept which, without the conditions of sensuous intuition, admits of a transcendental use only; hence, it is vain and useless. In the minor, however, we refer the same concept to the object of all internal experience, though without having previously established the condition of its application *in concreto*." [40] What then becomes psychologically of the notion *ego substance* upon which all rational Psychology is based? It is reduced to simple representation empty of all content, a representation of the I of which we cannot even say that it is a concept but merely a consciousness which concomitates all our concepts. "By this *I*, or *he*, or *it* (the thing) which thinks, nothing is represented beyond a transcendental subject of thoughts—an X which is known only through the thoughts that are its predicates, apart from them we can never have the slightest concept." [41] It is the logical not the real substance which the mind grasps. "Reason imposes upon us an apparent knowledge only by representing the constant logical subject of thought as the knowledge of the real subject in which that knowledge inheres; of that (*i.e.*, the real) subject, however, we have not and cannot have the slightest knowledge. Besides this logical meaning of the I, we have no knowledge of the subject in itself; the proposition that a soul is a substance signifies a substance in idea only, and not in reality." [42]

[40] *Op. cit.*, p. 325.
[41] *Op. cit.*, p. 282.
[42] *Op. cit.*, p. 285.

Rational Cosmology, which infers the existence of external or material substances, is just as fallacious as rational Psychology, because we have no intuition of pure substances prescinded from the phenomena which are supposed to manifest them. Moreover, we can prove, Kant continues, that the affirmations of rational Cosmology imply antinomies which show plainly the inanity of metaphysical speculation. The principal antinomy is pointed out in the following thesis and antithesis: *Thesis:* Every compound substance consists of simple parts, and nothing exists anywhere but the simple or what is composed of it. In effect, if all composition is suppressed in thought, there would be no substance at all, which is absurd. *Antithesis:* No compound thing in the world consists of simple parts, and there exists nowhere anything simple. Hence, it follows that all external relations, and consequently all composition, are possible only in space; the number of parts of the compound is equal to the number of parts of space occupied by the substantial compound. Space is indefinitely divisible; that is, not one of its parts is simple. It follows that no part of material substance can be absolutely simple. Therefore, nothing simple exists in the world.

From these and other arguments Kant concludes that all metaphysical affirmations are sophistical. The idea of substance for him is but an *a priori* condition of knowledge, which enables us to think of permanence of phenomena in time, and which renders all determination of time possible. Kant bases his proof on the so-called synthetic *a priori*

judgments. Only such are of scientific value.
Analytic as well as synthetic judgments, he claims,
are useless for scientific purposes: the former, because they are purely tautologous or, in other words,
because the attribute is already contained in the
notion of the subject and extracted therefrom; the
latter, because the nexus between the subject and
predicate is not universal and necessary. This is
due to the fact that particular synthetic judgments
are derived from experience, and nothing which is
universal and necessary can come from experience.
On the contrary, in such judgments as these,
"Everything that begins to be must have a cause"
or "Between two points the straight line is the short-
est," the subject is bound to a predicate which is
in no way contained in its notion. It is not the intuition which renders the synthesis of the subject
and predicate possible, since experience is always of
the particular, whereas the above judgments are universal and necessary. Such judgments, therefore,
are simultaneously synthetic and *a priori*. How are
such judgments possible? They result, Kant explains, from the application of the *a priori* forms
of the understanding to the sensibility given us in
experience; and from the fact that by means of these
judgments we organize the manifold of experience it
follows that we also introduce order and regularity
in the phenomena which constitute nature.

Kantian doctrine may be criticized from a twofold point of view. We may either attack the principles upon which it is grounded, namely, the so-
called synthetic *a priori* judgments, or show directly

that the antinomies or the contradictions of pure reason are only illusory and pseudo-contradictions.

In our criticism we shall confine ourselves to the former in view of the fact that synthetic *a priori* judgments constitute the corner-stone of his system. In his *Critique*, Kant repeatedly states that apart from sensible intuition there is no objective knowledge, and that a concept which is not immediately and wholly derived from sensible intuition must be held to be *a priori*. According to this principle, the substance of the soul as well as of the external bodies is never given in experience or sense intuition. Therefore, Kant concludes, the notion of substance must be exclusively the product of the understanding, namely, an empty *a priori* form. In these postulates, Kant takes for granted exactly what is in question, namely, that there is no intellectual intuition, and that all knowledge is either derived from sensible intuition or that it is exclusively produced by the understanding. This assumption, upon which the entire *Critique* rests, is for Kant a *postulate* of an absolute certitude, though he has never made an attempt to justify it.

This postulate is based on a theory of knowledge in which sensibility and understanding are not only two distinct faculties, but are moreover separated and unrelated. Thus, Kant cannot explain how sensation and the objects of sensations conform themselves to the *a priori* forms of the understanding. These two distinct sources of representation must somehow be harmonized by Kant, as their union is an empirical fact. Even in the absence of all justification, Kant is forced to postulate this harmony of sensibility and understanding. His whole edifice rests upon it, and without it neither experience nor thought would be possible. The *petitio principii* is here but too evident. Such are the results of Cartesianism and Empiricism; Descartes bequeathed to his successors the insoluble problem of the communication of substances, the latter made sensibility the only source of objective knowledge.

The true explanation of this important point is contained in the Scholastic axiom, *"Nihil est in intellectu quin prius fuerit in sensu."* By this the Scholastics simply claim that the intellect, though immaterial, is united to a body and to sensible faculties, hence, intellectual knowledge cannot be exercised without images or sensible representations. However, it is absolutely unwarranted to infer from this axiom that the senses are the total and adequate cause of cognition. On the contrary, sensible images become actually intelligible only in virtue of the active intellect which by its abstractive power prescinds them from their individualizing conditions. In this operation the intellect apprehends in things exactly what the senses cannot apprehend, namely, their essence.

What we wish to emphasize here is the persistent empirical criticism of the notion of substance inherent in the Kantian theory. To show the inconsistency of the notion of substance, Kant suggests that the whole procedure is the work of the imagination, consisting in divesting a thing given in experience of all its attributes and then concluding that nothing remains. If substance be a thing which by hypothesis has been deprived of all properties, Kant is more logical than Descartes in concluding that substance is but an *a priori* form devoid of all empirical content. Undoubtedly, substance divested of all its accidents would pass into the domain of the abstractions.

Our criticisms directed against the empiricists and idealists apply also to Kant. The paralogisms alluded to in this "Transcendental Dialectic" are paralogisms only from the point of view of the Kantian *Critique*, which rests on postulates absolutely devoid of foundation. Kant does not offer a single element in the criticism of the notion of substance. However, Kant pushes the Cartesian and empirical principles to their ultimate conclusions.

C. From Kant to Our Own Day [43]

It is both strange and interesting that during the year 1927 a volume of almost two hundred pages, in seven lectures dealing exclusively with the "problem of Substance," [44] should have come to light from the University of California Press. Such an event must be looked upon as extraordinary in our age and country, implying as it does a revival and examination of a doctrine supposedly of the Dark Ages and tolerated only *"patientia Dei et stultitia hominum."* After all, has not Lady Substance al-

[43] This section is a reproduction and expansion of two articles by the author which appeared in *New Scholasticism*, Vol. II, pp. 115-127, 236-249 (1928).

[44] *University of California Publications in Philosophy*, Vol. IX (1927).

ready performed her office; has she not blossomed, flourished, and prospered in her own day, and finally undergone a natural death? Dead and buried, her eternal sleep should not be disturbed; it should rather be respected and revered. What, then, could have led men of science to visit this forgotten tomb, to uncover its remains, to dig up and analyze its fossilized bones? It would be little short of a crime to suspect modern men of scientific culture of any base and unworthy motive in this matter, or to impute such a task to abnormal or sadistic tendencies. A more noble and worthy ideal must be assigned to this undertaking. It may be that, as post-mortem examinations are carried out whenever suspicion of some dark crime surrounds the demise of a person, our investigators also were prompted by similar motives of justice. They might have thought that substance after all did not die a natural death. For the story of her life shows only too well the intense hatred with which she has been pursued by her implacable enemies, envious of her fame, her splendor, and her undisputed power. It was to be expected that she should have been maligned or misrepresented by such antagonists as Descartes and Locke. Thus humbled and shorn of her splendor, it was supposed that Berkeley deprived her of one half her patrimony and Hume of the other half, leaving her an outcast and a destitute dying of starvation. Lastly the end came. Kant performed the last sad rites, and her tomb was sealed!

Happily, however, it never occurred to the gladiators of modern thought that the remains of their supposed victim were not genuine, that they were instead the relics of a fake and worthless substitute! For it was not the real and genuine Substance that has been exhumed, analyzed, and weighed in the balance of scientific thought in the year 1927, but only its poor and base substitute. And now we may ask: "What are the results of this extraordinary process? Has Substance been reinstated in her rightful place? Has justice been done by this new tribunal?" Our answer is *no*. This modern jury has again denied to Substance her rights; her possessions are declared worthless. And why? The answer is simple enough. The jury failed to deal with her real problem.

The results of this recent symposium on substance are best described by Professor Muirhead, one of the contributors to this volume, as follows:

"When the subject was proposed for consideration, I confess that I had some apprehension on this score. I feared that the end of it, as at the end of some other more material banquets, there might not be much left of the bill of fare. Substance and therewith any problem anent it, might prove to have largely disappeared. Some of the contributors still permit us to hold to the existence of substance, but deny that we can have any knowledge of its nature; others hold that even its existence is questionable, and must be taken at best as a great 'as if'; others deny even this, and would relegate the whole idea to the museum of philosophical antiquities. Only one voice seems to have been raised for substance, the whole substance and nothing but the substance. But even he, as I understand him, has confined himself mainly to the field of

sense perception, and went far in the direction of
asserting the existence of something in the end unknowable that lay behind it, as the substance of substance" (p. 174).

The question of substance is the chief problem
of these lectures; and since this is discussed in the
light of Logic, Epistemology, and Metaphysics, it
obviously implies all the abstruse difficulties of these
branches of knowledge. In this short discussion, a
detailed account and criticism of the various views
cannot be expected; for such a task perhaps several
large volumes would be required. Our purpose and
aim, therefore, will be centered around the metaphysical problem of substance; its logical and epistemological aspects shall merely be alluded to. After
a brief summary of the fundamental views contained
in the lectures, we shall by way of contrast and
criticism advance and defend the Scholastic teaching on the following points: first, the scientific value
of Metaphysics against those who regard Metaphysics as a conjecture, hypothesis, or guesswork;
secondly, an analysis of the Scholastic concept of
substance; thirdly, its objective existence directed
against those who are loud in denying it; and lastly,
its knowability.

After these preliminary remarks let us enter
upon our task. "Subject and Substance," by
J. Loewenberg, is the first topic of the symposium
under review. Owing to the loose and ambiguous
usage of the terms in question, Professor Loewenberg sets out to crystallize them by means of a
thorough analysis. Accordingly, the term "subject"

is considered from a logical, epistemological, and metaphysical point of view. Hence, he says, "the subject of a proposition may be everything and anything without restriction or modification; the very term 'nothing' is not excluded by the generous and democratic logical use of the subject." [45]   Epistemologically, "subject" is a knower, but not everything is a knower. Against Mr. Alexander's doctrine of the universality of the cognitive relation he emphasizes the uniqueness of the cognitive situation. "The peculiarity of the situation consists in the fact that the subject of knowledge is not merely together with it, but is aware of this togetherness." [46]   Hence, "everything under the sun may, indeed, be a logical subject, but only a certain kind of thing, the thing capable of awareness, can be an epistemological subject." [47]   So far we are in perfect agreement with Dr. Loewenberg.

With the question, in what does the reality of the knower consist, the metaphysical issue is introduced. To this two answers are given: according to philosophic Naturalism, "nature is the substance of all that is"; according to the Metaphysics of mind, "there is nothing ultimately real save the self."

"Substance, too, has its logical, epistemological and metaphysical uses," [48] and the nature of relation between substance and subject is made dependent upon whether the former signifies a *category*, a *thing*, or *self-existence*. As category, "substance

45 P. 4.
46 P. 5.
47 P. 6.
48 P. 9.

may be said to be a formal instrument of discourse applicable to anything and everything." [49]   Definite limitations, however, are imposed upon substance as an epistemological concept.   According to this view, "a thing is a substance when only specific characters are conjoined in a specific way." [50]   Again, things "owe their substantiality to the fact that properties, though universal, are concretely never found save in various concatenations." [51]   At the metaphysical level, the Spinozean concept of substance is compared with that of Santayana, with the result that "in either case it (substance) is the *underlying* reality which asserts itself in all things, and can be known only through its manifestations, none of which can define or exhaust it." [52]   Since self-existence is the ultimate criterion of substantiality, Professor Loewenberg concludes that we know its existence but not its essence.   The Kantian noumena are also included under the metaphysical interpretation of substance.

The relations between the logical subject and the categorical use of substance are summarized as follows: "Like subject, substance is elastic in application, but differs from the former in being preeminently an existential category.   At the epistemological level, subject (or knower) and substance (or thing) cannot be assimilated to each other, but must be viewed as the different partners in the interplay

[49] P. 10.
[50] P. 11.
[51] P. 12.
[52] P. 13.

of which consists the situation called knowing." [53]
At the metaphysical level, however, subject and substance are engaged in a vital warfare, where "one
must somehow swallow the other." This is the
struggle between Realism and Idealism, implying in
Dr. Loewenberg's words the denial or the affirmation of the supremacy of the mind, since, "for realism, mind has a reality which is derivative and not
pivotal; for idealism, it possesses a primary and
central reality." In his view, substance is the *lion*
of the situation. Metaphysically, substance is "a
name for the *absolute* ground of things, for the
reality *underlying* whatever appearances or manifestations we may anywhere discern." [54] In this
notion of substance Dr. Loewenberg seems to discover the basic argument for the Realism of science,
inasmuch as "the mind is a manifestation of something else, and not everything else a manifestation of
substance . . .; reality is independent of its being
known, because substance is prior to its appearances." Of course, "it is not *unqualifiedly* true that
reality is independent of knowledge; for being
known, for example, objects actually or ideally depend upon subjects capable of knowing them. The
important thing is, not independence of whatever is
'accidental,' and not independence in the sense of
freedom from relations, but independence in the
sense of exemplifying a particular kind of relation,
the relation of priority." [55] Unfortunately, however,

[53] P. 16.
[54] P. 23.
[55] P. 24.

this Realism of science does not rest upon solid foundations, for "the substance of science may, for all we know, be the accidents of a deeper reality," [56] which at the present stage of knowledge the human mind cannot fathom. Perplexed by this apparently insurmountable difficulty, Professor Loewenberg concludes with Locke, though for different reasons, that "the intrinsic nature of substance is unknown, and that of substance we can only say that it is, and not what it is." [57] This profession of faith is again and again emphatically reiterated. "Substance is always with us. We revolt against its mysterious nature. We hope and plot to enter into its inner citadel. This is our privilege as knowers." [58] And again: "What is problematic is the essence of substance, not its existence. The appearances that impel our minds to look in that direction cannot serve as knowable signs of the essence of substance." [59] At this juncture, what is said of substance applies also to the metaphysical subject. Here we have obviously the central theme of Dr. Loewenberg's thesis.

Leaving minor details aside, we shall elsewhere take issue with Dr. Loewenberg on two points—first, as regards the definition of substance, and second, as regards its knowability.

"The Logical Substantive" by D. W. Prall is the topic of the second lecture. According to the previous account the term substance has been analyzed from its logical, epistemological, and meta-

[56] P. 24.
[57] P. 25.
[58] P. 29.
[59] P. 30.

physical aspects; the analysis here made is on the first or lowest of these levels. "My point," he says, "is to indicate from logical theory itself the necessity for discourse to include the substantive as one of its essentials." [60]   The analysis and function of the logical substantive proper show the following results: "That the logical theory requires the category of substantive proper, the meaning of reference or application, over and above the meaning of content; that the enunciation of propositions about the world depends on the functioning of this category; that the elementary processes of demonstrative inference assume it; and that probable inductive inference obviously demands it and rests upon it. Thus, logic requires the specific function of the substantive, and this function is simply *the designation of items, the pointing to reality, the reference to the world about which we pretend to speak and hope to know.*" [61] The tenor of these last words clearly indicates the skeptical attitude of the author concerning the knowability of reality. That such is his attitude, Professor Prall does not hesitate to emphasize. He says: "Our whole logical analysis indicates that we never even refer to the real as such; . . . we can never demonstratively know anything to be really true at all." [62]   And again: "We must admit that we are in a position not to know substance as it is. . . . What we call knowledge is natural faith, inadequate and incorrect in exactly the measure in which it is really

[60] P. 42.
[61] P. 55. Italics mine.
[62] P. 57.

applied freshly to the world and is not merely habitual response or usual representative ideas." [63]   It is really strange that, in spite "of this inadequacy and incorrectness of knowledge," Professor Prall's belief in substance should remain unshaken. To give up our reliance on the substantive as indicating substance would seem to be abandoning man's greatest philosophical achievement; "and if we are to rely upon such knowledge as science offers, we should in all candor admit our faith in substance, though this faith be warranted not by demonstrative reason, nor by reason at all for that matter, but grounded in a natural instinctive trust." [64]   It does not take great intellectual acumen to perceive the many inconsistencies involved in the foregoing statements, but perhaps this may be pardonable for one who indulges in mere guesses, and who claims that Metaphysics is faith and that it may be developed also into poetry and religion.

In the third article of the series "Substance and Substantive," A. S. Murphy undertakes to destroy the elaborate work of the two previous lectures. In these articles, "metaphysical" substance has been defined and its existence accepted, though on faith only. In Professor Murphy's view, there neither is nor can be anything answering to the above definition. Hence, the problem of substance must be included among "those issues which are insoluble, because they rest upon false and arbitrary assumptions." [65]   For

63 Pp. 58-9.
64 P. 59.
65 P. 65.

metaphysical substance, which is the most bankrupt of entities, he substitutes the notion of substantive with its correlatives, adjective and relation. While his contempt for the absolute knows no bounds, he worships before the shrine of the relative. The idol substantive is described as "that of which characters are predicated, but which is not itself predicated of anything further." [66] Next he points out very logically the confusion resulting from the fallacy of bifurcation which is committed by the absolutists. "To bifurcate reality is to separate off some aspect which in fact is relative, and to treat it as though it were absolute." [67] He shows that, while disaster follows bifurcation, this can be avoided on a strictly relativistic view.

According to Mr. Pepper's lecture on the "Fiction of Attribution," we live in a qualitative world, the textures of qualities being ontologically ultimate.

Next we come to Dr. Dennes who, in his paper on "Primary Substance," takes up the defense of that Aristotelian view of substance which is held by the "ordinary man." The Aristotelian doctrine is condensed in the words of Professor Ross thus: "The substance is the whole thing, including the qualities, relations, etc. . . . . . It implies qualities, but these are not something outside it, which it needs in addition to itself. A quality, on the other hand, needs supplementation by a substance if it is to exist. Ob-

[66] P. 66.
[67] P. 68.

viously, if this is the meaning, Aristotle must be thinking of substance as the individual thing." [68]

The basic argument for the existence of substance in Dr. Dennes' view rests on direct experience, for "every quality is concretely experienced as a quality of an occurring and existing individual, whether perceived or imagined." [69] From the fact that the category of substance has such a solid basis in experience, he concludes that it is not and cannot be deduced *a priori*. So convinced is he of the value of this direct experience that he does not personally attach any great weight to the ontological argument, which may be stated as follows: if accidents or attributes exist, there must also be substances in which they inhere and of which they are attributes. "As far as *reason* goes, it seems to me quite satisfactory to suppose that they are attributes of something not themselves." [70]

As a predicate, substance has this peculiarity, that "it is applicable to every individual occurrent, whereas the application of all other predicates is limited. Every existent that occurs is substance or a substance, but not every existent is red or sweet or square." After thus proving the existence of substance and distinguishing it from its predicative function, Dr. Dennes challenges the thesis "that there is contradiction in calling substance self-existent and yet knowably qualified. To say that a thing could not be without qualities, and could not be

68 P. 130.
69 P. 135.
70 P. 131.

itself without its own determinate qualities, certainly does not deny its self-existence, if its qualities are a genuine part or phase of itself. It can hardly be meant, then, that qualification as such is incompatible with self-existence—that all determination is sheer negation, that *being what it is* negates the being of substance." [71] Not only that, but in union with Aristotle and Hegel he maintains that substances could not exist without having a determined nature, and that only qualified or modified substances can become objects of our knowledge. That we have some knowledge of substance, however partial and inadequate this knowledge may be, seems to be beyond doubt; for "to assert that perception and categorical knowing falsify things known is to assert the complete inaptitude of all knowledge and to throw the assertion itself under suspicion." [72] Therefore, it cannot be denied that known qualities are the qualities of substance, though we are willing to admit that our knowledge of the nature of substance is imperfect, partial, and incomplete. "If this were not so, our experience would supply us with no basis whatever either for the assertion, or for the ontological inference, of self-existent substance. And since all that we know and think begins with experience, we should consequently have to abandon *all* metaphysical conceptions at once." [73]

The problem of the plurality of substance is taken up with special diffidence, though it appears

[71] P. 138.
[72] P. 139.
[73] P. 141.

that such a conclusion is unavoidable. For once we admit the fact that substance could not exist except as something determined and particular, and once we make a real distinction between the knowing subject and the object known, it obviously follows that sub-stance is not one but many. If this were not so, "we should be able to achieve no utterly intelligible ex-planation of the experienced existence and otherness of things, of the fact of their changing accidents, and of the fact of their coming to be and passing away." [74]

As we have already remarked, our purpose here is devoted almost exclusively to the problem of meta-physical substance. At this juncture, however, we are confronted by a very learned analysis of "Physi-cal Substance" by V. F. Lenzen. It is with regret that we have to pass over this excellent dissertation as being outside the scope of this chapter. With re-gard to the knowability of ontological substance Mr. Lenzen's attitude is out-and-out skeptical.

In the last paper of the series on "The Self and Substance," Professor Muirhead, in agreement with Dr. Dennes, admits both the reality and the know-ability of substance. The threefold division of the lecture contains, first, his own view of the true idea and place of substance; next, the application of this view to the self; and lastly, the chief issue of the problem, namely, the knowability of substance. After an open admission of the manifoldness and hierarchy of substances, Professor Muirhead feels justified in "distinguishing what might be called

[74] P. 147.

formal substance (the substantiality which a thing possesses, if not in any strict sense 'on its own right,' yet in virtue of being a concrete whole or unity of differences) and its material or essential substantiality; *i.e.*, the degrees in which it reflects the character of the whole." [75] This he does with the view of excluding any merely pluralistic and any merely monistic interpretation of the world. This definition is applied to the self as follows: "Wherever we have anything that we call a self (and this holds of it at all the levels at which the word may be applied: the organized body, the psychical matter of feeling habits, etc., the rational will), we have *in the first place* something corresponding to what I have called formal substantiality, particular activities pervaded by some unity of principle both in their simultaneous and their successive exercise; and *in the second place* a certain degree, as compared with other substances, of the inclusiveness which I have called essential substantiality." [76]

Though placing the self on a higher plane than other beings, this description does not differentiate the substantiality of selves from the substantiality of other things. The essential difference consists in the fact that the self is conscious, in virtue of which it becomes something transcendent and obtains the power of self-projection. Here again he finds himself "between the apparent Scylla and Charybdis of one-sided Pluralism that seeks to establish the substantiality of the soul on the basis of its independence

[75] P. 181.
[76] P. 188.

and self-containedness and a Monism that leaves no room for anything but an adjectival existence for it." [77] He tries to get beyond both in this manner: "With one we shall agree that the self is or at any rate may become a substance both in the formal and in the essential sense. We shall only deny that there can be any talk of independence, self-subsistence, and self-containedness. With the other we shall agree that the self, as we know it, is a finite and partial embodiment of something that transcends it. But again we shall deny that there can be any talk of its mere adjectivalness; in so far as it is self-unifying it is self-substantializing, and we cannot rob it of its substantiality without robbing it of its selfhood." [78] Concerning the third point, or the knowability of substance, more shall be said later on.

I hope that in this brief summary I have been fortunate enough to present the essential features of the learned "guesses" of these lectures. The utterance of such an epithet here might seem rash, arrogant, and derogatory, indeed, but that such is not the case will clearly appear upon further consideration.

In the first place, we find some of the contributors themselves branding their own opinions and those of their colleagues as "guesses"; while others voice in no ambiguous terms their skeptical attitude as regards everything metaphysical; hence, the "guesses" in problematic and hypothetical results.

In addition to what has already been said the

[77] P. 189.
[78] Pp. 191-2.

following excerpts will corroborate our contention. Dr. Loewenberg is of the opinion that "the characterization of substance as problematic involves a vindication of all the different types of metaphysical generalizations, to each of which may belong a measure of truth. But what is truth? Is truth merely human? Are there degrees of truth? And on what basis may we accord to one metaphysical theory more truth than to another?" [79] According to Professor Prall "metaphysics is faith and it may be developed also into poetry and religion." [80] Mr. Lenzen concludes his lecture in the following words: "Rational knowledge is founded upon measurement, and the method of measurement leaves an insoluble residue as a basis of skepticism in metaphysics." [81] The same trend of thought pervades even more emphatically the pages of Professors Murphy and Pepper. These skeptical views are obviously the natural offsprings of Positivism and Kantian philosophy, which have rejected Metaphysics as vain in its object and erroneous in its conclusions. What other results, except "guesses," could be expected from such principles? Our purpose, however, is not to criticize these systems but simply to make some remarks on the scientifiic value of Metaphysics.

Metaphysics is generally defined by the Scholastics as the philosophical science of things that are *negatively* or *positively* immaterial. This is the inquiry into the ultimate nature of being. It is also

[79] P. 32.
[80] P. 60.
[81] P. 170.

called the science of being as being and of the highest determinations of being—in other words, the science of the first principles. Its aim obviously is the completion, unification, and systematization of sciences. As natural and empirical sciences deal with the proximate and immediate causes of phenomena, so Metaphysics deals with the ultimate and remote causes, principles, and determinations of things. Particular sciences give the general laws for the various groups of phenomena, whereas Metaphysics endeavors to bring the manifold sciences to unity and so to engender order.

Although the etymological acceptation of the term denotes a science which comes after and is above Physics, Metaphysics must not be understood as being purely evolved without a basis in reality from the depths of our inner consciousness, as the spider spins its web out of itself. Rather it is a study of reality and an endeavor to penetrate to the very core of reality. It considers the same objects as considered by other sciences, but from a higher and different point of view. Metaphysics is accordingly the most abstract and the highest expression of experience. In Scholasticism we achieve a complete synthesis of knowledge by reducing the particular sciences under the fundamental ontological laws—such as causation, sufficient reason, substantiality, etc. Only Metaphysics, for instance, can critically establish the objective value of the principle of causality, which is employed in other sciences but tested by none. Hence the dictum: no Metaphysics without Physics and no Physics without Metaphysics. In the light of

Scholastic philosophy, the relation between Metaphysics and the natural sciences may be compared to the relation of soul and body in man. It is rightly stated that sciences without Metaphysics are like a body without a soul, and Metaphysics without sciences is like a soul without a body. In order that we may have an adequate and complete system of the universe both are required. It may be observed here that the Metaphysics of the *philosophia perennis* rests on the solid rock of the theory of moderate Realism, the only true theory of knowledge which vindicates the validity of both sensory and intellectual cognition.

That we are naturally led by intellectual curiosity to inquire into the ultimate causes—into the why and the whence, the what and the whither of things—no one will seriously doubt. Doctrine must answer these questions; true philosophy must show and explain to us the origin, the nature, and destiny of cosmic things. Of course, all sciences do not reach so far. They teach us, for instance, the particular laws of motion or of some other natural phenomena, but they do not make known to us the general laws, the first principles of things and their final end. This is the privilege of Metaphysics, a privilege as far above all particular sciences as the universal is above the individual.

This Metaphysics which for centuries ruled as queen of sciences, and before whose throne were seen prostrate the greatest minds, has in modern times met powerful adversaries who, jealous of her power, are disputing her primacy and trying to deprive her of her most precious jewel—that is, scientific value. In this matricidal struggle Positivism, Phenomenalism, Relativism, and their allies have been vainly wasting their efforts and time worthy of a nobler use. Though differing on practically all points of doctrine, these modern philosophical heresies agree perfectly among themselves on one sole point—in waging a continuous war against the queen of sciences, denying not only her supremacy but even a dark corner in the republic of sciences. Why is this?

The basic principle of the contemporary heresiarchs of thought denies the possibility of metaphysical knowledge. According to them, experience is the only criterion of true cognition; only knowledge acquired by internal and external experience is possible and scientific. "We cannot go beyond facts and the laws of facts," is the universal cry. Away then with the suprasensible, the intellectual, the metaphysical!

Does such an attitude find even a shadow of justification? We are of the opinion that there cannot be even a possibility of justification. Does not experience deal exclusively with the particular *this* or *that*? How can *this* and *that* explain itself without transcending itself? Obviously, any interpretation of experience must of necessity go beyond the immediate data given in experience. Hence, willynilly, we are forced into the domain of Metaphysics and the metempirical whenever we attempt an interpretation of experience. Thus, Positivism and Phenomenalism are not entitled even to talk about the laws of facts, for in doing so they actually transcend the factual and the empirical.

Indeed, we live in a world rich in facts, but these facts must be analyzed, correlated, classified, and synthesized. However, these laborious operations cannot be carried on successfully without the metaphysical means of abstraction and generalization, for whatever intelligibility is found in positive science is derived from the application of ontological principles. The same may be said about the process of classification and subordination of sciences.

As experience is concerned only with the concrete and the particular, so science must deal with the general and universal. The object of all metaphysical speculation is the universal nature. Therefore, a philosophy such as Positivism and Phenomenalism, which rejects all metempirical knowledge, is vain and erroneous, because it not only cannot reach its objects but must even abandon all attempt at expressing the laws of facts; it must confine itself strictly to *this* and *that*. From the above remarks it follows that, if the general notions of Ontology are invalid, no notion of the particular and concrete can be valid, for the fate of the particular is indissolubly bound up with the fate of the general. Thus, we are justified in concluding that, if Metaphysics is not a real branch of knowledge, no other science can be real, since the latter must be based on the ontological principles of contradiction, sufficient reason, and causality.

We come now to what in our opinion is the crucial point of the problem, namely, the analysis

of the idea of substance.   In reference to the ontological notion of substance, we believe that Dr.
Loewenberg derived his concept of substance from
Spinoza, which same view is entertained by some of
the others.   As in Spinoza, his thesis rests or falls
with the definition of substance.   In approaching our
contention we wish to say that, whatever good reasons
we may have for the existence of an absolute ground
of things, we do not know it either by sense or intellectual intuition, and that it is upon our knowledge
of the world, the world we experience here and now,
that we must build our philosophical edifice.

This pluralistic world of ours consists of a collection of individual substances which, although related to other beings, are complete in themselves in
the sense that we can think of them as independent
of any other individual.   The most ordinary observation upon the objects of our experience shows that
these individual substances are endowed with various
accidental modifications, such as color, size, figure,
hardness, extension, etc., which do not exist by themselves and independently but have their being in
another.   Hence the Scholastic division of contingent
reality into substance and accident.   This brings us
to the Thomistic doctrine of substance.

Although substance is distinguished from accident, to which it is opposed in that it has its *esse
per se* or *in se* and not *in alio*, nevertheless substance
cannot really be said to be a being *in se* or *per se*,
but rather "an essence or thing to the nature of which
it is due that it should not exist in a subject."[82]

[82] *Quodlib.*, 9, a. 5, ad. a.

Aquinas frequently noted, and forcefully inculcated, the fact that in case substance should be regarded as being *per se,* this being could be conceived as genus. For if substance be regarded as being *per se,* then, inasmuch as being is opposed to accident, in that case substance and accident would be referred to being as species to their genus, and being would be divided into being *per se* and being *in alio.* "To exist *per se,*" St. Thomas notes, "is not the definition of substance, because thereby its quiddity is not indicated." [83] The note (characteristic) *per se* or *in se* whereby the essence of substance is distinguished from accident (to the nature of which it is due that it should exist in a subject), must be taken not positively but by way of negation, namely, in such a manner as to deny that the *esse* substance should have a subject of inhesion. This suggests that the nature of substance is essentially negative. But that this is not really so may be shown as follows.

The nature of contradictory notions must refer to an identical reality, so that what one of them affirms, the other denies, and vice versa. But concerning being, which is the principle of the categories, only not-being can be denied, for the reason that being is the first notion of the intellect, is derived from no other notion, and is the source of all other concepts. Thus, Aquinas properly remarks: "Being is the first intellectual concept: hence, to being nothing can be opposed by way of contrariety or privation, but only by way of negation; for, as being is not based in any other notion, so also its opposite,

[83] *Ibid.,* I, 8, a. 5.

for contradictories refer to the same thing." [84]   Now, that which is essentially denied in the definition of substance is inherence (*i.e.*, to be in another as in a subject of inhesion). But the notion of inherence is itself negative; for that which inheres in another, as in its subject, has its being not through itself but through the subject of inhesion. The notion of inhesion contains in itself the negation of subsistence, namely, the *in se*. As a consequence, what is essentially denied in the definition of substance is negation. Negation of negation, to use the Scholastic phraseology, is affirmation; for instance, if one denies that an animal is irrational, he simultaneously affirms that it is a rational animal. Therefore, the notion of substance is as a matter of fact positive, not negative.

But if the concept of substance does not properly include negation, negation is, however, included in the manner whereby we understand and denominate it. The proportioned objects of the intellect are material things. Since material things have for constitutive principle the essence and the accidents which inhere in the constituted essence, the intellect reflecting upon objects first perceives the accidents as being more known, and then, perceiving that accidents cannot exist apart from a subject, the mind infers that there must be something as the subject in which accidents inhere and which does not itself inhere in another. This something, or *hoc aliquid*, which is apprehended as the subject of accidents, is named essence in the category of sub-

[84] *In Lib. I Sent.*, Dist. 19, q. 5, ad ult.

stance. If substance is perceived by way of negation, it is necessary that it should be named negatively; and, indeed, since words or terms are immediate signs of our concepts and only mediately signs of things we cannot depict, things as these are not in themselves but only in the manner in which we apprehend them.

Substance, then, may be considered either logically, in so far as it is the first mode by which the *esse* is understood to belong to the essence, or ontologically, inasmuch as it is the ultimate perfection of essence. "In the definition of substance there is no *ens per se*. For, from the fact that it is described as a being, it cannot be a genus; since it has already been proved that being does not contain the conditions of a genus. And again, from the fact that it is described as being *per se*, because this seems to implicate only negation, since it is said to be a *per se* being through not being in another (*in alio*), which is pure negation. And this cannot satisfy the conditions of a genus; for then a genus would not express what a thing is, but rather what it is not. Substance, then, must be understood as that to the nature of which it is fitting not to be in a subject." [86]

But the Angelic Doctor himself frequently asserted that this definition of substance is not a strict definition but rather a description, on the ground that it is impossible to define substance strictly and logically; for, if substance should be logically defined, the essence would constitute its genus, and the *non esse in alio* its difference. This cannot be the

[86] *Cont. Gent.,* I, c. 25.

esse, because essence which is determined into categories considered in itself is nothing else but a general and abstract notion of being. Such a being, as we have previously demonstrated, cannot be a genus. Moreover, the concept of difference is not actually contained in the genus. But the concept of the *non esse in alio* is not outside the concept of essence, for the concept of essence denotes here a concept of the most widely abstract being. If this concept were really outside the concept of essence, it would follow that it would denote merely not-being. Therefore, the *non esse in alio* which is placed in the category of substance cannot be the *differentia.* St. Thomas writes: "We must conclude that this definition cannot be of substance, substance being that which is not *in alio*; for being is not genus, the negation is not, does not posit, anything in the subject." [87] This being granted, we must hold that substance does not admit a strict definition but only an exposition or description.

As the Spinozan doctrine of substance plays such an important part in the first two lectures, it becomes imperative here to review the definitions of substance formulated by Spinoza. We find him basing his philosophy, after the manner of geometricians, upon definitions and axioms, defining substance as follows: ʏ"By substance, I understand, that which is in itself and is conceived through itself; in other words, that, the conception of which does not need the conception of another thing from which it

[87] *In Lib. Sent.,* Dist. 8, a.2, 4.

must be formed." [88]   Hence, he deduced that one substance cannot be produced by another substance, for, if two things have nothing in common with each other, one cannot be the cause of the other.   From these and other postulates he concluded that there must be only one infinite substance, namely, God.

It is obvious that, in his concept of substance, Spinoza first failed to distinguish the essence from the existence (*i.e.*, from the mode whereby essence exists in the category of substance) ; and secondly, he did not accept the phrases *in se* and *per se* as denoting merely non-inherence in another subject, but in such way as to exclude every notion of any efficient causality distinct from the being of substance itself. This being the case, substance, in Spinoza's view, is said to exist and to be conceived *per se*, not, however, on the ground of not having its being in another subject but on the ground that it has its being *ex se*. Failing to distinguish the essence of substance from the mode of its existence, he maintained that substance is a self-determining cause, thus including existence in itself; hence, he logically deduced therefrom the existence of one infinite substance, God, in whom essence and existence are identical.

But it is not difficult to see how Spinoza corrupted the notion of substance.   In the first place, Spinoza accepted the possibility of a strict or logical definition of substance.   And, indeed, there cannot be a shadow of doubt that Spinoza accepted his definition of substance in a strict and logical sense. Following the geometric method, he explained the

[88] *Ethics,* Part I, Def. III.

notion of substance, together with other definitions
and axioms, in the beginning of his *Ethics*; in like
manner he also drew from them certain propositions
and corollaries.

The Scholastic view, on the other hand, maintains that the notion of substance cannot be comprehended in a logical definition, since being in general
(*i.e.*, being as being), as it was proved, cannot be
taken as genus for the single reason that there is no
difference outside being to divide it.

Moreover, Spinoza confuses substance with the
Absolute; and consequently, since from the definition
of substance he deduced that only God is substance
consisting of infinite attributes, it would clearly follow that the Absolute cannot be logically defined,
for, according to Spinoza himself, the Absolute is
simple. It would, therefore, be impossible to distinguish what constitutes genus in Him and what constitutes *differentia*.[89]

In considering the Thomistic doctrine of substance we feel justified at the risk of repetition in
recalling the more salient points discussed in previous
chapters. As substance is composed of two elements—namely of essence and of a mode of being
(*esse*) not *in another*—it will be worth while for the
elucidation of its notion for us to consider it in relation both of the essence to the being, and also of the
being to the essence. If we consider substance inasmuch as its being is related to the essence, its chief
characteristic consists in not having its being in
another, as its subject; for when *to be not in another*

----

[89] For further criticism see pages 104-107.

is added to the essence, we thereby denote that the essence which *of itself* is indifferent (whether to have being in another or not have being in another) is contracted or determined to that sort of being which is not in another. If, on the other hand, substance be considered inasmuch as the essence is related to the being (*esse*), its essential characteristic will consist in being the subject of accidents.

And indeed, when the essence is confined to the being, to whose nature it belongs *to be not in another*, it becomes opposed to the essence, to whose nature it belongs to be *in another*. But this other cannot be anything else but substance. For, if this other were not substance, it would be accident, since between substance and accident there is no medium, and since every accident requires ultimately a substance in which it may inhere; otherwise we would have to admit a process *ad infinitum*, which is absurd. Therefore, from the very fact that the essence is determined through its non-being in another, it becomes the subject of accidents. As we have already explained in discussing the two elements of which substance is composed, the essence to whose nature it belongs to be not in another is called substance. Regarding the first of these elements, the essence, inasmuch as it is determined through its being not in another, is less in extension than essence from the absolute point of view; or, as Scholastics would say, it is referred to essence in general as the lower is related to the higher. But the lower in the series of those things which are predicated stands under the higher. But the essence which is determined through its not being in another is precisely what we mean by substance.

As to the second of these elements, the essence, to whose nature it belongs to be not in another, is the subject of accidents because it receives these into its own being. But the essence in which the accidents inhere is understood to be *under* the accidents, or the subject of the accidents. Therefore, the essence which is determined by its being not in another, and also from the fact that it is the subject of accidents, vindicates to itself the name of substance. Hence, the essence, to whose nature it belongs to be not in another, is called substance, both because it is a special determination of the essence absolutely taken, and also because it is the subject of accidents. Essence considered in the first sense is also called subsistence from the fact that it has its being *in se* and not in another; hence, it is said to subsist.

Although this characteristic of substance, as a special category, is due not only to the fact that it has being not in another but also to the fact that it is the subject of accidents, the notion of substance consists essentially in the fact that it is an essence to whose nature it belongs to be not in another. This can be corroborated by many arguments, the most important being the following. In the first place, the notion of a thing should properly be placed in that by which the thing is constituted; but substance, as we have previously remarked, is constituted not because it is the subject of accidents but because of its having its being not in another. Moreover, the notion of substance undoubtedly consists

in that which differentiates it from the accident, inasmuch as it is opposed to the accident through the
first division of being.   But the differentiation of
substance from accident results from the fact, not
that it is the subject of accidents, but that it has its
being *in se* and not in another.

Again, some collaborators in the symposium are
inclined to regard substance as a permanent subject
of changes or something which, amid all variations,
continues unchanged.   Against this view we advance
the following arguments.

The characteristics of permanence and mutability are not the first two modes of determination of
a contingent entity.   As a matter of fact, we cannot
understand the permanence or invariability of a being without first understanding the *inseity* of such a
being.   On the other hand, the changeableness and
variability of a being cannot be understood without
first understanding its characteristic of *inaleity*.
Therefore, even if permanence and mutability were
the modes into which being is divided by means of
categories, these two modes would undoubtedly not be
substance and accident, inasmuch as the two modes
into which being, the principle of the categories, is
contracted are rather *inseity* and *inaleity*.

Furthermore, permanence and mutability are
not the mode of being denoted by the term category,
for the reason that predicaments are those modes
of being whereby contingent being is determined.
But immutability and variability do not denote the
peculiar modes of such determination, since they of
their own nature require a being already constituted

and determined. It follows, then, that permanence and mutability are so far from being the first two categories that they cannot even be included in their number. Finally, it is beyond doubt that the notions of substance and accident consist exactly in those notes by which they are differentiated. But substance is not distinguished from accident because it is subject to change, nor is the accident distinct from substance because the latter is permanent and invariable. As a matter of fact, some accidents, especially those which flow from the essence of a thing, may also possess such characteristics. In conclusion, we repeat once more that the nature of substance consists in *inseity* and not in permanence under successive changes.

So far we have been concerned with Dr. Loewenberg and others who admit the reality of substance, although their conceptions of it are rather arbitrary, erroneous, or inadequate. We have analyzed and examined these notions and, to the best of our ability, pointed out their weak points. We have done this without neglecting our chief thesis, which is to vindicate the clearness, completeness, and reasonableness of the Scholastic doctrine. Our task, however, is still unaccomplished. Here we find ourselves confronted by Professors Murphy and Pepper who, although in perpetual disagreement between themselves, invariably agree in denying the objectivity of substance, regarding it as something useless, inert, and superfluous. For these thinkers such concepts as being, unity, goodness, truth, potentiality, actual cause, etc., have no meaning, for the

simple reason that all our knowledge must be limited
to observation and experimentation; hence the impossibility of supra-sensuous knowledge.   These errors
might well be traced to epistemological sources and
discussed from that point of view.   However, it will
be sufficient for our purposes to show that, although
their criticisms are well directed against the Spinozan concept of substance adopted by Dr. Loewenberg and Professor Prall, yet these criticisms in no
way affect the Scholastic doctrine.   To refute the
contentions of Professors Murphy and Pepper and
to make the Thomistic doctrine on this point still
more explicit, it will be sufficient to restate the arguments against Hume and Locke.

Obviously, the Scholastic definition of substance
as *ens in se et per se* does not of itself and in its abstract form imply the notion of activity, but this
static order is that of the concept and not of the
concrete substance.   Concrete substance is active, inasmuch as it is never apprehended without accidents.
In other words, we mentally distinguish between substance, nature, and essence.   In the real order every
substance is simultaneously essence and nature, that
is to say, affected by a proper individual and specific
dynamism.

On the other hand, *permanence* is not of the essence of substance any more than *succession* or *non-
permanence* of accidents is of their nature.   According to Hume, we cannot think of a succession of
phenomena except under the form of persistence of
an object in time; hence, he infers that permanence
of the constituted object is the only formal basis of

substance. Such an erroneous conception may be traced to naïve Realism, of which Empiricism is but a consequence. Though we readily ascribe to substance a *relative* stability in the sense that it can survive the disappearance of one or more accidents, still duration is not essential to its definition; whereas the accident, being an *ens entis*, must necessarily cease to exist with the cessation of the substance it modifies. A substance would have been a substance though its duration had been but for an instant.

To conceive substance as a thing which subsists without accidents, is to render it unintelligible. In nature only individual substantial beings endowed with divers properties and activities exist. Isolated from these modifications substance would be reduced to the mere concept of essence, for that which is conceivable without accidents is not substance but essence or a pure abstraction. Still, this abstraction is founded in reality, of which it expresses an aspect. Only concrete substantial being has real existence. Though accidents and properties do not enter into the abstract definition of substance, they must nevertheless form part of its concrete existence and description. A substantial composite, in so far as it denotes an individual essence, is by nature inseparable from its accidents; therefore, it can neither be conceived nor *a fortiori* imagined without them. There is, however, a real distinction between them. But this distinction implies simply that the concrete individual, remaining essentially what it is, is capable of receiving new modifications; it is not the concrete reality but the essence or abstract substance which is immune from change. Hence, the opposition between permanence and non-permanence which Empiricism and atomistic philosophy are unable to solve is simply fictitious. There is nothing immutable in contingent substance; whenever accidents undergo change—and change is perennial—it is the whole substance together with the accidents that undergoes mutation within the boundaries of the essence by which it is circumscribed. Of course, we may speak of the *permanence of substance* provided we have reference not to concrete substance but to the essence which defines it.

If this were not so, if change concealed an absolutely permanent substratum, generation and corruption would be impossible and unexplainable, because from a mere phenomenal change nothing warrants us to infer a substantial change. In conclusion, there is nothing more repugnant to the genuine notion of substance than to conceive of it as the permanent *substratum* isolated from its phenomenal manifestations. In the investigation of the nature of reality experience must be our guide. But every man experiences the consciousness of his own substantial reality and of his personal identity. Consciousness clearly testifies that we are the *subjects* of our acts; it also manifests that all these acts converge to and emanate from the same principle, namely, the soul which becomes actually conscious of itself in its operations and activities.

The objectivity of substance and its knowability has been energetically defended by Professors Dennes and Muirhead. For a more detailed account of these problems we refer the reader to the sixth chapter of this book. It is enough here to say that Scholastics do not claim that our knowledge of substance is adequate or complete. But, as Dr. Dennes remarks, "the fact that we have no complete knowledge of the nature of substance hardly allows the inference that qualities manifest in our experience do not reveal the character of substance at all." [90] And again: "To assert that perception and categorical knowing falsify things known is to assert the complete inaptitude of all knowledge and to throw the assertion itself under suspicion." [91] According to the Scholastic principle *operari sequitur esse* (acting follows being), it would follow that a substance without qualities or activity would be altogether unknowable, meaningless, and unthinkable.

The wise maxim of the Roman sage has been admirably applied to substance by Dr. Muirhead: "Cast out the idea of substance with your epistemological fork, it will ever recur."

Before closing this chapter mention must be made of two recent views on this subject. In unison with virtually all modern thinkers, Eddington directs his attacks on the reality of substance. "Physicists," he says, "have chased the solid substance from the continuous liquid to the atom, from the atom to the electron, and there they have lost it." [92] And again: "Substance belongs to our everyday world, because the mind put it there; it is a fancy projected by the

[90] *Op. cit.*, p. 139.
[91] P. 139.
[92] *The Nature of the Physical World*, p. 318.

mind into the external world." [93]   Jeans speaks in
the same tenor: "Science gives us no knowledge of
the real essence of substance. We have no knowledge
of substance. Everything is reduced to mathematical fomulæ; hence, the universe is somehow mathematics. For substantiality is purely a mental concept measuring the direct effect on our sense of
touch." [94]   We may observe in this regard that it is
not necessary to give up the philosophical idea of
substance, even if we accept the kinetic theory of
gases which are reduced to an aggregation of
material points.

Moreover, we do not hesitate to say fearlessly
that Eddington, Jeans, and the host of modern
thinkers take part, unintentionally perhaps, in the
conspiracy against truth. They attack a notion
without studying its true meaning, and accept for
cash value the phenomenalistic tenets of Hume. No
wonder that they take refuge in Idealism. For the
objectivity of substance once eliminated, the reality
of accidents *ipso facto* disappears. *Cessante causa
cessat effectus* (The cause ceasing, the effect ceases).
It seems to us that the rejection of substance is not
the result of Idealism, but rather that Idealism is the
result of this rejection. Many scientists will admit
that phenomena must have a cause. But all kinds of
phenomena or accidents which obviously cannot exist
in themselves postulate an adequate cause for their
mode of existence; this cause cannot be other than
substance. It is not necessary to reproduce here all

93 *Ibid.,* p. 318.
94 *The Mysterious Universe,* p. 138.

the arguments advanced by the Scholastics for the objectivity of substance. The reality of substance is a natural and objective inference from sense perception. Only one blinded by Sensism, by Empiricism, or by Skepticism will deny the objective value of this important notion. In a word, the malignant attitude of modern thinkers on this point may be best described in the words of the poet: "*Hoc volo, sic jubeo, stat pro ratione voluntas*" (Thus I wish, thus I command, be my will sufficient reason).[95]

[95] Juvenal, *Sat.*, 4.

CHAPTER VIII

THE CATEGORY OF QUANTITY

Quantity First of the Nine Genera of Accidents.—Controversy on This Point.—Essence of Quantity.—Critical Analysis of Various Views.—Divisibility the Ontological Essence of Quantity.—Measurability the Logical Essence of Quantity.—Elucidation and Proof of These Doctrines.—Division of Quantity into Discrete and Continuous.—This Division as Specific.—Fundamental Characteristics of Quantity.

∴

THE SIXTH CHAPTER OF this book was devoted to the explanation of the nature and objectivity of accident in general. Before passing on to the problem of this chapter, it may be well to note that there are various kinds of accidents due to the various principles according to which something is said to belong to another. This gives rise to the various modes of inherence. This question has been stated by St. Thomas in these words: "We must consider that in each of the nine genera of accidents there are two points for remark. One is the nature belonging to each one of them considered as an accident, which applies to each of them as inherent in a subject, for the essence of an accident is to inhere. The other point of remark is the proper nature of each one of these genera." [1]

[1] *Sum. Theol.*, I-II, q. 28, a. 2, c.

The problem before us is which of these nine genera of accidents should be considered first. At the outset, it is important to keep in mind that, as our knowledge originates in sense experience and finds its completion in the intellect, we must study the categories as they exist in material natures and are objects of sense perception before investigating their immaterial essences. In the first place, it is plain that the various genera of accidents result from the various modes by which their essence is determined in the existential order. Secondly, it is also apparent that our mind by abstraction elaborates the notion of the categories from the contemplation of sensible realities. Finally, it is clear that the first category, substance, being inaccessible to the senses is the last one to be attained by means of abstraction. From this it can be readily seen that quantity and quality are the first two categories in the class of accidents. Since quantity is related to matter and quality to substantial form, they are in a more intimate contact with substance than the remaining accidents. This is due to the fact that matter and form constitute the essence of bodily substances. But what is closer to the substance of a thing is last in the order of knowledge. Consequently, quantity and quality are prior to other categories in the line of accidents. We have taken this argument from St. Thomas who says: "Any accident is so much prior to others, according as its accidental form is in closer contact with the substance."

The question whether quantity is prior to quality or vice versa, was debated amongst the ancients.

The author of the work on categories was of the opinion that quality is prior to quantity, because it is related to substantial form which is the principle of specification. This formal principle, being the source of all the qualities and perfections of the substance, must in his view be prior and nobler than the material principle which is the source of quantity.[2] Aristotle, on the other hand, seems to have held the contrary opinion, for he discussed quantity immediately after substance.[3] It is not our purpose to investigate which is the nobler, but which is the source of the others. Although substantial form (being the source of qualities) is nobler than prime matter (whose basic property is quantity), in the order of nature the latter is prior to the former. Matter must exist before the form is added to it, nor can it be conceived how, in the generation of things, a form could precede matter. Wherefore, whether we consider things themselves or the manner in which we apprehend them, we shall always perceive that the category of quantity is prior to that of quality. This opinion, widely held by the ancients, was also accepted by Albertus Magnus, Aquinas, and other doctors of the Middle Ages.[4]

Making this last view our own in the exposition of categories, we shall treat of quantity, asking at the outset in what its notion consists. This question divided the Scholastic camp into various groups, each claiming St. Thomas on its side. Many held that

---

[2] *Apud Simplicium.* In Road's *Aristot. Comm.*

[3] *Categoriæ,* c. 6, p. 92 ff.

[4] St. Thomas, *In Lib. IV Sent.,* dist. 12, q. 1. Also Alb. M., *Lib. de præd.,* tract. 3, c. 1.

the essence of quantity consists in the extension of parts. To obtain a clear grasp of this doctrine, we must keep in mind that there is a twofold extension of parts: an extension *in ordine ad se,* or intrinsic, and another, *in ordine ad locum,* or extrinsic. By the first or intrinsic extension is meant the entitative existence of the part outside (or better, distinct from) part; for example, in man the head, neck, or shoulders are distinct from each other and the other parts of the body, without however having any reference to the place in which these parts are extended. By the second or extrinsic extension is meant the position of parts outside parts in space; for instance, when we say that the head occupies the highest part of space, the shoulders the middle part, and the feet the lowest part. Now, many scholars both of the Thomist (such as Goudinius)[5] and of the Scotist school (such as Boyvinius)[6] maintained that intrinsic extension constitutes the essence of quantity, and appealed to their masters as having taught the same. Another group held the opinion that the essence of quantity should be really placed in measurability, or in that whereby substance can be measured. Others, finally, thought that this essence consisted in divisibility. Capreolus maintained that this was the genuine doctrine of St. Thomas.[7]

As far as modern philosophers are concerned, we shall pass over the opinion of those who, following in the footsteps of Leibniz, Boschovich, and

[5] *Log. mai.,* pars I, q. 3, art. 1, concl., pp. 285 sqq.

[6] *Log.,* part. I, disp. 2, sect. 2, pp. 230 sqq.

[7] *In Lib. II Sent.,* dist. 19, q. 1, ad 2.

Kant, have denied real quantity to bodily substances, and have attributed to them only phenomenal or apparent quantity. These views are the logical inference from the various doctrines these philosophers taught concerning the essence of bodies. However, we must take into special consideration the opinion of Descartes and his followers. According to these philosophers bodies are made up of atoms or extended corpuscles. They not only ascribed real quantity to these atoms, but even maintained that the essence of quantity consisted in the extension of parts outside parts in space.

Our task shall be to defend a view which in our opinion best harmonizes with that of the Angelic Doctor. We contend that the essence of the category of quantity, if regarded from an ontological point of view, consists in divisibility; if however it be regarded from a logical viewpoint, its essence consists in the capacity of being measured or measurability. Before taking up the defense of our contention we shall subject to criticism the various opinions which were already mentioned.

In the first place, it is not probable that the notion of quantity consists in the intrinsic extension of parts (*in ordine ad se*). To have a clear understanding of this, it is well to bear in mind that the plurality of parts in the material substance is neither *actually* there, nor that it can be conceived without division. Although extended substance is made up of many *quanta*, parts as parts are not actually therein, there being but one continuous extension under which parts are potentially contained. The parts out of which the extended substance is composed are essentially the same (*as* many *quanta*), but they are so conjoined and united that no distinction remains amongst them. Consequently, their union simply constitutes a *quantum* or *continuum*, in which the entity of all these parts is contained. Hence, it appears that the parts of quantity, if their essence be considered, do *actually* exist in quantity, inasmuch as they constitute the essence of quantity; but, if they be regarded as parts, they are not *actually* but only *potentially* in quantity, inasmuch as quantity is capable of division, and because it is only through division that parts are distinguished from one another. While we cannot think of quantity as extended without conceiving many extraposited parts actually inherent and conjoined in it, this phenomenon must be ascribed to the fault of our imagination; for reason cannot compel us to think that there are *actually* many parts as parts in quantity.

If in the material substance there should be many parts *actually* distinct, its quantity would not be a real *whole* but only a whole of aggregation. For, if the parts of quantity which are *actually* distinct one from another were so many distinct quantities, it would follow that quantity would be made up of the aggregation of many quantities. But the quantity of any substance can be but one, as St. Bonaventure says: "It is impossible that there should be in the same subject two accidents of the same species, because an accident receives its number through the subject in which it inheres." [8]   It

[8] *In Lib. II Sent.*, XIII, a. 3, q. 2.

is, therefore, repugnant that there should *actually* be many parts in a material substance.   Moreover, the parts, one of which is actually outside the other, are *contiguous* because parts outside parts cannot be conceived forming a whole otherwise than by mutual contact of one with the other.   But from contiguous parts, not a *continuum* (whole) but only a contiguous whole can be effected. Therefore, to say that in quantity there are *actually* many parts is to confuse the contiguous with the continuum. As a consequence, it must be admitted that the multitude or plurality of parts in quantity of a material substance is found therein not *actually* but only *potentially.*

From what has been said it may easily be inferred that the multitude of parts in quantity cannot actually exist, except through the division of quantity.   "Division," Aquinas remarks, "causes multitude, because those things which are in no wise distinct are one." [9]   But the distinction through quantity, as everyone will admit, cannot be effected otherwise than by the division of the same quantity.   Consequently, a multitude of parts cannot actually exist in quantity unless quantity be divided. Hence, Aquinas again says: "All plurality follows division." [10]   Since the actual multitude of parts cannot exist without division of quantity, it follows that we could not even understand the potential multitude of parts without apprehending the fact that quantity is capable of being divided into parts. For, as potency and act are correlative notions, the es-

[9] *Qq. dispp., De Pot.,* q. 9, a. 7, c.
[10] *Sum. Theol.,* I, q. 30, a. 3, c.

sence of potency must be proportioned to the essence of the act.

Such being the case, it can be concluded logically that the essence or formal reason of quantity cannot consist in the intrinsic extension of parts (*in ordine ad se*). This intrinsic extension of parts distinct from part denotes the potential multitude of parts, because quantity, as it was shown, contains many parts not *actually* but *potentially*. But, for argument's sake, let us assume with the ancient as well as modern Atomists that there is in it an actual multitude of parts. It will be beyond doubt that in neither case does multitude of parts constitute the essence of quantity. To prove this point we advance the following argument: since multitude of parts requires the division of quantity, either actual if the multitude is actual, or potential if the multitude be potential, it follows that the notion of division is prior in the order of knowledge to the notion of multitude. "Division is the cause of multitude, and is prior in the mind to multitude." [11]   But what the mind first perceives in a thing as the *objective root* of whatever this thing has, is undoubtedly its essence. Therefore, the essence of quantity cannot consist in the extension of parts *in ordine ad se*, whether this multitude of parts be actual or potential.

If it is probable that the extension of parts *in ordine ad se* does not constitute the essence of quantity, it seems to be less probable to make it consist in the position of parts outside parts in space, as Descartes and the ancient Atomists maintained. In

[11] *Qq. dispp., De Pot.*, q. 9, a. 7, ad 15.

the first place, the essence of a thing must be placed in what it is considered in itself, and not in what it is with regard to something else; for, as St. Thomas wisely remarked, whatever belongs to a thing with regard to something else, belongs to it not absolutely but only relatively.[12]   But the position of parts distinct from parts in space does not belong to quantity considered in itself, but to quantity with regard to something else; for space has reference to quantity, not as (*qua*) quantity, but inasmuch as it has a determined nature through which it is in space.   Consequently, the essence of quantity should not be placed in the fact that it occupies space or in the position of extraposited parts in space.

In addition, we cannot conceive the parts of quantity as co-extensive with the points of space without conceiving them as parts measuring place, so that *quantum* is in a definite place, as it were measuring it, in the same way as a whole is in a whole or a part in a part.   But it cannot be perceived how quantity can occupy a certain place by way of a measure without perceiving its dimensions. It follows, then, that we must think of quantity with its dimensions before we can apprehend how these parts are posited in space.   "We must say that no body can occupy place except through the dimensions of quantity; and, therefore, wherever a given body is in place, its dimensions are coterminous with the local dimensions." [13]   Since the dimensions of quantity are quantity itself, we must consider the

---

12 *Sum. Theol.*, I, q. 82, a. 3, c.
13 St. Thomas, *Cont. Gent.*, lib. IV, c. 87.

position of parts outside parts in space as something superadded to the constituted essence of quantity. Now, whatever is superadded to the constituted essence of quantity, must undoubtedly be outside its essence. Hence, we may conclude that the essence of quantity does not consist in the extraposition of parts in space.

With the elimination of these two opinions we may pass over to the defense of our view, contending that the essence of quantity from an *ontological point* of view consists in divisibility, and from a *logical viewpoint* in measurability. Armed with this distinction, it will not be a difficult task to harmonize the various passages of Aristotle, St. Thomas, and other learned men, who at different times placed the essence of quantity now in the fact that it can be divided, now in the fact that it is a measure. Such passages, needless to say, gave rise to many controversies.

At the outset, we wish to state that it seems quite clear to us that, ontologically considered, the notion of quantity consists in divisibility. All the properties—or, as Scholastics would say, all the *passions*—of quantity have their foundations in the extension of parts either *ad se* or *ad locum*. But extension, no matter in what light it be considered, implies either an *actual* or *potential* multitude of parts. A multitude of parts can neither exist nor can it be thought of apart from division, either potential if parts exist potentially in quantity, or actual if parts are actually divided. Therefore, divisibility is prior to any other characteristic which is found in quantity; it is the source of all, since from it all the other properties can be inferred. As that which is primarily apprehended in the thing itself, and is the principle or the objective source itself of whatever there is in a thing, constitutes the notion or essence of that thing, it follows that, ontologically considered, the essence of quantity consists in divisibility. Very appropriately Aquinas says: "The notion of quantity in general consists in a certain divisibility." [14]

Undoubtedly, such must have been the opinion of Aristotle, so clearly explained by Albertus Magnus, St. Thomas, Scotus, and others. For the Stagirite in his *Metaphysics*, discussing the categories from an ontological point of view, stated that quantity consists "in that which is divisible into those parts which are included in it, of which any and each is potentially one and *hoc quid*," [15] that is, is capable of existing as an individual. Here he evidently teaches that quantity is divisible into those characteristics which are essentially in it, to signify that those parts into which quantity can be divided are in quantity not *virtually* but *really* before all *division*. Whatever there is in quantity cannot of itself be a specific whole or an individual thing prior to division; each one is in quantity in such a manner that after division it becomes a specific whole. The additional words in the definition, "of which any and each is potentially one and *hoc quid*," serve to describe how the inexistent parts of the

[14] *In Lib. I Sent.,* dist. 19, q. 1, a. 1, ad 1.
[15] Lib. IV, c. 13.

quantum are discriminated from the elements in the compound, the matter and the form, which are not each potentially "one and *hoc quid*." These two characteristics belong to quantity in a special manner. In the first place, as the parts of quantity constitute the essence of the same prior to division, it is necessary that they inhere in quantity according to that essence. Secondly, as each part of quantity retains its whole essence after division, it follows that each part of quantity when segregated from the rest becomes of itself (*per se*) some sort of *quantum*.

Trendelenburg calls into question [16] the Aristotelian definition on two grounds. On the one hand, he contends that the cognition implied in the Aristotelian definition is taken for granted, because anyone who does not know what *quantum* is must necessarily ignore the parts constituting the *quantum*. On the other hand, he claims that the property of divisibility belongs not only to the notion of quantity but also to all substances consisting of matter and form; and because matter and form constitute the essence of a composite, they must come within the province of divisibility.

Trendelenburg, though in other respects a very learned man and a most able interpreter of Aristotelian philosophy, was unquestionably mistaken in this point. As to the first objection, he himself would have sheltered Aristotle from such an imputation had he followed the right method whereby the mind attains to the knowledge of the categories. For, as was previously remarked, the categories as such,

16 *Hist. of Categories*, p. 79.

regarded in the light of Logic, are in the mind and not in *rerum natura*; the mind, however, aided by the consideration of objective reality may come to the knowledge of the former, because it is necessary for the mind to begin with the cognition of sensible things before it can obtain the first or second notions. Let us take an instance from the very category of quantity with which we are now concerned. Knowing that substance can be divided into parts and that each of these in isolation is itself a body, the mind will infer that every bodily substance is made up of potential parts. As every act is referred to *potency*, it follows that material substance could not be divided into actual parts if it did not contain them potentially before division. Hence, whenever we apprehend this accident of bodily substance (whereby these can be divided into parts), we infer that quantity belongs to material things, that it consists in the divisibility into parts inherent in bodies, and that each of these parts becomes after division a specific whole or an individual. As a consequence, this shows not only our ability to know but our actual knowledge of the parts from which *quantum* results, which knowledge is logically prior to that of quantity itself. Then, because we experience material substances undergoing division, we form the notion of quantity which is apprehended as the category of bodily substances.

The second objection may be answered as follows. The genus and species are implied in every strict or logical definition in the same manner as parts of quantity inhere in quantity; yet, genus pre-

scinded from the species does not connote the complete essence of a thing, and the same may be said of
species prescinded from genus. On the contrary,
every part of quantity separated from others retains
the complete notion of quantity, because, as St.
Thomas observed, in the part of every quantity there
is one and the same essence.[17] On which account both
quantity and the complete essences consisting of
genus and species agree in the fact that in both their
constitutive parts are essentially included; they differ, however, in the fact that each part from which
quantity is derived retains its complete essence in the
state of separation; whereas genus prescinded from
species and species prescinded from genus do not
denote the whole notion of a thing. In this connection it is worth while to hear Albertus Magnus who,
explaining the Aristotelian definition of bodies, says:
"In such (quantities) the complete essence of each
remains in the parts as in the whole. The case with
quantity is not the same as in natural substances.
Flesh ceases to be flesh when cut off, as also a hand
separated from the body is no longer a hand; if
the continuum, however, be divided into parts, each
will retain the entity and unity of continuity as the
whole. And if a number be divided into unities, each
remains a unity, and has its unity in the division." [18]
Aquinas also taught that the parts into which substance is divided on the basis of quantity are of a
different nature from the parts resulting from the
division of substance into matter and form, because

17 *Qq. dispp., De Pot.*, q. 7, 10, c.
18 *In Met.*, Lib. V, tract 3, c. 1.

these latter are the constitutive principles of bodies.[19]

Although the capacity of being divided into parts of the same nature constitutes the essence of quantity from an ontological point of view, we are of the opinion that this definition cannot be applied to quantity considered from the viewpoint of Logic. As frequently happens in the world of speculation, the view just expressed by us has been challenged by some learned Thomists (*e.g.*, Javellus)[20] who maintained that such was not the genuine doctrine of the Angelic Doctor.

It is beyond all dispute that the essence of this category logically considered does not consist in that which constitutes the essence of quantity in an absolute sense. The logical conception should rather denote the relation of quantity to other concepts of the mind, and describe the mode in which it can be predicated of substance. Logically, the categories or predicaments are the most widely generic classes or groups of predicates applicable to an individual subject, and denote, therefore, the order which the mind effects among various concepts. Regarding the category of quantity in such light, it is clear that its essence cannot be placed in divisibility but in measurability. In so far as we know that quantity consists in the capacity of being divided, our cognition refers only to what constitutes its essence in an absolute sense. But what belongs to each category from such a point of view pertains to its ontological essence. Divisibility, therefore, belongs to the essence of

---

[19] *In Lib. III Sent.*, dist. 8, q. 1, a. 2, ad 1.
[20] *In Lib. II Sent.*, dist. 20, ad 2.

quantity ontologically considered. It must, however, be borne in mind that we arrive at the notion of quantity in no other way than by thinking of it as a whole composed of parts into which it can be divided; we first apprehend parts added to parts successively, and then from these parts we perceive that a certain and definite quantity is effected (as number is made up of unities). The mind analysing the continuum into its parts must necessarily reach a last part, the terminus of analysis. True it is that matter, as we shall show in the sequel, is potentially divisible *ad infinitum*, yet its division cannot actually be infinite, since it is repugnant that an infinite multitude of parts should actually exist. As all synthesis or composition begins at the point where analysis or resolution ends, so the mind striving to establish the same continuum anew must perceive as the principle of quantity the last part as first, to which others are added one by one. Hence, it may be seen that although we attain the notion of number (being itself a quantity) by division of the continuum, the continuum can be apprehended in no other way than by the number which consists of many units as of many parts. As unit, being the principle of number, is the measure of number or discrete quantity, so the last part which marks the resolution of the continuum is apprehended as the measure of the continuum. Although the last part into which the analysis of the continuum is made is not indivisible as a unity, it is nevertheless the minimum which we understand of continuous quantity. In that respect it approaches the simplicity and indivisibility of unity, which is the principle of number. As we call a number greater or less according as more or fewer notes are added to unity, we likewise call a continuous quantity greater or less accordingly as this quantity comes nearer to or departs farther from the ultimate resolution of the continuum. We have taken this whole line of argument from Albertus Magnus and Aquinas. The former maintained that every quantum is known by the minimum of substance inherent therein, and that such minimum is conceived as something ultimate and something into which the analysis of the quantum is made.[21] Hence he points out that the essence of measure belongs properly to unity which is the principle of number, and also that it belongs to the minimum which is the principle of continuous quantity, for the minimum of the continuum imitates in a certain way the indivisible unity. This leads us to conclude that the essence of quantity logically considered is *measurability*.

If, however, we regard quantity logically as a measure, we refer it to substance exclusively as that whereby substance is measured. As the function of the intellect is to predicate something of something else, it is clear that one thing is predicated of the other in so far as it is in relation with the other. Thus, we predicate quantity of bodily substance, because through quantity and other remaining accidents bodily substance is distinguished from other substances. For this reason the essence of quantity, as a predicable, should be based on the fact that its

21 *In Met.*, lib. 1, tract. 2, c. 3.

function consists in distinguishing one bodily substance from another.   But this distinction is accomplished on the basis of quantity by taking the minimum in every species of it.   By comparison we discover that in one substance more parts, and in another fewer parts, can be added to their least part
(*minimum*), which is the principle whereby the various quantities of substances are measured.   Such
being the case, St. Thomas rightly concluded that
quantity logically is the measure of substance.[22]

That the opinions embodied and defended in our
dissertation represent the genuine teaching of Albertus Magnus and St. Thomas seems to be beyond all
doubt; moreover, it is also certain that they derived
these doctrines from the works of the Stagirite.
Aristotle in the sixth chapter of the *Categories*, discussing the nature of quantity from a logical point
of view, stated more than once that he regarded
quantity as the measure of substance; in the thirteenth chapter of Book Four of his *Metaphysics*, the
concrete quantum is described as "that which is divisible into the parts included in it, of which any
and each is potentially one and *hoc quid*."

Since the essence of quantity logically consists
in the measurability of corporeal substances, it follows that we must distinguish as many kinds of quantity as there are modes according to which we derive
quantity from the unit, the latter being its principle
and its measure.   The parts constituting quantity
may be added to the unit which is its principle in a
twofold manner—that is, engendering two kinds of

[22] *Sum. Theol.*, I, q. 28, a. 2, c.

quantity, namely, discrete and continuous. Discrete quantity consists of parts actually distinct and each having its own boundary or extremities; it forms a whole whose unity is purely mental; in reality, it is a multitude or number, since its parts are actually distinct. Continuous quantity is made up of parts not distinct but so united to one another that the boundary of one is identical with that of the next. The boundary or link which connects each and every part of continuous quantity is known as *common* boundary or link, since it does not belong properly to any of the parts which it binds; it is, however, the limit of the preceding and the beginning of the following part. Such being the case, the common boundary must undoubtedly be the limit of quantity; hence its task does not consist only in connecting each and every part but also in determining quantity itself. On this account St. Thomas praised Euclid for "mentioning a point in the definition of a straight line, as the limit in the definition of that which is limited," [23] and he said that the essence of a line would be destroyed were it not limited by a point.

It is obvious that the division of substance into discrete and continuous is the first and the most important. As the first division of being is made by way of affirmation and negation, namely, into being and non-being, it is clear that in all kinds of things that division should be considered first which is made by affirmation and negation, that is, by two propositions, one of which affirms what the other denies.

[23] *Sum. Theol.*, I-II, q. 35, a. 8, ad 2.

But such is the division of quantity into discrete and continuous because in the former it is affirmed that parts have their own limits, whereas in the latter this is denied. Therefore the division of quantity into discrete and continuous is ultimate and most fundamental.

Many other sub-divisions of both these quantities have been devised and explained by various philosophers. Our aim, however, is to eliminate here any further divisions and to confine ourselves to the general discussion, explanation, and comparison of discrete and continuous quantity.

Our beginning must be made with the continuum. The genuine and useful method of philosophizing requires that in the attainment of knowledge we should proceed from what is first and better known to us to what is less known. Although continuous quantity, as Aquinas remarks, is in the order of nature subsequent to discrete, yet in the order of knowledge it is first and better known to us than the latter because we arrive at the knowledge of discrete quantity through the division of the continuum. This is mentioned to justify our method of procedure.

In the concrete quantum which essentially belongs to bodily substances, there are three dimensions of continuous quantity, namely, length, breadth, and depth, as every body possesses these essential characteristics. Although these three dimensions exist united simultaneously in bodily substance, we are able to think of longitude exclusive of breadth and depth, and of latitude exclusive of depth, because any of these notions are contradictorily opposed. Thus, when we inquire how long is the road that leads from Chicago to St. Paul, we inquire only about length; and when we seek the area of a field, we are concerned only with the length and breadth. Length without breadth and depth is that quantity which is called *line*; breadth and length constitute *surface*; the quantity which possesses all these three properties is named *body*. By the term *body* is here meant not a solid or physical but a mathematical body, namely, the three dimensions simultaneously united and prescinded from sensible matter. Even though the dimensions of quantity cannot exist *in rerum natura* apart from sensible matter, they can be thought of apart from it. On this account we bestow the term body upon all these dimensions of quantity, whether they be considered as simultaneously present in or prescinded from sensible matter. This is briefly stated by Aquinas as follows: "The word *body* is used to denote a genus of substances from the fact of their possessing three dimensions themselves; in which sense body is said to be a species of quantity." [24]

It is not our purpose to investigate how the mind obtains the notion of these quantities, and how they concur in effecting a mathematical body; we leave such inquiries to mathematicians. The only thing necessary for us to explain is how the parts of continuous quantity constitute quantity itself.

It must be remembered, in the first place, that that which fulfills the task of the common term or

[24] *Sum. Theol.*, I-II, q. 18, a. 2, c.

link in continuous quantity must be something in a
certain way indivisible; if not, this would denote not
something which connects and limits the parts of
quantity, but something which itself exists as a part
of it.   How the common boundary, which must always be something material, is in a certain sense
indivisible shall be explained in the sequel. It suffices
here to remark that the indivisible element which
limits the line from both extremes and joins its parts
is called *point*. And, indeed, that which *limits* the
line from both extremes must be devoid not only of
breadth and depth but also of length; for if it had
length it could not be the principle and the end of
line, but it would itself be a line. Now, this is what
geometricians call line, maintaining a point to be
something indivisible belonging to a body which,
while *per se* deprived of parts, is the principle of all
continuous quantity; because, as St. Thomas says,
from the motion of a point results line, from the
movement of a line surface, and from surface we
often obtain a body.[25]   Hence, that indivisible something which limits line from both extremes is point.
St. Augustine says: "That I call the beginning of a
line from which length proceeds, which (beginning)
I want you to consider apart from any length, for
if you attend to length you will in no wise understand whence length itself proceeds. This is what
excludes division and is called point." [26]   The point
being both the principle and the limit of line, it is
necessary that it should connect each and every part

25 *In Lib. IV Sent.*, dist. 41, q. 1, a. 1.
26 *De quant. anim.*, c. 11, n. 18.

of the line as their common boundary or link. We cannot apprehend a line resulting from the movement of a point, itself being the principle and the end of the line, otherwise than by apprehending the point as connecting all the parts of a line in such a way that the limit of one is identical with that of the next. It seems that there is no other way of conceiving the connection of extreme parts of the continuous quantity which constitutes the whole or continuum. This implies that the point is the common link whereby each part of the line is joined with the others; hence, if one were to cut the line into many parts, the various lines effected by the cutting would also terminate in one point. This is substantiated by St. Augustine: "A line begins and ends in the point itself. . . . Hence, whenever the line can be divided, it is divided through a point since a point in no way admits of division." [27]

What has been said of line may be applied also to surface and body. As that which limits line through division is point, so that which terminates a surface is line, for just as we apprehend line from the movement of a point, in like manner we apprehend surface from the movement of a line. In other words, as the point limits a line and conjoins its parts as a common boundary, so line terminates surface and unifies its parts as a common boundary. Finally, body is limited by the surface, just as the surface by lines and the line by points; hence, from the projection of the surface arises depth, from the

[27] *De quant. anim.*, c. 12, n. 19.

expansion of line to the side results surface, and from the motion of the point proceeds line.

At this point we must observe that the common boundaries of continuous quantity are contained therein actually, and those conjoining its parts only potentially. On the one hand, quantity can actually exist without being measured by certain limits, for what determines quantity must actually be in it. On the other hand, since the constitutive parts of continuous quantity are in it potentially, that which connects its parts must be potentially therein. Hence Aquinas taught that in a line there are two actual points, but at the same time an infinity of potential points because it is capable of being divided *ad infinitum*. This, besides being consonant with reason, is also proved by experience. For in every line we perceive two points which are its extremes; in every oblong surface four lines, of which one is above and the other below, and one on the right and the other on the left; in every cube six equal square faces. But if a line or an oblong surface or a cube be cut in two parts, each of the two lines resulting from the cut will have two points, each of the two oblong surfaces four lines, and each of the two resulting solids six sides. But there could not result two points from the division of the lines, neither four new lines from the division of oblong lines, nor six new surfaces from the division of the cube, unless these were contained potentially in the line, in the oblong surface, and in the cube; for if "an act," as Aquinas says, "has reference to potency," [28] a thing can be

28 *Con. Gent.*, lib. II, cap. 55.

called into an act only in so far as it is there in potentiality. Therefore, the common boundaries of continuous quantity which conjoin each and every part have potential existence in quantity.

Discrete quantity was described above as made up of parts really distinct and each having its own limits. This, if we are right, is effected in the following way. Unity (the principle or source of discrete quantity), being itself a finite quantity, cannot engender parts in such a manner that each should be simultaneously the end of one and the beginning of the next, for a finite quantity cannot be conceived as the limit of one part and at the same time the principle of the next. But the common boundary denotes that which in each and every part of quantity is the limit of one and the beginning of the next. Therefore, the parts of discrete quantity cannot be connected by any common boundary.

Although the parts of continuous quantity are joined by a common boundary because its principle is something absolutely indivisible, it must be admitted that the parts of discrete quantity cannot be united by any common boundary because its principle is unity or a finite quantity. It seems that this must have been the view of Albertus Magnus, who teaches that the material indivisible element is the essential principle of continuity, and that unity is the essential principle of discreteness. What has been asserted *a priori*, the Universal Doctor proved also *a posteriori* as follows: "This may be proved inductively and by way of example. If five particles are placed beside other five particles to number ten, these ten have no common boundary which would be the end of one part and the beginning of the next: for the unity which terminates the first five is not the same as the unity which engenders the other quintet, because the first group possesses its terminating unity separately and discretely from the incipient unity of the following quintet. The parts of ten are always discrete regardless of grouping." [29]

This may be corroborated by another indirect argument which leads *ad absurdum*. If it be said that a certain common boundary connects the parts of discrete quantity, such a boundary could be no other than that which is called unity in a strict sense, because the parts of discrete quantity are units. But it is manifest that strict unity cannot bind the parts of discrete quantity as a common boundary. What fulfills the task of a common boundary does not increase the parts, for the reason that it is the limit of one and at the same time the principle or source of the next; and as long as the parts are not interrupted, the common boundary is not distinct from them. But if a strict unity should be placed between the parts of discrete quantity, its parts would be increased, for any unit added to a finite number changes its species. For instance, if a unit be placed between seven and three or between five and five, we should have as a consequence no longer the number ten but rather the number eleven. We must conclude, therefore, that the parts of discrete quantity are not bound by any common link.

From the fact that the parts of discrete quan-

[29] *Cat.*, I, c. 1.

tity are not joined by any common boundary, as is the case with the parts of the continuum, it must be admitted that the parts exist in the continuous quantity in a manner different from that in which the parts exist in the discrete quantity. As was shown, the parts of continuous quantity being connected by a common boundary can exist in quantity in no other way than potentially. On the contrary, the parts of discrete quantity, being deprived of the common link and distinct one from another, are in the quantum in a certain respect both actually and potentially. If they be considered in so far as they are not continuous but are separated one from another, or in so far as they do not combine to constitute a certain number (for instance, ten), their existence in quantity is actual: for anything which is perceived to be segregated from all others or disjoined must have actual existence. But if these parts be regarded as constituting a certain species of number (*e.g.*, a quantitative whole), they exist therein potentially; for, the essences of things being simple, this whole cannot be thought of as divided without destroying the essence itself. For instance, if we consider the number three in itself, we perceive it as actual, inasmuch as it is perceived as a number distinct from others; but if it be regarded as a constitutive part of ten, then it exists therein potentially; for one apprehending the number three disjoined from seven does not apprehend ten but rather two distinct numbers, namely, seven and three.

The species of a number is determined by the ultimate unit. "The addition of unities constitutes

species." [30] And, indeed, since we apprehend number to be generated by adding unities to the first
unit (this being the principle of number), it is obvious that the units from which number results constitute its matter, and that the ultimate unit constitutes its form, because the species of number is
determined by the ultimate unit. For example, the
sixth unit gives the species or essence to the number
six; if this unit be subtracted from it we have the
number five, and if a seventh be added to the sixth
unit the number seven would be engendered. "In
numbers," says Aquinas, "the addition or subtrac-
tion of a unity changes the species." [31]

Such being the case, it follows, first, that the
parts of discrete quantity, as Albertus Magnus observes, though distinct from one another for the lack
of a common boundary, form an essential unity (a
unum per se), because they are bound together under
one specific form of separation which is the ultimate
unity of the aggregate. Secondly, the parts of discrete quantity, in so far as they constitute quantity,
are contained therein potentially, although in a somewhat different manner than in continuous quantity.
Aquinas contends that such parts cannot exist in
any other way in discrete quantity. For if there
were actual parts in discrete quantity, the *unum per
se* which is the essential characteristic of every *quantum* would not exist, but only the *unum per accidens*.[32] Thirdly, discrete quantity, as long as it re-

30 *Qq. Dispp., De Virt.*, q. 1, a. 2. c.
31 *Cont. Gent.*, lib. IV, c. 41.
32 *In Lib. VII Met.*, lect. 3.

mains in its species, is one and undivided, although the units constituting its matter are divided; consequently, the division of discrete quantity destroys its species.

From what has been said we are enabled to appreciate the wisdom of Aristotle in teaching the difference between that kind of quantity whose parts have position among themselves, and that kind whose parts are deprived of such a position.[33] By saying that quantity has parts having position among themselves, is meant that it has such parts so that each is related to the other as having its own place; hence, we say this part is in that place, or in front, or behind, or above, or below. In order that the parts of quantity should be so related, according to both Greek and Latin interpreters, three conditions are required. First, they should be in a place—namely, in a certain subject, as the parts of a straight line are in a plane, or as the parts of a surface are in a body. This is beautifully and elegantly exemplified by St. Augustine in the following: "Nor in fact can there be any bodily substance, which is not less in part than in whole, or which can possibly have one part in the place of another at the same time; but, having one thing in one place and another in another, its extension in space is a substance which has distinct limits and parts, or so to speak sections." [34] Secondly, the subject in which they inhere should be continuous; for if such were not the case, surely it

---

[33] *Categ.*, I, c.1.
[34] *Against the Epistle of Manichæus*, Chap. XVI, Vol. IV, p. 137.

could not be said that such a part is in front or behind, or that it is up or down. Thirdly, they should
be simultaneously permanent, for if one were destroyed upon the arrival of the other, it could neither
be said that one is in the other, or that one is here
or there, above or below the other. It is already
plain that the parts of any discrete quantity have
no position among themselves, for, as it was shown,
they are deprived of the common boundary of continuity and are considered as separate; hence, it is
impossible that they should all inhere in a continuous subject.

On the other hand, in all species of continuous
quantity, time being excepted, there are parts having position among themselves. Evidently the parts
of time do not enjoy such prerogatives, for one part
of time ceases to exist upon the arrival of the other.
But the parts of line, surface, body, and place, which
are the remaining kinds of continuous quantity, have
position among themselves. Apart from the fact of
their permanence, they are always found in some
continuous subject according to the manner and condition of their nature. Thus, line must be in a surface, surface in a body, and body in a place. But
surface is a continuous subject, and the same may
be said of body and of place. Hence, no matter on
what plane a line be drawn, we can always show
where each part is posited, and indicate that in such
and such a place is the beginning, the middle, or
the end. In like manner, no matter on what body a
surface may be found, we can indicate that such and
such a part is above, below, first, last, middle, or

extreme. Again, this same may be said of a body, for it is easily shown of such a stone, for instance, as it is in the wall, what its upper and what its lower side is.

From the foregoing we may clearly perceive the difference between point which is the principle of continuous quantity and unity which is the principle of discrete quantity. Although the former as well as the latter is an indivisible something and a measure of quantity, the first has a certain position. This should not be taken to mean that the point consists of parts having position because, being only a principle and not a specific kind of quantity, it cannot have parts. But as point is the beginning of line, it must necessarily have a certain relation to the parts of the line which themselves have position.

After these considerations it will not be difficult to solve the controversy which so violently agitated the Scholastic world, namely, whether the division of quantity into discrete and continuous is specific or analogous. Bearing in mind the doctrine of Albertus Magnus and St. Thomas, which we have explained and defended, we find that the division of quantity from an ontological point of view is that of genus into its own species, and from the logical viewpoint is that of analogy. The notion of quantity taken ontologically consists in its capacity of being divided into parts. But as the parts into which any quantity can be divided are either continuous or discrete, it follows that its having discrete or continuous parts constitutes the *differentia* whereby quantity is determined. Quantity which has continuous parts is magnitude, and discrete quantity *multitude*. The consequence is that quantity onto-logically considered through its *differentiæ* is divided into magnitude and multitude. But such a division is that of genus into species, for the capacity of being divided into parts is found equally in magnitude and multitude, the difference between them being due to the fact that the parts of the former are continuous and those of the latter discrete. Therefore, onto-logically regarded, quantity is divided into magni-tude and multitude as genus into its species. The continuity and discreteness are the *differentiæ* by means of which it is determined into the species of magnitude and multitude.

Measurability, as was shown, is the essence of quantity from the viewpoint of Logic. But quan-tity so considered is not divided into discrete and con-tinuous in the same manner as genus is divided into the species, but in an analogous way, since the note of measurability is strictly and properly applied to discrete quantity alone. We say this because mea-sure taken in its strict and proper sense has unit as its principle, and because the unit is not the primary principle of continuous quantity. Therefore, the characteristic of measure belongs primarily and more properly to discrete than to continuous quantity. And, as such a mode of predication is analogous, we must say the same of the above division.

In conclusion, we may say that not only is ma-terial substance affected by the accidental form of quantity but that all the other accidents are measurable at least *per accidens*, as when we predicate of them much and little.   St. Thomas makes all the accidents "related to their subjects by the medium of the dimensive quantity, as the first subject of color is said to be the superficies." [35]

[35] *Sum. Theol.*, III, q. 27, a.2.

CHAPTER IX

THE CATEGORY OF RELATION

Nature of Relation.—Division of Relation into Real and Logical.—The Three *Fundamenta* of Real Relation.—Two Modes of Logical Relation.—Refutation of False Doctrines.—Relation as a Special Category.—Distinction between Absolute and Relative Accident.—Division of Relation *secundum Dici* or Transcendental and *secundum Esse* or Predicamental.—Certain Characteristics of Relational Terms. ..

WE SHALL NOW ADVANCE the Scholastic doctrine of relation. In his *Organon* Aristotle placed not only quantity but also relation ahead of quality, although in his *Metaphysics* this order is reversed. As we have often stated, whenever there is question concerning the acquisition of truth, we should proceed not from what is prior in nature but rather from that which is prior in the order of knowledge. But relation becomes known to us before quality or the other categorical accidents; for in discussing quantity we have encountered such concepts as small, large, many, few, and other such things which imply certain species of relation. It is our purpose to limit the scope of our inquiry to the following questions: first, what is the nature and kinds of relation; secondly, whether relation is a special category, and in what light it must be considered to belong among the categories; thirdly, what are its chief properties as a category.

The solution of the first question is without doubt of the greatest importance. Since relation as a category is itself a certain species of relation, it follows that we cannot comprehend its nature without considering the generic and differential elements which constitute it.

In its general acceptation, relation properly denotes that whereby something has reference to something else. The complete essence or notion of relation consists in the order of one thing to another. This definition obviously implies several terms either really or logically distinct from one another. Since relation denotes a certain order, its notion must necessarily contain at least two terms, namely, one of the thing which is referred to another, and one of the thing to which reference is made. Furthermore, the mental activity in predication implies relation. Whatever be the nature of the terms between which relation takes place, relation exists in them potentially, having actual existence only in the mind. Nevertheless, the nature of relation must be derived not from the nature of the intellective action but from the nature of the terms, for the nature of the intellective action does not depend on the action itself but on the nature of the object with which it is concerned. The object of the intellect referring one thing to another is the entity of the terms. Therefore, the nature of the intellective action in this referential process must be derived from the nature of the terms, and we may easily infer that there are as many different kinds of relation as there are diversities of terms. This diversity of relational terms is due to the fact that not only objective realities but also mental conceptions can be referred to one another; for example, with regard to objective realities, father and son are related to each other in such a manner that the intellect refers sonship to paternity and vice versa. The *entity* of things in nature being real and the *entity* of concepts being logical, it is clear that the *entity* of the terms which are the objects of relation may be either real or logical—real if the term be referred according to the order of existence, logical if according to the order of knowledge. St. Thomas says: "Relation in its proper meaning signifies only what refers to another. Such regard to another exists sometimes in the nature of things, as in those things which by their own very nature are ordered to each other and have a mutual inclination; and such relations are necessarily real relations. Sometimes, however, this regard to another, signified by relation, is to be found only in the apprehension of reason comparing one thing with another, and this is a logical relation only: as, for instance, when reason compares man with animal as the species with the genus." [1]

As this first and most important division of relation is not only useful in philosophy but absolutely necessary, it will be wise to devote some time to its elucidation. Taking real relation for our starting point, it is to be observed, first of all, that this relation requires two things, namely, that the terms be

[1] *Sum. Theol.*, I, q. 28, a. 1, c.

real and that they should be mutually related
through a real principle. With regard to the first,
as the nature of relation depends on the nature of
the terms, it is clear that it cannot be called real
unless its terms denote realities existing in nature.
As to the second, if any of the terms be related to
another, not through something in the thing itself,
but through mere mental consideration, neither the
order between the terms nor the relation itself would
be real. For instance, the relation existing between
knowledge and the known object cannot properly be
called real, for there is nothing in the known object
whereby this object is referred to cognition; the mind
makes it intelligible. Moreover, every real relation,
as was observed by the Scholastics, is mutual; for
whenever it is found, the order between the extremes
is reciprocal; since relation essentially consists in
order, and since real order is in both extremes, the
relation itself must be consequently mutual—for example, there is mutual relation between father and
son, because the father is related to the son and the
son to the father. Not only is every real relation
mutual, but no other relation is mutual except the
real. And because the terms of real relation are always extra-mental realities, it follows that the order
existing between terms of real relatives is diverse
according to the diversity of the principle which engenders this order. Relations must be diverse according to the diversity of the order existing between their terms, because relation consists in the
order one thing has to another. Therefore, we must
distinguish as many real relations as there are prin-

ciples engendering this order. The principle engendering the order between the terms of relation was called by the Scholastics *fundamentum*, the ground or foundation of the relation.

A thing may be related to another for three principal reasons. First, a thing may be related to another on account of some essential property; for instance, when one thing is referred to another in such a way as to constitute a certain genus or species. In this manner primary matter is related to substantial form; for example, the human body is not that of brutes, because it is animated not by an animal but by a human form or essence. Secondly, one thing may be referred to another on account of the principle of causality; for instance, as effect is to the cause or vice versa. Thus, father and son are mutually related, because paternity is the cause of filiation and filiation is the effect. Thirdly, a thing may be referred to another on account of some accidental characteristics, as when that by which one thing is related to another is outside its essence. For this reason two white walls are related to each other by way of similitude of whiteness, which is the accidental quality. Beyond these three principles there are neither more nor less from which real relation is effected.

In this connection it is important to make two remarks about real relation. The first, which we have learned from St. Augustine, relates to the fact that sometimes the order of relation is in both terms of the same essence, and on this account the relation in both is denoted by a single term; at other times this order not being essentially the same, two distinct terms are required to denote the relation. Of the first type is the relation of similitude, which exists between two white objects; there being the same order of whiteness in both, each is called white. Of the second type is the relation existing between father and son; the relationship of the son to the father is different from that by which the father is related to the son, this relation being called paternity in the father and sonship in the son. As this difference cannot be described in clearer terms than in the words of St. Augustine, we quote the whole passage without comment: "(Which) relative terms at times are identical and at times different. They are identical, as for instance, the relation of brother to brother, of friend to friend, of neighbor to neighbor, of brother-in-law to brother-in-law, and such like whose number is wellnigh infinite. For in these cases the relation of the first to the second is the same as the relation of the second to the first. They are different as the relation of the father to the son, and of the son to the father, of the father-in-law to the son-in-law and of the son-in-law to the father-in-law, of the master to the slave, and of the slave to the master. The first is not related to the second as the second to the first, and although both are men, the relation is different, not the nature. For if I consider the relation of one to the other, the first is not related to the second in the same way as the second to the first, because the first is father and the second son, the first is father-in-law and the second son-in-law, or the first is master and the second slave. If, however, you consider each one as he is in himself, one is what the other is, because the one is a man as the other." [2]

The second point, which was frequently inculcated by St. Bonaventure and Aquinas, has reference to the fact that the specific multiplication of relations should be derived from the diversity of the *fundamenta* which are causes of relations; and that the numerical multiplication should be drawn from the number of subjects in which they exist, neither one nor the other being derived from the multiplication of terms. In the first place, as the specific nature of relation consists in an order to something else, it results that, the *fundamenta* (in virtue of which one thing is related to another) being multiplied, the specifically distinct relations are also multiplied. For instance, if one is both father and a master, paternity and dominion constitute specifically distinct relations, because the *fundamenta* or causes from which they are engendered are specifically distinct. In the second place, if many subjects are related on account of the same *fundamentum*, the relation in them is specifically one because of the unity of *fundamentum*; it will, however, be numerically manifold because of the multiplicity of subjects in which it is found. For instance, if a father has many sons, the relation is specifically one, namely, filiation in all the sons, there being but a unique cause whereby they are related to the father; but numerically there are many relations in them according to the number of sons. Thus, in the father there is

2 *Epist. clxx*, n. 6.

essentially and numerically one unique relation, namely paternity, by which the father is related to many sons, for in this case both the principle and the subject are one. In like manner, there is only one relation in virtue of which the son is related to his parents; not only because the son is a unique subject, but also because the *fundamentum* is one.

After the explanation of real relation, let us now pass on to the logical. This, as St. Thomas observed, may have four diverse modes. The first is had when one of the terms of relation has *fundamentum in re*, and the other only in the mind. Such relation, for instance, is that existing between knowledge and the known object. This relation has a real foundation in the subject acquiring knowledge, for the subject by the acquisition of knowledge attains a new mode of being; but it has no real foundation in the known object, as the object apprehended by the intellect does not undergo any change. The knowledge, however, is in the thing through the instrumentality of the intellect, for the mind apprehending a certain thing as an object of knowledge refers it to the mind.

A second mode is obtained when two related terms are in reality one and the same term, which term is apprehended mentally by two distinct acts. To obtain a clear understanding of this, we must note that the mind, which is one, can at different times actually exercise its powers, and that the intellect can apprehend one and the same thing by many distinct acts in such a manner that what is actually one may be mentally manifold because of the number of acts by which it is apprehended. "For reason apprehending one thing twice regards it as two, thus it apprehends a certain habitude of a thing to itself." [3]

Therefore, there may be a relation whose term is really one and the same, and which is apprehended by the mind by two distinct acts. It is obvious that such a relation is merely the work of the mind, and hence purely logical. Every relation requires diversity of terms. But a diversity of terms in relation whose terms are really one, is not really in the terms themselves as is the case in the terms of real relation. Hence, in this process the intellect combines two things which in reality are one, not only apprehending their diversity but also creating it. St. Thomas speaking of the relation of identity says: "Now, it is clear that the relation of a thing to itself is not a real relation." [4]

The third mode consists in the relation existing between two extremes, one of which denotes being (*esse*) and the other non-being (*non esse*). Although non-being cannot be the term of real relation, it may have logical relation to the being with which it is compared. Since the intellect knows that non-being is the negation of being, the intellect relates the former with the latter. But a relation in which one term has order to the other in the conceptional sphere, is logical. Therefore, a relation in which one term denotes being and the other non-being is logical. Thus, when we say that we are prior to those who are to exist in the future, this

[3] *Sum. Theol.*, I, q. 13, a. 7, c.
[4] *Ibid.*, I, q. 42, a. 1, ad 4.

priority is a logical relation, for what does not actually exist cannot be the term of a real relation.

Finally, the fourth mode of logical relation is that whereby one term of relation is understood to have order to another. Since all relation by its very essence must have order to another, it obviously follows that the mind perceiving the reference of one thing to another should simultaneously perceive the relation of the relation itself. But this perceiving of the relation of relation is not real but logical.[5]

What has been said of real and logical relation is in our opinion in perfect harmony with St. Thomas' teaching which may be summarized in his own words: "Sometimes from both extremes it is an idea only, as when mutual order or habitude can only be between things in the apprehension of reason; as when we say a thing is the same as *itself*. . . . Now, there are other relations which are realities as regards both extremes, as when for instance a habitude exists between two things according to the same reality that belongs to both; as is clear of all relations consequent upon quantity; as great and small, double and half, and the like; for quantity exists in both extremes; and the same applies to relations consequent upon action and passion, as motive power and the movable things, father and son, and the like. Again sometimes a relation in one extreme may be a reality, while in the other extreme it is an idea only; and this happens whenever two extremes are not of one order; as sense and science refer respectively to sensible things and to intellectual

5 *Con. Gent.*, lib. II, c. 13.

things; which, inasmuch as they are realities existing in nature, are outside the order of sensible and
intelligible existence." [6]

The first of these three relations has been called
by recent Scholastics logical, the second real, and the
third mixed (that is, partly logical and partly real).
It is, however, important to bear in mind that this
last one was named by Aquinas now logical, now
non-mutual, as indicated by the following extract:
"Relations which result from the mental operation
alone in the objects understood are logical relations
only, inasmuch as reason observes them as existing
between two objects perceived by the mind. Those
relations, however, which follow the operation of the
intellect and which exist between the word intellectually proceeding and the source whence it proceeds, are not logical relations only, but are real relations; inasmuch as the intellect and reason are real
things, and are really related to that which proceeds from them intelligibly; as a corporeal thing is
related to that which proceeds from it corporeally." [7]

From the fact that some relations are real and
others logical, it is easy to see the mistake of those
philosophers who held either that all relations are
logical or that all are real. It seems that the first
opinion was held by Zeno of Elea and by almost all
ancient philosophers before Plato and Aristotle.
Their arguments may be summarized as follows.
Relation is not a special categorical accident, but
is something common to all the categories, due to the

6 *Sum. Theol.*, I, q. 13, a. 7, c.
7 *Ibid.*, I, q. 28, a. 1.

fact that relation does not exist in things, since it is an order established by the mind between concepts. It is the mind which contemplates the natures of things, which arranges them in a certain order. But what is due purely to intellectual activity is logical, not real. As a consequence, all relations are logical. St. Thomas, explaining the opinion of such philosophers, said in a few but concise words that in their opinion "relation is neither a certain genus of entity, nor something existing *in rerum natura,* but only a certain *aspect* found in all entities, and that relations belong to second intentions, which have no existence outside the mind." [8]   The ancient Sceptics under the leadership of Ænesidemus accepted this doctrine most eagerly, and arrived at the conclusion that no certain knowledge of the nature of things was possible; because, if no other order or aspect of things be known to us except the one which is intellectually conceived, it follows that objective knowledge would not be possible, because being ignorant of the real order of things we should necessarily be ignorant of the natures of things themselves.

A few sentences from Sextus Empiricus are apropos: "Whatever is referred to another, being mental construction, has no real existence. . . . That relation is only in the mind, is a teaching resulting from the confession of the Dogmatists. For they unanimously teach that by relation is meant that which is referred to another. But if it (relation) had extra-mental existence, they would not have

[8] *In Lib. I Sent.,* dist. 26, q. 2, a. 1.

defined it in this manner—rather they would have said that relation is that which co-exists with another (*quod alteri adexistit*)." [9]

The same teaching has been advocated by the modern Sceptics, especially Hume. Notwithstanding his abhorrence for Pyrrhonism, Immanuel Kant, following in the footsteps of ancient and modern Sceptics, divested relation, as well as the remaining categories, of all objective value and considered all relation to be purely logical.

On the other hand, many have taught just the contrary, namely, that all relations are real.[10] St. Thomas makes frequent mention of those who followed the leadership of Plato. According to Plato,[11] among the most universal Ideas are being and not-being, like and unlike, unity and number, the straight and the crooked, and other relations which have foundation in quality and quantity; universal ideas alone have real existence independently of human intellect, and they alone are perfect, unchangeable, eternal, indivisible, imperishable; the individual objects of the phenomenal order participate in these ideas, so that each individual object has part in the Idea corresponding to it which participation makes it to be what it is. All of which justifies us in concluding that Plato considered every relation to be real.

These two mutually exclusive opinions, whether considered in themselves or in their consequences,

---

9 *Adversus Logicos*, lib. VIII, sect. 453.
10 *Sum. Theol.*, I, q. 32, a. 2, c.
11 *Theæt.*, pp. 184, 186.

cannot be accepted.   Since we are concerned with a controversy of great importance, it is necessary to elucidate this point.   That there are real relations is beyond all doubt, inasmuch as relational terms denote realities existing in nature.   Moreover, the *fundamentum* which gives rise to such relations is also real, because relation must be of the same nature as the principle engendering it.   It is certain, in the first place, that there is a certain order or habitude between existing things.   It is also apparent that the perfection of extra-mental realities arises not only from what belongs to them in an absolute sense, but also from the relation they have one to another. Secondly, the source of this order must also be real, because order is based upon the natures of things. As a consequence, it is certain that there are real relations.   Let us hear St. Thomas: "Moreover, the perfection and goodness which are in extra-mental realities must be considered not only in the light of something absolutely inhering in things, but also in relation of one thing to another, as in the order of the different parts of an army consists the goodness of the army.   The Philosopher in the X *Met.* compares to this order the order of the universe.   Then there must be a certain order in the things themselves; but this order is a certain relation." [12]

However, it is false on this account to deny logical relations and to maintain that all relations are real.   Considered in itself, relation does not require that its terms be either real beings or logical entities

[12] *Qq. Dispp., De Pot.,* q. 7, a. 9, c; *Sum. Theol.,* I. q. 13, a. 7, c.

(*entia rationis*). In this respect relation is indifferent to both. Consequently, if order exists not only in the extra-mental world but also in the conceptual domain (*i.e.*, between concepts and the objects of reference), we are compelled to admit not only real but also logical relations. But a certain order may actually exist both among the concepts themselves as well as between concepts and the objects of reference, for the intellect in virtue of its reflective power can establish such order. For instance, the intellect, comparing the concept of a stone which it actually considers with the concept formerly entertained of the same stone, apprehends that one is identical with the other and posits between them the relation of identity. Therefore, besides the real we must admit also a logical relation.

Furthermore, these two mutually exclusive opinions culminate in the utter ruin of all knowledge. As regards the denial of real relations, it opens wide the doors to Scepticism. For, if no other relations be known to us except those conceived by the mind, it would follow that all order is subjective without any basis in extra-mental reality; and, if we cannot obtain the knowledge of the order existing among extra-mental realities, it would result that knowledge of extra-mental things themselves would become impossible. This obviously leads to Scepticism. The same may be said also of the other opinion. If all relations were real, it would follow that the human mind could neither know the relations existing between its concepts nor the relation between concepts and the objects represented by them. However, the perception of this order is necessarily required for the attainment of knowledge, which cannot be obtained otherwise than by knowing the manner in which it is acquired; but this manner cannot be known without apprehending both the order of concepts as well as the order existing between the concepts and the extra-mental reality represented by them. Hence, Scepticism is also the consequence of this opinion.

In addition to what has been said, it would be well to examine the foundations upon which the two doctrines are based. In every real relation two things must be taken into consideration, namely, the nature of the order existing between the things and that which is the source of this order. The nature of order constitutes the entity of relation in the mind, for, although there is order in nature, the essence of this order cannot be apprehended except by the intellect. St. Augustine says: "But if there were not a man, that is some substance, there would be no one who could be called relatively a master; or if there were no horse having a certain essence, there would be nothing that could be called relatively a beast of burden." [13]

Some philosophers, however, failed to perceive the *fundamentum in re* in the relations which we call real, and in considering them merely as relational functions of thought concluded that all relations are logical. On the other hand, others rejecting logical relations as mental figments taught that all relations are real.

[13] *De Trin*, lib. 7, c. 1, n. 2.

The foundations upon which our opponents based their doctrines are very defective. Although every relation has its being in the intellect, it does not follow that it cannot have a *fundamentum* in the realities to which it is referred. The concept of relation *per se* merely prescinds from such corollaries.

From such an analysis of relation it cannot be inferred whether there are any real relations. However, we have often remarked that there are relations in which both terms are real (*i.e.*, denoting real existences), and that there are in them certain characteristics in virtue of which they are related. St. Augustine says: "Therefore, when a man is called a master, man himself is essence, but he is called a master relatively; for he is called man in respect to himself, but master in respect to his slave. But in regard to the point from which we started, if essence itself is spoken of relatively, essence itself is not essence. Add further that all essence which is spoken of relatively, is also something, although the relation be taken away; as, for example, in the case of a man who is a master, and a man who is a slave, and a horse that is a beast of burden, and money that is a pledge, the man, and the horse, and the money, are spoken of in respect to themselves, and are substances or essences; but master and slave, and beast of burden and pledge, are spoken relatively to something." [14]

Likewise, the doctrine of those who deny logical relation does not rest on a solid foundation. Logical relation is in no way repugnant to the notion of rela-

[14] *De Trin.*, lib. 7, c. 1, n. 2.

tion in general. Although the entity of these relations has no *fundamentum* in reality, they are not a
mere figment of reason and consequently nothing.
Notwithstanding the fact that both terms of such relations are logical or *entia rationis*, they still must
have some *fundamentum in re*, if not an *immediate*
and *proximate* one (as in the case of real relations),
then assuredly a *mediate* and *remote fundamentum*,
because the intellect derives these concepts from the
natures of things. If one term is real and the other
logical, the relations have a proximate foundation in
the fact that the real term is referred to the logical.
Since logical relations have some *fundamentum* in
things, whether this be remote or proximate, they
obviously are not a mere figment of reason. If
logical relations were but a useless figment of the
mind, they would be altogether useless in the acquisition of knowledge. However, logical relations
are not only useful but also very necessary for knowledge, and consequently cannot be considered as a
vain figment of reason. There is no difficulty in
proving the truth of our assertion. In logical relations in which both terms are logical, if the intellect
derives the concepts between which a certain order
is established from the nature of things, it is apparent that the intellect can derive a great advantage
in the processes of cognition. For if logical relations are principles aiding the mind in knowing the
order of things, they must be necessary for the attainment of knowledge, because the latter cannot be
obtained without knowing the existing relation. We
are aware of the fact that the Sceptics at this point

will emphasize the inability of the human mind to know whether any extra-mental reality corresponds to our mental concepts. However, on this point we will quarrel, not with the Sceptics, but only with those who, while not denying our ability to know the essences of things, nevertheless contend that logical relations are impossible. With regard to relations in which one term is real and the other logical, the case is clearer than in the former. Such relations teach us that a thing which is the real term depends on another which is the logical term.

Having explained the notion of relation and enumerated its species, we go on to our next point of inquiry: whether relation constitutes a special category. This question implies two parts. Since relation may be regarded from various points of view and is on that account manifold, every one will see that, if we consider relation as a special category in itself, it must further be inquired under what respect it is a category.

To understand the origin of this controversy, it must be remembered that categories are an object of Logic in so far that they are certain supreme concepts to which all other concepts are reduced; that they also signify the highest classification of realities existing in the natural order, according to which the mind apprehends a determined entity in every nature of thing. Relation, though in a different degree, is found in all categories. It is, indeed, found in substance, as the relation of father or son, master or servant, and such like; in quantity, as that of equality or inequality; in quality, as that of likeness and dissimilarity, and so on.   From this it might seem that relation is not a special category, but a certain modification in all categories apprehended by the intellect.   Accordingly, some, not only among the ancients but even among the lesser lights of the Scholastics themselves, rejected relation as a category; while, on the contrary, some modern philosophers reduced all the categories to the one category of relation.

It is clear that the first of the two views was taught by Zeno and those others who admitted only logical relations; since they regarded categories ontologically only and not logically, they obviously could not include relation among the number of categories.

The second view, refuted by St. Thomas, was recently revived by Renouvier.[15]   If we are not mistaken, this view was also advocated by Hume and Ænesidemus.   For if the mind according to their teaching cannot know the essence or nature of things except in so far as they are referred to the intellect, it necessarily follows that relation is the supreme concept of the mind to which other concepts must be reduced.   Kant came very close to this view.   Although he taught that relation is a special category, he must have regarded the categories only as diverse modes of predication, because he derived all his categories from the analysis of judgment.   According to Rosmini, dialectical categories consist in diverse relations of identity of the predicate with the subject.   It appears that these categories are not

15 *Essai de la Critique Generale,* p. 86.

real things (beings), but only mere modes of pred-
icating concepts, for an attribute *qua* attribute is
a mental act.[16]   But as Aristotle and all the famous
Doctors of the School regarded relation as a special
category, we shall defend their teachings.

Relation is a special category if it possesses a
special mode which determines realities existing in
nature, and if it denotes a special concept which cannot be reduced to any other.   Such is the case with
relation. As regards substance, the thing is obvious,
because substance being an entity *per se* and relation
an entity *per aliud* (namely, through substance), it is
plain that the entity of substance is not the entity of
relation, and that relation is a genus of being which
cannot be included under the genus of substance.
Appropriately St. Augustine says: "It is absurd
that substance should be spoken of relatively, for
everything subsists in respect to itself." [17]   With regard to other accidents relation has in common with
them the characteristic of inherence (*i.e.*, to be in a
substance as in a subject); this is the peculiarity of
every being whose entity is opposed to the entity of
substance.   However, relation is discriminated from
the remaining accidents, because these remain as it
were in the subject (*i.e.*, by modifying the subject
without referring it to something else), while relation
remains in the subject by modifying it by reference
to something else. For instance, both quantity
and quality which are accidents of wood remain in
the wood, with this difference, however, that while

16 *System of A. Rosmini,* pp. 46-47, *passim,* 330.
17 *De Trin.,* lib. VII, c. 4.

the former only extends the wood, the latter places the wood in relation to something else. To perceive more clearly the force of this argument, we should observe with Aquinas two things in every genus of accidents—namely, what they have in common with each other and what differentiates them. That in which they agree is nothing else than the common characteristic of inherence or inaleity; that whereby the accidents differ from one another is but a special mode according to which this inherence is determined in each one. For example, quantity and quality agree in the fact that they are in substance as in their subject; they differ from each other because quantity is in substance as its measure, quality as its disposition. Among the peculiar and various modes whereby inherence is determined, is also that mode in virtue of which the subject has a certain order in relation to another; for example, paternity not only denotes the entity which is in the father as in its subject, but also produces in the father a certain relation to the son. Let us hear the Angelic Doctor: "We must consider that in each of the nine genera of accidents there are two points for remark. One is the nature belonging to each one of them considered as an accident: which commonly applies to each of them as inherent in a subject, for the essence of an accident is to inhere. The other point of remark is the proper nature of each one of these genera. In the genera, apart from that of relation, as in quantity and quality, even the true idea of the genus itself is derived from a respect to the subject; for quantity is called the measure of substance, and quality is the disposition of substance. But the true idea of relation is not taken from its respect to that in which it is, but from its respect to something outside. So if we consider even in creatures relations formally as such, in that respect they are said to be assistant, and not intrinsically affixed, for in this way they signify a respect which affects the thing related and stands from that thing to something else; whereas, if relation is considered as an accident, it inheres in a subject, and has an accidental existence in it. . . . Gilbert de la Porrée considered relation in the former mode only." [18]

From the preceding we may infer the reason for the Scholastic division of accidents into absolute and relative. Relative accident is that which affects the substance in such a way as to refer it or ordain it to something else. While some accidents inhere in substance *per se*, others inhere only through the instrumentality of another, so that substance becomes the proximate and immediate subject of certain accidents, and only the remote or mediate of others. For instance, whiteness which is an accident of the category of quality does not inhere in substance except through the medium of quantity; hence, substance is the proximate subject of quantity and the remote subject of whiteness. St. Thomas assigned for this a weighty reason. Since all categorical accidents flow from the essence according to natural order, they must necessarily flow one after another according as one is nearer to substance than another; for example, as the first is the cause of all, so that

[18] *Sum. Theol.*, I., q. 28, a. 2.

which is nearer to the first is, in a way, cause of those
which are more remote. But if accidents flow from
the essence successively, one must inhere in the substance by means of another according as one is
nearer to substance than another. Therefore, some
of the accidents inhere in the substance immediately,
and others mediately through other accidents. Relation is an accident of the latter type, because it requires not only the entity of substance but also the
entity of some other accident by means of which substance is placed in relation to another. Hence, two
things cannot be called similar except on account of
a quality common to them (*e.g.*, two white things are
similar because both possess the quality of whiteness) ; and two given things cannot be said to be
equal except they are so on account of an equal
quantity in both. Absolute accident, on the other
hand, through which relation inheres in substance,
is either quantity, or action, or passivity. For instance, Peter is said to be father of Paul because of
action; Paul is said to be son of Peter because of
passion; one is said to be larger or smaller than the
other because of diversity of quantity which is in
them. Relation, being an accident inhering in substance through another accident, requires three conditions: first, a subject for inherence, which is called
the remote *fundamentum* of relation; secondly, a
certain principle in the subject on account of which
it may inhere in the subject, which is the proximate
fundamentum of relation; thirdly, an accident of
another subject effecting the term of relation, which
is called correlation. Thus, when we say "virtue is

more precious than gold," virtue is the subject of the relation; gold is the term to which it is related; and precious expresses the foundation of the relation (*viz.*, price or value).

It is apparent that those who regarded relation not as a special category but as a certain mode of categorical accidents confused the *fundamentum* of relation with relation itself. From the fact that relation is not in substance except through some absolute accident, it does not follow that the entity of relation is the entity of the absolute accident itself, but only that the entity of some absolute accident is the principle of relation belonging to substance with the result that it is the proximate *fundamentum* of relation. The entity of relation certainly is distinguished from the entity of the accident through which relation belongs to substance. For as the absolute accident, St. Bonaventure says, is taken in a relative sense, not *per se*, but on account of a certain order or respect that it has to another, it must be understood as something added to its entity. But what is added to another must necessarily be distinct from the entity to which it is added. Therefore, the entity of relation should not be confused with the entity of absolute accident. This also may be proved by an argument leading *ad absurdum*. If every accident which belongs to substance through another should be identical with this other, it would follow that no categorical accident would inhere in substance through another, but every categorical accident would *per se* inhere in the substance as in its subject; such a conclusion is absurd; consequently, it also is absurd to confuse the entity of relation with the entity of the accident. Therefore, from the fact that relation belongs to substance through a categorical accident it cannot be inferred that relation is not a special categorical accident.

Though it is clear enough that the entity of relation is really distinct from the entity of absolute accident, we shall nevertheless advance additional arguments. In the first place, if relation denotes a mode distinct from other accidental modes, the entity of relation is distinct from the entity of every other category through which relation belongs to substance. The antecedent, as we have proved, is true; hence also the consequent. Moreover, two things of which one remains the same while the other is multiplied, cannot be identical. But relation may be multiplied while the categorical accident remains one (*e.g.*, from one whiteness may arise innumerable similitudes). Those things are not identical of which one is intensified while the other is extenuated, and vice versa. Such is the case with relation and the absolute accident through which the former inheres in a subject; *e.g.*, Peter and Paul are now equally warm, but if Peter goes nearer the fire, he undoubtedly becomes warmer than Paul according as the degree of heat is increased in Peter and is decreased in Paul; hence also the likeness which exists between them is decreased. Therefore, the two accidents are not identical. The same may be said of two things of which one remains while the other ceases to exist. But frequently, while the categorical accident which is the *fundamentum in re* remains in one subject, the other ceases to exist. In this same way the relation ceases to exist. Let us follow the example just given. Should Peter remain warm while Paul grows cold, obviously the categorical accident of heat remains in Paul, and the relation of similitude between the two ceases. Hence, the entity of relation is clearly distinct from the entity of the accident which is its *fundamentum*. Finally, if a relation were identical with the categorical accident (through which it inheres in a subject), it would follow that its two opposites would be identical. In such a case the subject through which an absolute accident is referred to an opposite one would *ipso facto* be referred to the other; for example, a subject which is white would be similar to another white subject and dissimilar to a black subject. As a consequence, if relation were not really distinct from categorical accident on which it is based, two opposite relations would be identical with the categorical accident; for instance, likeness and non-likeness which are based upon whiteness would be identical with whiteness itself; and since two things which agree with one and the same third thing must agree also with each other, the consequence is that two opposite relations would be really one. Such being the case, we must conclude that relation is a special category, and not a certain mode whereby the intellect considers all the other categories.

With regard to the views of Rosmini and Renouvier, it must be observed that, although relation has its entity in substance, its essence does not really consist in this but rather in the fact that it places the substance in relation to something else. While we agree with them that the reason for which something is predicated of a subject consists in the relation of identity, we contend that not everything which is predicated of a subject places the same subject in relation to something else. A thing can inhere in another either in the order of permanence or in the order of reference; hence, it is necessary to know not only that a thing inheres in another, but also that it is referred to another. Therefore, although every accident is predicated of the subject from the fact that it inheres in the subject, the essential characteristic of relation may be wanting therein, for, as Aquinas says, "the true idea of relation is not taken from its respect to that in which it is, but from its respect to something outside." [19]

We may add that, if relation consisted exclusively in the reference of the predicate to the subject or in the reference of anything to its supreme genus, we should be forced to admit no other relation but logical. For, as we have frequently noted, the logical synthesis of the predicate with the subject, as well as the reduction of any thing to its genus, is purely an intellectual process. "It is in the power of our intellect to form enunciations." [20] Thus, it is only a logical relation, when our mind compares man to animal as the species to the genus.

According to Rosmini and Renouvier, categories denote the diverse modes whereby the predicate is referred to the subject. They may not, how-

[19] *Sum. Theol.*, I, q. 28, a. 2, c.
[20] *Sum. Theol.*, I, q. 14, a. 14, c.

ever, have perceived that such relation is not real but logical only. Logical relation cannot contribute in any way to the knowledge of the subject without having a basis in the very nature of the subject. Hence, we are unable to know in what manner a predicate is referred to a subject without knowing the manner in which the entity denoted by the predicate inheres in the subject; neither can we know all the modes whereby the predicate is related to the subject unless we know the modes of things as they exist in nature. If the diverse modes whereby the predicate is referred to a subject have their *fundamentum* in the diverse modes according to which being is predicated, we are justified in concluding that the principle of categories is not relation but being upon which relation is based. Hence, St. Thomas aptly notes that "every relation is based upon quantity, action and passion: it presupposes the distinction of other genera." [21]

As a corollary to what has been said, we may infer the solution of the second question proposed by us, namely, whether every or only a certain species of relation is a category. If every category must denote a special mode whereby being is determined in divers natures of things, no other kind but relation, strictly and properly so called, would constitute a special category. For, as only real relation has real terms and a real foundation by which one thing is referred to another, this alone denotes a special mode by which being is determined in things. Hence, we must hold with St. Thomas that

[21] *Qq. Dispp., De verit.*

no logical relation is a category, because logical relations are not reduced to an ultimate genus of things
but are applied to all kinds of entities, while on the
contrary real relation is a special category because
it denotes a determined genus of being.

After these considerations our task is to give a
genuine definition or rather description of relation
as a category, since every category denotes a certain
supreme genus which strictly cannot be defined.
Aristotle has formulated two definitions: one at the
beginning of the seventh chapter of the *Categories*,
the other at the end of the same chapter, as well as
in the seventeenth chapter of the Fourth Book of the
Metaphysics. The Scholastics of the Middle Ages re-
tained both descriptions, contending however that the
second description was more appropriate and complete. This gave rise to that subtle Scholastic division of relations into *secundum dici* and *secundum
esse*—otherwise known as transcendental and predicamental relations. This division seems to be both
consonant with truth and very useful to distinguish
the category of relation from any other. The relation *secundum dici* is something absolute which acquires a certain order in relation to another, in such
a manner as to denote primarily an absolute accident
and secondarily a certain habitude to another. Such
relation, for instance, is science; for this primarily
denotes a quality inherent in a subject as effecting
knowledge, besides implying a certain order to the
known object. Such also would be the relation of
part to the whole. The other relation is nothing else

but the reference one thing has to another. For example, paternity does not denote something which absolutely belongs to the father, but something by which the father is related to the son. St. Thomas has a brief summary of this division in the following words: "Some relative names are imposed to signify the relative habitudes themselves, as master and servant, father and son, and the like, and these relatives are called predicamental (*secundum esse*). But others are imposed to signify the things from which ensue certain habitudes, as the mover and the thing moved, the head and the thing that has a head, and the like, and these relatives are called transcendental (*secundum dici*)." [22] St. Augustine, who inculcated this division, wisely remarked that there is a distinction between the relative terms of both kinds due to the fact that the former always imply a certain modification in the subject to which they refer, and that the latter are referred to a subject not involving modifications. Hence, he called the first relative accidents in the proper sense, and the second accidents in a relative sense. "Those things are relative accidents which happen in connection with some change of the things of which they are spoken. As a friend is so called relatively; for he does not begin to be one, unless when he has begun to love; therefore, some change of the will takes place, in order that he may be called a friend. And money when it is called a price, is spoken of relatively, and yet it was not changed when it began to be a price; nor again when

[22] *Sum. Theol.*, I., q. 13, a. 1, ad 1.

it is called a pledge, or any other thing of the kind." [23]

Accordingly, we are justified in placing the relation *secundum esse* among the categories, because such relation by its nature denotes a special mode whereby a being is determined in nature. Thus, relation in so far as it is a special category may be defined or rather described as an accidental mode of being or a certain accident whose essence consists in an habitude to another. This definition serves to distinguish the category of relation from the category of substance due to the fact that relation cannot be understood otherwise than as a certain accident. "Relations," Thomas Aquinas says, "have a dependent entity, as their entity is other than the entity of substance; hence, they have a special mode of being according to their essence, as is the case with the remaining accidents." [24]

The additional words, "whose essence consists in a certain habitude to another," signify that the essence of relation is constituted, not from the fact that its entity is in the subject, but from the fact that through its entity the subject is related to another. And indeed, when we apprehend relation as having its entity in the substance as in its subject, we only perceive that its essence is accidental, or, in other words, that relation is one of the accidents. On the other hand, when we consider the entity which relation has in substance as effecting the order whereby substance is referred to another, we perceive that

[23] *De Trin.*, lib. V, c. 16.
[24] *Cont. Gent.*, lib. IV, c. 16.

the entity of the accident called relation is distinguished from the entity of other accidents, not only because it inheres in substance as the remaining accidents, but also because it places the substance in reference to something else. But that which serves to distinguish a certain thing from others belonging to the same genus or analogue, constitutes its essence. This is the source whence we have drawn our argument. "If we consider relations formally as such, in that aspect they are said to be assistant, and not intrinsically affixed, for in this way they signify a respect which affects the thing related and tends from that thing to something else; whereas, if relation is considered as an accident, it inheres in a subject, and has an accidental existence in it." [25]

It is very important at this point to explain certain characteristics of the relational terms in order to obtain a more comprehensive knowledge of the category under discussion. As every relation necessarily implies at least two terms, it is plain that no one can have a complete understanding of it without the knowledge of these terms. The terms between which relation exists may be considered either materially or formally. And indeed we must carefully distinguish in related terms that whereby they are simply certain things, from that whereby they are related. Since relation is an accident inhering in a subject whereby this subject is referred to another, obviously the entity of the related thing is different from the entity whereby that thing is referred. The former entity constitutes the matter, and the latter

[25] *Sum. Theol.*, I, q. 28, a. 2, c.

entity the form of the relation. Thus, if you consider Peter who is father of Paul, not in so far
as he is the father of Paul, but only in so far as he
is such an individual, you consider the father of
Paul materially. If, however, you regard Peter not
as this or that individual but in so far as he begot
Paul, you regard the father of Paul formally, because you regard Peter according to relational form,
namely, paternity. If things are related on account
of the relational form inhering in them, it follows
that we must examine these formal properties of
related terms.

In the first place, it is clear that the relational
terms are such that the concept of one implies
the notion of the other. St. Augustine says: "All
things that are said relatively arc said reciprocally."
And indeed, as the essence of relation consists in
habitude to something else, it follows that no term
can be understood as relative without perceiving it as
having a certain habitude, for whatever is known,
is known through its essence. But we cannot apprehend a thing as having reference to another without
apprehending this other to which it is referred.
Hence, a relative term cannot be understood without
the other; but in the definition of a relative term
the other is not necessarily included, because the
function of a definition is to explain the essence of
the thing defined. The essence of a relative term
consists in having a certain respect to another term.

Secondly, each related term is defined through
the other. *Proof*: No matter what kind the relation
is, it is nothing else than the order of one term to

another. As that which has reference to another is determined by and is dependent upon that to which it is referred, it follows that in every relation two things must be considered, namely, the order of one to another and the determination of this order. The first constitutes the genus of relation, the second the difference; for that whereby something is determined is known as differentiation, whereas that which is determined by difference is called genus. Since everything must be defined through genus and difference, every relative term must be defined by the correlative.

It is beyond doubt that the terms of a categorical relation are simultaneous by nature. Since the terms of relation in so far as it is a category are both real, it necessarily follows that in each term there should be a certain entity whereby reference to the other is made. But in a relation considered as a category each term has order to the other through its real entity. As a consequence, one cannot be affirmed without the other, or one denied without involving a simultaneous denial of the other. Thus, if there is someone called father, there must also be someone called son; in like manner, if there is no father, there would be no son, nor without son could there be a father. On the contrary, if the related terms be such that one is real and the other logical, as is the case in non-mutual relation, they obviously would not be simultaneous by nature. As non-mutual relation does not necessarily and simultaneously require a real term, the terms between which there is a non-mutual relation are not necessarily simultaneous by nature. Again those relatives are not simultaneous by nature when the affirmation of one does not necessarily imply the affirmation of the other. But in a non-mutual relation, the logical term being posited, it is not necessary that a simultaneous real term should be posited. This may be illustrated by the non-mutual relation existing between knowledge and the object of cognition. Only those relatives are simultaneous by nature in which the denial of one implies the denial of the other, while the affirmation of one implies the affirmation of the other. If the object of knowledge be taken away, knowledge itself is destroyed, because there is no such thing as cognition without a known object; on the other hand, even if the object of knowledge be there, cognition does not necessarily follow, for the object may be without a knower. In like manner, in the absence of a sensible thing, there would be no sensation, as sensation without the thing sensed would involve contradiction. It is, however, not repugnant that there should be bodies without the existence of sentient beings; therefore, in positing the sensible, it is not necessary to posit a subject of sensation. It is apparent that both cognition and its object, as well as sensation and the object sensed, are terms of relations which are not simultaneous by nature. In this regard Aquinas very appropriately says: "To know whether relations are simultaneous by nature or otherwise, it is not necessary to consider the order of things to which they belong, but the meaning of the relations themselves. For, if one in its idea includes another and vice versa, then they are simultaneous by nature; as double and half, father and son, and the like. But if one in its idea includes another, and not vice versa, they are not simultaneous by nature. This applies to science and its object, for the object knowable is considered as a potentiality, and the science as a habit, or as an act. Hence, the knowable object in its mode of signification exists before the science, but if the same object is considered in act, then it is simultaneous with science in act; for the object known is nothing as such unless it is known." [26]

We conclude that relation in the light of Scholastic philosophy is not merely an invisible and mysterious link which somehow connects two things and makes them one. In science as in other matters we may know a relation without being able to discover completely the nature of the entities it relates. Nevertheless, we do know something about them. We know that they exist, that each has a certain nature, and that it is on account of this nature that the relation between them arises. We cannot know a relation, therefore, without knowing something of the things which it relates, for a relation presupposes its "terms." Hence, the universe cannot consist of relations only, but must be composed of things in relation.

[26] *Sum. Theol.*, I, q. 13, a. 8, ad 6.

CHAPTER X

THE INTELLIGIBILITY OF RELATION

Criticism of the Relational Functions of Thought.—
Sources of Difficulties.—Relation as Constitutive of
Reality.—Criticism of the Monistic View.—Examination of
the Monadistic Conception of Relation.—Intelligibility of
Relation.—Bradley and Taylor.—An Answer to the
Processes *ad Infinitum.*—Conclusion.

∴

EVEN IN A SUPERFICIAL consideration of the proper
nature of thought, it seems that its first and fundamental function is that of relation, that is, of referring the elements of reality to one another, or of
studying these relations in themselves. Whether we
describe, classify, explain, or predicate something of
something else, our thinking reveals itself as implying relations. Although at times we seem to affirm
only the existence of an object independently of the
fact that such an affirmation always implies a relation between thought and reality, the affirmation of
the existence of an object always implies the reference of the object itself to other objects or to a
mind.

This characteristic function of thought has not
been immune from doubts and criticisms. The questions have been asked: "Is relation *per se* really in-

telligible? How must we understand its reference to the terms? What sort of reality are we to attribute respectively to the terms and to the relation proper? And to what extent does the relational function of thought express or reproduce the ultimate nature, the *in se* of reality?" These are questions, as it will be seen, that make the epistemological problem so closely connected with that of Metaphysics that the former cannot be solved without first coming to a determined conception concerning the structure of reality. Perhaps there is no other epistemological problem that has such a fundamental metaphysical import as the present one.

The problem of the intelligibility of relations is not an artificial problem; it emerges from the difficulty which confronts thought in understanding multiplicity in unity and in reconciling the one with the many. From the time of the Ionian and Eleatic schools up to the present time, philosophical speculation has been largely engaged in this problem. It is, then, of great importance to solve these questions by a rigorous analysis of the true nature of relational function.

There was a time when only the relations between two terms were thought possible. But recent researches in Logic and Pure Mathematics have demonstrated the possibility of relations between many terms, which relations present their special properties. For the sake of simplicity, we shall confine ourselves to relations between two terms, since the number of terms does not in any way change the nature of our problem.

How does this problem arise? When we posit a relation, we obviously define one element or one aspect of reality by means of another; in other words we establish a connection whereby we seem, on the one hand, to define the reality of a term and, on the other, to transcend it, inasmuch as we feel the necessity of referring it to something else. Hence arise the questions: "Does or does not relation transcend the reality of the terms? Is it a mode of conjoining the content or a mode of getting out of it?" But this is not all. From another point of view a new difficulty presents itself. Relation has no meaning without presupposing the reality of the terms; the terms themselves also can never be found outside of a relation; and, in the last analysis, the reality of these terms is exhausted in the complexity of relations of which they are terms and by means of which we define them. This explains how some have been led to reduce relations to certain qualities of things; others to reduce terms to complexities of relations; and some others to consider relations as characteristic of phenomenal reality alone. We shall analyze these various views respectively.

Is it possible to reduce qualities to relations? The basic argument of those who maintain the unintelligibility of relations, so long as we attribute to the terms a reality distinct from references, is the following. If the qualities A and B are such as exist independent of the relation between them, the relation is then something extrinsic and arbitrary; hence, it has no meaning for reality. We shall never succeed, they say, in determining a quality without referring it to some other, nor shall we ever succeed in apprehending the reality of an object except by means of relations in which its nature is revealed; take away these relations and the object disappears. To be real, or reality, consists in having reference or relation to something else; in other words, relation constitutes reality.

For the present, we shall consider simply the difficulties confronting the view which does away with the terms *in* relation. We claim that things are in themselves what they are independently of their relation. Obviously, before anything can have reference to something else, it must exist. Things can be considered absolutely as they are *in se*. A relation requires that the terms should be something additional and distinct from their relations.

This line of argument applies not only to complex entities but also to the most simple entities. It is self-evident when I say that A is father of B; that A and B are real, and that their reality is distinct both from the reality of their relation and from the reality of the respective qualities which make relation possible. The same may be said of two most simple qualities that are related to each other in the most simple manner, namely, by the relation of distinction. When I say that color A is distinct from color B, it is obvious that what is proper to one and to the other is not inferred from their relation, and that color A is more than merely its relation with B; because, if A is different from B, it is clear that there is in A something which is not in B, a something which cannot merely emerge from the relation with B. Every relation by definition implies distinction of terms, and this distinction implies the transcendence of terms with regard to relation; but if terms were reduced to relation, the terms would become identified with each other, because relation is essentially a unity. Reduce, then, as long as you wish a reality into a sum of qualities, making each of these a term of one or more relations; every quality will always remain distinct from every relation of which it is a part, and the object at first considered as something simple will always appear, in so far as it is the subject of its qualities, as a unity which has a determined relation with its manifold qualities, which unity will be distinct from these and all other relations. Continue as long as you like to reduce complex objects into relations, you will find yourself always before the terms of a relation, but never before relations exhausting and, as it were, creating the reality of their terms.

The term is always something which transcends relation—a something which cannot be resolved simply into a relation or into a complexity of relations. Consequently, the quality a of a real A, definable by means of relation R between A and B, is always something distinct from R. As a matter of fact, a belongs to A in a different sense than the relation R belongs to A. If a were reducible to R, evidently B would be present in A in the same manner as B is essentially present in R. But in such a case every element of reality would be all-inclusive; that is, it would not be possible to assign to the universe a reality other than that of the single element A.

Thus, A would no longer be a microcosm, but a macrocosm, *i.e.*, the great universe.

Incidentally, this observation throws light on the problem of the nature of space and time. It is easy to see how the absolutistic and the relativistic views differ; the former shows a tendency to consider space and time as constituted respectively of points and real moments conceivable as so many absolute positions; the latter shows a tendency to consider space and time as systems of relations. The latter conception, however, will always be confronted by the following difficulty: if the point A (and the same may be said of temporal relations) is reduced to a number of relations, all extension will be contained in the point A, because relation is all-inclusive to such an extent as to exhaust the whole of space. Although spatial and temporal points are not intelligible apart from relations, they must, nevertheless, have in themselves a peculiar form of reality without which space and time would lose every character of intelligibility and reality, whatever this reality may be.

But the strongest argument against the reducibility of qualities to relations is that of the so-called asymmetrical relations of Russell. A relation xRy is called asymmetrical when it excludes the relation yRx.[1] Thus, the relation, Paul is father of Peter, is asymmetrical. He who denies a distinct reality of the terms of relation must consider as real only the relation which mediates between the two terms. This has been called the monistic conception of re-

[1] Russell, B., *The Principles of Mathematics*, p. 218.

lational thought; the relation xRy (x is with y in the
relation R) is interpreted as if it were (xy)R. But
the monistic formula (xy)R gives no reason for this
difference between the relation xRy and the relation
yRx; this formula would represent equally well the
relation of x to y or that of y to x, which relations
are as a matter of fact different. The monistic conception will never be able to account for the fact that
from the relation, A is to the right of B, we must infer the other, B is at the left of A. The monist is
misled by the formula because he assumes the relation itself as a reality in which both terms are comprised and from which they derive their reality.
Moreover, he is not aware that relation has no meaning except for the fact that the two terms remain
distinct from each other and from the relation itself.

This becomes even more evident if we consider
the relation between the part and the whole. To say
that A is part of B, will be for the monist the same
as saying that the whole AB presents this relation,
whereas the whole AB is different from B. If this
relation presented by the whole AB be not a relation
of the part to the whole, we shall be unable to say
anything of relations between the whole and the
parts, and we shall be led to consider, as a monistic
view would require, the relation between part and
whole as something predicable of the whole. If in
the last resort the monist should insist that the whole
consisting of A and B is not distinct from B, and
then should define the whole as the sum of parts, he
would not only be contradicting his monistic views
but also representing as symmetrical the relation be-

tween the whole and parts, when such is certainly not the fact.[2]

Moreover, the monist does not give in any way at all an interpretation of relational thought. For, when we change the proposition, x is in a relation R with y, into the affirmation of a whole (xy)R, we are but entifying the relation; that is, we transform it into something which is no longer a relation, because it ceases to possess terms in the true sense. The attempt to absorb the terms into a relation will force us to transform relation into an entity. In such a case the question would be whether such an entity is affirmable *per se*, or whether it becomes intelligible without becoming a term of a new relation. As a consequence, the monistic conception, if it is to be truly logical and rigorous in reducing the reality of the terms to relation, and if it is to hold that *to be real (esse reale)* has no other meaning than *to be referred to*, will be occupied constantly and exclusively in proceeding from one relation to another. It will be engaged in a successive ramification of relations without ever arriving at a *terminus ad quem*; in which process every concrete term would evaporate just at the time when the monist believes that he is about to grasp it. Such a condition would recall to our minds the situation of one who, according to the caustic remark of Schopenhauer, should find himself without knowing how in an altogether unknown society of which each member would introduce to him another member as a friend or an acquaintance; the unfortunate man, although expressing himself

2 Cf. Russell, *op. cit.*, p. 225.

happy at every introduction, at every instance would feel prompted to ask the question: "How in the devil shall I ever come to the beginning of all this re-union?"

Opposed to the monistic view there is a certain monadistic conception of relations which considers as real only the terms with their qualities, relations themselves being only a certain mode produced in conceiving the qualities themselves. According to this view, reality would belong only to that which is *in se* (*e.g.*, as an absolute position), and that which is *in se* would exclude the relation to other entities, the latter being but an exterior mode of their appearance in our consciousness. It is claimed that, if the relation R should really affect the terms A and B, the respective qualities of A and of B between which relation is placed would be real only in so far as they emerge from relation; and the same may be said of whatever characterizes A and B; so that at the end A and B would never be strictly real. Here we have a metaphysical conception containing an aspect of truth which must be taken into consideration.

Can this view render relation intelligible? It is well to note that, if the order between two terms A and B be purely subjective, that order presupposes a relation between the two terms themselves and the subject; such relation must be real. On the other hand, it is possible to admit that relation is but a mental connection or a subjective point of view. The qualities which constitute the foundation of relation must also be referable; and this reference is already a relation. These qualities before all must be distinct, and distinction is a relation. Moreover, if relation is solely a subjective conjunction, it is clear that the real qualities must be different from those which appear to us in relation; or, to be more precise, their objective reality must remain outside that *quid* which is the terminus of all the relations. This, however, implies that we can have no knowledge whatever of such a reality, and that we cannot avoid placing a relation between such a reality and its phenomenon, a relation which enters as a term in all our relational judgments. Here, too, we are confronted by the absolute impossibility of rendering an account of all forms of relation.

According to the precise definition of the monadistic interpretation of relation as given by Leibniz, the proposition, "Line L is greater than line M," may be understood as a relation of the greater line L to the smaller M, or as a relation of the smaller M to the greater L. We have, therefore two propositions: (1) "L is greater than M," in which "greater than M" is an adjective of L; (2) "M is smaller than L," in which "smaller than L" is an adjective of M. This description or interpretation of relational judgment would reduce relation to a mode of qualification of terms; it would be but a unique expression equivalent to two judgments whereby the two terms of relation are respectively qualified. Obviously, if we consider both L as well as M, *per se* and absolutely, we do not find in either of them separately taken anything that would differentiate them. Difference or qualification begins with reference, and it is clear that, when we attribute

to L the adjective "greater than M," this adjective
has no meaning except in so far as it implies a relation. In this case we would be substituting an adjective as a means in making the relation intelligible,
and we would be transforming a relational judgment
into a predicative judgment; in this manner relation
is attached to the predicate, and does not really
change the substance of the judgment.

If we put the relational judgment in this form,
we are no longer able to explain many of the characteristic and essential properties of relations. From
the judgment, L is greater than M, we can obtain
the judgment, M is smaller than L, only if we consider L and M as two distinct terms between which
mediates a relation; but from the predicative judgment, L is greater than M, I can obtain only those
judgments which the laws of immediate inference
allow by placing under another form the order between the subject L and the predicate "greater than
M." I shall never be able thus to obtain the relation
between M and L as it is expressed by the judgment,
M is smaller than L, unless I surreptitiously presuppose a relational judgment between the term L
and the term M.

Although this monadistic view is philosophically
superior, because it saves *the real* from annihilation
by Monism, nevertheless it is not immune from grave
metaphysical difficulties. On the one hand, Monism
wishes to save the system of reality and does this by
annihilating the reality which it ought to render intelligible; Monadism, on the other hand, attempts to
reduce real being to an aggregation of single entities,

deprived of reciprocal relation, and out of which it is
impossible to establish an order or a system. Monadism does indeed save reality, but it compromises
its intelligibility, and consequently the possibility of
its being recognized by thought. The best proof of
this consists in the fact that Leibniz himself, after
having conceived his monad without doors or win-
dows, was forced to introduce the preëstablished harmony, itself being a form of relation. Here again
all the difficulties involved in such a concept recur in
a more complicated manner. As for the remainder,
to hold with Leibniz that one monad is representative of the others, in effect means positing a relation
—a relation which he attempts to present as something extrinsic, but which *de facto* is always intimate
enough to define the proper nature of the monads.
Leibniz himself, in investigating the problem of
the relation between body and mind, was forced to
make even a more explicit concession to the relational
nature of reality. Although in this respect he leans
more to Spinoza than to Descartes, yet, in explaining activity and passivity, and the various degrees
of clearness of perceptions of one monad with reference to the perceptions of another, Leibniz does
but reëstablish the reality of interaction and of the
mutual dependence of monads. Surely, the concept
of inter-independence of monads has its basis in the
fact that substance is conceived by Leibniz as a
unity of causal series, a unity which must have in itself *ab æterno* all its predicates; such determinations
according to him are definable apart from relations.
If *to be in se* is an essential note of the definition of

the real, to be *cum alio* and *per alium* is another essential note which must not be overlooked, if we do not wish to make of reality an unthinkable category.

The conclusion of what has been said is, first, we cannot conceive relations independently of terms, and, secondly, there are no real beings that are without relation. The more logical view would consequently consider reality as constituted of terms *in* or *with* relations. However, even this view appears to some unsatisfactory and even contradictory. Bradley (especially in the third chapter of his *Appearance and Reality*) and also Taylor (in the fourth chapter of his *Elements of Metaphysics*) are opposed to this view. The main or rather the only serious argument which these writers bring against the relational conception of reality is the following: Relation leads to an infinite process; also it is impossible to reconcile effectively the reality of terms with the reality of relation. If we consider the problem from the point of view of quality, they contend, we shall discover that this quality must be the support, the presupposition, and, at the same time, the result of relation. If A is in a relation r, this A presents two aspects: one, which is presupposed by r and which we may call a; the other, which results from the relation and which we may call A. In consequence, A must be simultaneously the one and the other. This, however, requires that a should be related to A, and that this A again should be partly a_1 and partly a_2; the same must be also said of a. Thus, the unity of A begins to be broken up into an infinite series of qualities in relations, one being implied in the other. If, on the other hand, we consider the problem from the point of view of the relation itself, we shall discover that this relation cannot be a nonentity with regard to qualities, since in that case these qualities would no longer be related; while, if it be an entity as regards qualities, this entity must be a new relation, and so on. Here, too, we are under the tyranny of an infinite regress, which renders relation unintelligible.

This argument, however, is by no means decisive against the legitimacy of relational thought. We do not believe that the interpretation of reality as a system of real things in relation leads necessarily to an infinite regress. We must note, in the first place, that the first of the two regresses *ad infinitum*, discovered by Bradley, is directed against an hypothesis which is not the one that Bradley intends to combat with such an argument. To say that A is simultaneously *a* and A—*a* in so far as it is presupposed by the relation, and A in so far as itself presupposes the relation—has no meaning for one who maintains that the reality of A cannot be assumed outside of its own relations. In such an hypothesis the constitutive elements of reality stand in relations which cannot be reduced and eliminated, because these relations are part of their reality. To presuppose in such elements a part prior to these relations is perfectly arbitrary. Bradley advances this example: A is distinct from B; therefore, A is at the same time *a* (inasmuch as it is something which renders possible the distinction), and it is also A (that is, it is itself, inasmuch as it is distinguished from B). Bradley, however, is not aware of the fact that the *a* which is the foundation of distinction is itself already the A distinct from B. If red is distinct from green, it would be vain to seek in the red something that should be the foundation of distinction without being itself distinct from the green. This process *ad infinitum* is, therefore, artificial.

No less arbitrary is the other process *ad infinitum* which Bradley and Taylor attempt to derive from the necessity of establishing an order between the relation itself and its terms. This argument arises only from a gross confusion between relation as such and the concept of relation *in se*. The whole demonstration of Bradley is based just on this: he takes relation as isolated from the terms, as divested of its character of relationship and of its special function; he makes relation an entity in itself, and then seeks for its relationship with terms between which it is placed. The concept of distinction between A and B implies this distinction; but it is not the concept that the differentiation, the relation of the two terms to each other as distinct, is something other than the concept of their difference. Therefore, when we place a new relation between the relation and each of its terms, we must not think that this new relation is necessarily implicit in the *meaning* of the first, but only that it becomes possible when we wish to make it the term of a relation by mere conceptualizing. The relation between A and B, inasmuch as it implies the reference of these two terms to each other, does not presuppose any relation other than itself. Hence, no other relation is required.

In conclusion, relation appears to be an indispensable condition for the intelligibility of the real. Those who consider the relational thought as intrinsically contradictory must, with Bradley and Taylor, take refuge in Mysticism. Since every relation implies contradiction according to them, we must come at last to a superior form of knowledge in which the manifold is done away with, in which the absolute is intuited in its fullness, not as a whole made up of parts, but as a unity without relations. It is hardly necessary to say that such a superior order of knowledge implies an utter elimination of knowledge. If the mystic wishes in some way to think of his absolute, he must, before all, distinguish it from appearances and the relative; in other words, he must discover determined relations. Even the absolute is thinkable, and as such it is not only a system of relations but a perfectly unified system of relations. Nor is it necessary to conceive the absolute as a whole constituted of parts. The whole of unity is one thing, and the whole of aggregation is another. What is of importance is the fact that the absolute should imply relations; otherwise, the absolute becomes unthinkable and ineffable in the strict sense of these words. To place the absolute outside all relations, to make it the object of a special form of knowledge, and to pretend that there is consciousness without distinction, implies the acceptation of what is contradictory. The mystic, consequently, must deny knowledge. The contradiction between the reality of terms and rejection of the value of relation as something objective arises from the refusal to consider terms as terms and relation as relation, and also from the obstinate will to make of relation a term; thus, it arbitrarily gives rise to a process *ad infinitum*. On the contrary, as terms are for thought a prerequisite for the intelligibility of relations, so also relations are an indispensable condition for the intelligibility of terms and for a rational and systematic constitution of the universe. Thought cannot renounce the category of objective reality without destroying itself, nor can it posit relations without postulating a support of these relations. While the elements of reality do not themselves necessarily consist in thought, they are, nevertheless, a necessary prerequisite of thought. A mediate thought without an immediate something or *datum* is an absurdity. On the other hand, as the *in se* or real elements cannot be such without being referable or thinkable, so the intelligibility which is essential to the definition of the real already denotes referability or relations.

CHAPTER XI

THE CATEGORY OF QUALITY

Distinction between Quality, Quantity, and Relation.—Various Meanings of the Term Quality.—Quality as a Category.—Definition of Quality.—Enumeration of Its Four Species.—Meaning of Disposition and Habit.—Definition of Powers.—Real Distinction between Nature and Its Powers.—Three Characteristics of Quality.

∴

So FAR WE HAVE been concerned with those accidents which affect substance in so far as it is substance—for example, quantity extending substance into its permanent parts, and relation placing it in reference to something else. Now we come to the explanation of that accident whose function consists in disposing the substance for its active and passive activities: this is called quality. It must be noted that these first three accidents, namely, quantity, quality, and relation, enable the substance to receive the remaining six. Quantity determines the entity which these six accidents have in substance; for instance, the amount of energy in virtue of which the substance acts or is acted on (*actio, passio*), the place it occupies (*ubi*), its duration in time (*quando*), the manner in which the parts of a body are disposed with regard to an adjacent body (*situs*), and that whereby a bodily substance is externally modified by another (*habitus*), as its dress, protection, or ornament. Through relation substance is affected in such a manner as to become enabled to receive into itself the where, the when, posture, and habiliment. Finally, by means of quality substance is enabled to act or to be acted upon.

That quality is a category (that is, a special accidental mode by which actual being is modified), was the teaching of Aristotle and the Scholastics. Recent philosophers, with the exception of Kant and his followers, regarding the discussion of categories as a useless and ridiculous endeavor of Peripatetic philosophy, paid either little or no attention to quality as a category. Some considered qualities as the sum-total of the constitutive characteristics of a thing; others made qualities consist in the accidental attributes added to the essence. Among others, Adam Frank contended that quality is not at all an accident in the Aristotelian sense; quality in his view consists in whatever constitutes the nature of a thing (*i.e.*, in all the permanent properties belonging to a thing). Hence, he divided qualities into the essential attributes of a thing (*e.g.*, impenetrability in bodies or unity in spiritual substances) and into the properties or faculties which are inseparable from the attributes (*e.g.*, figure and color in bodies).[1] On these grounds he severely criticized Aristotle and Kant for placing quality among the supreme notions or categories.

The Stagirite discussed quality not only in the

[1] *Dict. Phil.*, art, "Qualité," tom. V, pp. 312-314.

abstract but also in the concrete. There is this difference between quantity and quality: while the notion of the latter is purely abstract, that of the former is both abstract and concrete. To perceive this difference more clearly, it suffices to note that line, surface, and body are not only comprised in the notion of quantity but are *themselves* quantities; hence, we may say that such a surface is quantity. On the contrary, if two or three objects are connoted by the term whiteness, we cannot say of any of them that this is whiteness. It is apparent that quantity is an object of sense perception, whereas quality can be apprehended only by the intellect. As human knowledge has its origin in empirical data, Aristotle could explain the notion of quantity without making use of *quanta*, as of so many degrees; he was, however, obliged to proceed by concrete instances of qualities to its general notion.

It must be remembered that the term quality is used in various meanings. At times it denotes not only the categorical accident but also the specific or essential difference, because specific difference in determining the essence of a thing qualifies it. For instance, by adding the note of rationality to the notion animal we denote what sort of animal man is. The term quality likewise is used to signify whatever there is outside the essence of a subject, whether this is a *proprium* or a common accident, inasmuch as these properties are said to qualify the subject (*e.g.*, when we add to the notion of rational animal the characteristic of risibility). But all the categories, substance excepted, being the proper ac-

cidents of the subject qualify the subject in their
peculiar way. However, a quality alone exercises
this prerogative in the strict and proper sense, making the subject such and such (*e.g.*, black, white
sweet, sour, learned, etc.). It is by quality that we
are enabled to describe what sort (*quale*) anything
is. It is this accidental form which determines the
subject to a special mode of being. As the notion
is a simple one, it does not admit of a strict definition comprising the proximate genus and specific
difference. "Quality," Aquinas remarks, "properly
speaking, implies a certain mode of substance. Now,
a mode, as Augustine says,[2] is that which a measure
determines; wherefore, it implies a certain determination according to a certain measure. Therefore,
just as that in accordance with which the material
potentiality (*potentia materiæ*) is determined to its
substantial being is called quality, which is a difference affecting substance, so that in accordance with
which the potentiality of the subject is determined
to its accidental being is called accidental quality,
which is also a kind of difference." [3] Since the categorical accident modifies substance either *per accidens* or *per se*, we must admit two distinct accidental
modes of quality.

As there are three modes according to which
substance is qualified, it remains to inquire whether
quality is a category, and, if so, which of these three
modes constitutes it. These two questions are so intimately connected that the solution of the second de-

[2] *Gen. ad lit.,* 4.
[3] *Sum. Theol.,* I-II, q. 49, a. 2, c.

pends on the solution of the first. As soon as we discover that a certain mode of quality is irreducible to any other supreme mode of reality or category, it becomes apparent that quality must be a special mode of being constituting a special category.

It is beyond doubt that there is such a mode of being, *i.e.*, quality. There are certain accidents qualifying substance in such a way that these cannot be ascribed either to quantity, or to relation, or to any other of the remaining accidents. For example, science, virtue, whiteness, etc., qualify the subject endowed by science, virtue, whiteness; in other words, they make it such and such. And indeed quantity modifies substance in a peculiar manner so as to make it such and such a quantity; relation refers it in such and such a way. But those accidents which denote a mode of being which cannot be reduced to any other mode must be regarded as a special category. On the other hand, quality, in so far as it denotes specific difference, cannot be viewed as a special category, for specific difference together with genus constitute species (*i.e.*, the complete essence of a thing). What determines the essence of a thing contained in a genus is a certain predicable or categorema, and not a special category. Neither can quality have a special place in the categories, in so far as it is a mode common to quantity, relation, and other accidents; in these quality is not an accidental form, namely, that whereby the nature of the accident is constituted and differentiated from the remaining accidents, but it is, as it were, the material element in every accident. Thus, to take an example from the first two accidents, quantity and relation, we find quality in both. The quality in the former, however, is different from that in the latter, because in the first it is determined by quantity and in the other by relation. Hence, the subject cannot be said to be qualified in an absolute sense through quantity and relation, but only through this sort of quantity and this sort of relation. But an accident partakes of the nature of categories, not from its material, but rather from its formal element, because form or essence is that which makes the thing to be what it is and distinguishes it from all others. Therefore, quality considered in a sense in which it is common to other accidents cannot be a special category.

It follows, then, that quality is a special category in so far as it qualifies the substance *per se*, and in so far as it is predicated of substance; for instance, when we say the line is straight, the crow is black, the dove is white. We may, therefore, define quality in the words of Albertus Magnus, as "the sort of accident which completes the substance in its existence and activity (*accidens complens ac perficiens substantiam tam in existendo, quam in operando*)." [4] This definition distinguishes quality from other accidents clearly enough, notwithstanding the fact that other accidents also dispose and modify the substance in a certain way. The remaining accidents do not qualify substance in an absolute sense, except in so far as they give it a special mode of being; hence, it cannot be properly said that substance is modified and disposed by them. Although

[4] *In Præd.,* c. 1.

quantity extends substance, it does not modify or dispose it; it only gives substance parts which are capable of modification. Quality, on the contrary, disposes its parts in one way or another, so that they either engender a triangle or a circle or a square. Hence, to modify or dispose the parts of substance is the prerogative of quality and not of quantity. Furthermore, if anything is changed according to quantity, it is not called alteration but augmentation or diminution; if, however, there is a qualitative change (*e.g.*, in color or figure), we have alteration.

Having made clear the essence of quality in so far as it is a special category, we shall proceed to enumerate its various modes or species. Since the nature of quality consists in the modification or determination whereby substance becomes simply *qualified* (*i.e.*, of this or of that sort), it follows that there are as many species of quality as there are principles modifying substance in a strict sense. According to St. Thomas, there are four principles of such modifications: "The mode or determination of the subject to accidental being may be taken in regard to the very nature of the subject, or in regard to action and passion resulting from its natural principles, which are matter and form, or again in regard to quantity. If we take the mode of determination of the subject in regard to quantity, we shall then have the fourth species of quality." [5] Here we shall confine ourselves to the discussion of natural powers and of disposition and habit, inasmuch as these participate in the proper metaphysical abstraction.

[5] *Sum. Theol.*, I-II., q. 49, a. 2.

Substance can be disposed well or ill in itself or towards something else—for example, the body with regard to health or sickness, the intellect as to error or knowledge. If substance can be determined well or ill, quality must certainly be required to determine it. Thus, health disposes the body well, sickness ill. It is obvious that this species of quality is by nature prior to others, since it has its foundation in nature itself, which is the source of all activities and operations. The other species are subject to the first as to their subaltern genus. Some of the qualities belonging to the first class inhere firmly and permanently in the subject, others are transient; the first are called habits (*e.g.*, science, health, virtue, vice, etc.) ; the second are called dispositions (*e.g.*, well, ill, ready, unready, etc.). According to St. Thomas, "disposition properly so called can be divided against habit in two ways; first, as perfect and imperfect in the same species, and thus it is called a disposition, retaining the name of the genus when it is had imperfectly, so as to be easily lost; whereas, we call it a habit when it is had perfectly, so as not to be easily lost. And thus a disposition becomes a habit, just as a boy becomes man. Secondly, they may be distinguished as diverse species of the one subaltern genus; so that we call habits those qualities which by reason of their very nature are not easily changed, in that they have unchangeable causes (*e.g.*, sciences and virtues). And in this sense, disposition does not become habit." [6]

[6] *Sum. Theol.,* I-II, q. 49, a. 2.

From the above it appears that habit "differs from faculty or power, in that it enables one to act; but habit, presupposing powers, renders action easy and expeditious, and ready to come at call. We have a power to move our limbs, but a habit to walk or ride or swim. Habit then is the determinant of power. One and the same power works well or ill, but not one and the same habit." [7] That habit dwells only in such powers as are not determined to one mode of action is evident. If a thing is by nature determined to one and only one end and can act in only one way, any further helping of it to its end would be useless and impracticable; and it is not to be supposed that nature has made provision for the reception into our faculties of what would be useless to them in the work of attaining their end. Hence, such faculties do not admit habits. Sensitive powers can be imbued with habits, for inasmuch as they are subjected to the command of the will, they may be ordained for diverse purposes. Brutes can be trained by man to a certain mode of action, but "the habit is incomplete, as to the use of the will, for they have not that power of using or of refraining, which seems to belong to the notion of habit; and therefore, properly speaking, there can be no habits in them." [8] As Aristotle remarks, you may throw the same stone repeatedly in the same direction and with the same velocity; it will never acquire a habit of moving in that direction with that velocity. Hence, "the

7 Rickaby, J. S., *Moral Philosophy*, p. 64.
8 *Sum. Theol.*, I-II, q. 50, a. 3.

powers of material nature," says St. Thomas, "do not elicit their operations by means of habits, for they are of themselves (already adequately) determined to their particular lines of action." [9] We may add that "habit is a living thing; it grows and must be fed. It grows on acts, and acts are the food that sustains it. Unexercised, a habit pines away, corruptions set in and disintegration." [10]

Qualities of the first class are powers or faculties of action. The term potency in its widest meaning denotes possibility, and according to this acceptation of the term we divide being into actual and potential. Here the term potency or power is used in a more restricted sense as designating a certain species of quality. It may be defined as the proximate principle of an act, which principle is constituted and ordained by its very nature to the performance of such activities. In this definition the following remarks must be taken into consideration: (1) Power or faculty is called the proximate principle of operation, because the first and radical principle is the substance itself acting by means of faculties. (2) Under the term operation are included acts emanating from the faculty, whether those acts be transient (as striking) or immanent (as thought is in the intellect). (3) Power is called the principle of operation when regard is had not to its mode but to the act itself, for as regards the mode the act may depend also on other factors (*e.g.*, on habit).

9 *Sum. Theol.*, I-II, q. 49, a. 4, ad 2.
10 Rickaby, J., *op. cit.*, p. 67.

(4) Finally, power is called the principle which by its very nature is ordained to act, because if quality were not *per se* and primarily ordained for this purpose but only to preserve and perfect the subject, it could not properly be called power. For instance, such a faculty as the will without its acts would be entirely superfluous and altogether inconceivable. Incapacity or impotence in this connection does not mean the negation of the power of acting, but that the power is paralyzed or more or less hindered or inhibited in its exercise.

Very famous is the division of power or faculty into active and passive. Active power is the principle of change in another. Passive is the principle receiving change from another. As a thorough grasp of this doctrine would involve a lengthy discussion on the nature of causality, we must for the present be satisfied with the following annotation: (1) One and the same power or faculty may be active or passive at least in relation to diverse acts; for example, the intellect is an active power in so far as abstraction and attention are concerned, and passive inasmuch as it is informed by an idea. (2) By passive power is meant, not purely passive power (probably such power does not even exist in the genus of quality), but a power which cannot react without being acted upon, as is the case with sense faculties or power. (3) Active powers are either purely active or simultaneously active and passive. A purely active power is that which elicits its acts without receiving them in itself (*e.g.*, the power of locomotion in animals). Power is both active and passive when it elicits its act and also receives it, as is the case in human will. According to Leibniz, energy differs from active power in the fact that "power or faculty is nothing else than the proximate possibility of acting which nevertheless needs to be stimulated in order to respond. Active energy, however, contains a certain element mediating between the faculty and the act, it involves conation, thus eliciting an act by itself; nor does it require any help, but only the removal of impediments. This can be illustrated by the example of a bow in the state of tension." [11] This distinction, whatever the Leibnizian theories on the activity of bodies may be, should not be rejected as it seems very consonant with the natures of things.

Since power is ordained to act, it is obvious that the distinction of powers must be derived from their acts; for that reason they are not defined except through act. The diversity of acts is in its turn taken from the diversity of objects. Aquinas reasons: "Every act is either of an active power or of a passive power. Now, the object is to the act of a passive power as the principle and moving cause. On the other hand, to the act of an active power the object is a term and end. . . . Now, from these two things an act receives its species, namely, from its principle or from its end or term." [12] Thus, for instance, the acts of seeing and hearing differ from

[11] *De primæ philosophiæ emendatione.* Inter Leibnitii opera, Vol. II, p. 20.
[12] *Sum. Theol.*, I, q. 77, a. 3.

each other because the acts of seeing and hearing are
stimulated by diverse objects, namely, by ether vibrations or by air vibrations; so also the acts of speaking
and judging differ due to their tendency to diverse
objects, the first being directed to the manifestation
of ideas, the other to the composition of ideas. Here
we must also bear in mind another point inculcated
by St. Thomas: "Not every variety of objects diver-
sifies the powers of the soul, but a difference in that
to which the power of its very nature is directed.
Thus, the senses of their very nature are directed to
the passive quality which of itself is divided into
color, sound, and the like, and therefore there is one
sensitive power with regard to color (namely, sight)
and another with regard to sound (namely, hearing).
But it is accidental to a passive quality (for instance,
to something colored) to be a musician or a grammarian, great or small, a man or a stone. Therefore,
by reason of such differences the powers of the soul
are not distinct." [13]

In this connection arises the important Scholastic thesis of the real distinction of the soul from
its faculties. The vast majority of philosophers
agree in teaching that the soul exercises its activities
through certain faculties inherent in the soul itself;
their contention is whether these powers can be identified with the soul, or whether they are distinct from
its essence. Those who hold the first opinion teach
that the soul (or the ultimate source of all the activities in man) is simultaneously the *principium quod*
and the *principium quo* of its acts; hence, the soul

13 *Sum. Theol.*, I, q. 77, a. 3.

is not only the remote but also their proximate and immediate principle. The followers of the second opinion maintain that the essence of the soul is only the remote and mediate principle of its operations, and that the powers are the *principium quo* or the immediate and proximate modes of activity of the soul—for example, in the same way as the roots, though being the source and origin of the fruits, nevertheless produce them by means of branches.

Spinoza teaches that in the mind there is no absolute faculty of understanding or willing or loving. Hence, it follows that these and similar faculties are either absolutely fictitious or nothing else but metaphysical entities, that is, universal notions which we are accustomed to form from the particulars.[14] Schelling and Hegel maintained practically the same opinion. The real distinction of the faculties from the essence of the soul was denied also by the Nominalists. Influenced by the dictum, *entia non sunt multiplicanda sine necessitate*, they taught that the faculties are but terms denoting the various activities of the soul. Of course, no other opinion could harmonize with the Leibnizian theory of monads. As the essence of the soul, according to Leibniz, consists in the power of representation of all reality, it follows that no other faculties could be ascribed to the monad than the various transmutations of that unique energy.

A great number of Scholastics, on the other hand, were defenders of the real distinction. It seems that the arguments advanced by St. Thomas are of

14 *Ethics,* Part II, prop. XLVIII.

great weight. The first may be construed as follows:
"As power is to operation as its act, so is the essence
to being." [15] "For an action is properly the actuality of a power; just as existence is the actuality of
a substance, or an essence." [16] But being (*esse*) and
activity (*agere*) in the world of contingency are not
only nominally but really distinct from each other.
The essences from which being and the power of activity flow are also really distinct. There can be
no doubt that in finite causes being and activity
are really distinct. Moreover, the essence of the
soul is substance, whereas power is an accident.
Since power is ordained to action, it is necessary that
the power should belong to the same genus of reality
as the actions which flow from it. But actions do
not constitute the substance of a being; rather they
are something inhering in it, for otherwise the thing
and its action would be identical. Consequently, we
must say that power is not the substance of the soul
but something belonging to substance. "Since that
which is acted upon does not belong to the substantial
being of a thing, it is impossible that the principle
whereby action is performed should be of the essence
of a thing." [17] Therefore, as the accident is really
distinct from substance, so also is power really distinct from the soul.

If the faculties of the soul were identical with
the soul itself, the latter would be instantly and completely in activity, because the soul is essentially an

[15] *Sum. Theol.*, I, q. 79, a. 1.
[16] *Ibid.*, I, q. 54, a. 1.
[17] *Qq. dispp., De Anim.*, a. 12.

act. Now, if the powers of the soul were always in complete activity, the soul would simultaneously perform all the activities of which it is capable; it would at each instant feel, understand, will. But it is obvious from universal experience that the soul has power to act as well as to abstain from action, that it can do this or that. The soul does not simultaneously but successively perform these operations. Therefore, we must admit a real distinction between the powers and the soul.

The same conclusion is derived also from the consideration that, as the actions of the soul are generally distinct, they cannot flow from one unique principle; otherwise, no reason could be assigned for their diversity. Finally, if no real distinction be admitted between the soul and its faculties, one would not be subordinated to the other, nor would one depend on another.

Here a Nominalist might object to our doctrine on the ground that entities should not be multiplied without necessity. The answer to this is that we must of necessity admit such entities if we wish to understand the activities of the soul and avoid many absurd consequences.

It is not necessary to say much about qualities of the third and fourth class, for, as we have remarked, due to their material character they are outside the domain of Metaphysics. As to the power of causing sensations and as to the resulting modification of the sense, the former belongs as quality to the objects of sense, the latter to the senses that are modified. Shape or external form and figure of extended bodies constitute the fourth class. Aquinas insists upon the fact that this mode of quality (morphology) is the most certain index of the identity or diversity of species, especially in plants and animals.

It remains now to say something concerning the characteristics of quality. Aristotle enumerated three: (1) qualities have contraries: (2) qualities are the basis of all relations of similarity and dissimilarity: (3) qualities admit of varying degrees of intensity. According to the Aristotelian definition, contraries are "such as within the same genus lie as far as possible asunder." [18]

Contraries are, therefore, two positive things, because the positive is contrasted with the negative not as its contrary but as its contradictory. But these two positive entities are then not subsistences or substances, but they are rather inherences in an apt subject, for substances as such have no contrariety among them. The contraries are contained under the same genus either proximately or remotely, for contraries naturally inhere in the same subject. The transition from one contrary to another does not take place *per se* between those things which are generically distinct. If the same subject is capable of receiving both contraries at different times, this is due to the fact that contraries are included in a certain generic agreement. Elements of the same species cannot properly be contraries; for example, a degree of warmth added to a body does not destroy the preexisting warmth, nor does new knowledge destroy preëxisting knowledge. The distance between those

[18] Zeller's *Aristotle*, Vol. I, p. 224.

things which are opposed as contraries is the greatest; because the characteristic of contraries is that
they should be mutually exclusive in such a manner
that one should not have anything of the other.
Whenever there is a medium between contraries, this
medium participates in some way in both extremes;
hence, in so far as it is a medium, it does not perfectly
exclude either one of the extremes. The greatest
possible distance is that which exists between two
extremities of a given latitude—*e.g.*, the distance
between two extreme points of a line, which two
points are said to be opposed as contraries. Contraries are likewise mutually exclusive from the same
subject; this exclusion may be of two kinds, namely,
effective and formal. It is effective when the action
of one contrary upon the subject of the other contrary excludes the latter (*e.g.*, the acts of virtue exclude the opposite vice). It is formal when two
things cannot by their very essence simultaneously
exist, inasmuch as one implies the negation of the
other; for example, whiteness expels blackness, because whiteness is a quality of body by which all
colors become diffused, and blackness is a quality by
which all colors are absorbed. Contrariety requires
not only an effective but also a formal exclusion,
which exclusion is the characteristic of all contraries.
Hence, it is apparent why contraries are said to be
mutually exclusive, for formal exclusion is necessarily reciprocal. It also seems certain that not all
qualities have contraries. A figure cannot be more
or less triangular than another, though one man may
be wiser than another; and there is no contrary to

red, though just is contrary to unjust. However, health and illness, virtue and vice, science and error, and many other habits, are opposed as contraries.

In the second place, qualities admit of varying degrees of intensity. According to the teaching of Aquinas, in every reality capable of increase or diminution this increment or diminution can take place in a threefold manner. First, qualities admit of varying degrees of intensity according to form or the reality itself, in such a manner that the form becomes more perfect or more imperfect in itself. Thus, science of geometry, for instance, is increased when one learns a certain geometrical theorem of which one was formerly ignorant. Secondly, they admit of varying degrees of intensity according to the participation of the subject (*i.e.*, a reality being educed in a greater or lesser degree from the potentiality of the subject). Thus, as one mental assent may be more intense and firm than another, so also science itself is increased in man in proportion as he can more promptly and easily recollect the scientific conclusions. Thirdly, qualities admit of varying degrees of intensity according to number, that is, according to the plurality of subjects which partake of a certain form. This kind of increment is twofold: either when another subject having similar form is added to a subject having a certain form, as in the case where to a luminous body another luminous body is added; or when a certain part of one and the same subject receives a form which it formerly did not have, as warmth is increased in man affecting the members which were cold. If the form receives the first mode of increment, the form itself is called greater or less; if the second, the subject itself is called more or less (*e.g.*, more or less strong, wise, etc.) ; if the third, we should have to say (*e.g.*) that there are many or few luminous or heavy bodies, or that the same material substance is warmer or colder according to many or fewer parts.

We next have to examine what realities or forms are capable of increase or decrease in one way or another. Every form which by itself constitutes a certain species or essence is absolutely incapable in itself of increase or decrease. The essential constituents exclude subtractions and additions, because metaphysically the essences of things are immutable. For instance, whiteness cannot be *per se* more than other whiteness, or humanity be more than other humanity, or a substance more of a substance in the order of substance. However, things which receive their species from the end for which they are ordained can admit of increment or diminution in themselves; for example, the science of geometry is extensively greater in proportion to the number of theorems which it embraces, or rectilinear motion is intensively greater in proportion as the velocity is increased though it is specifically the same motion.

If we consider forms or perfections inasmuch as they are participated in by a subject, this participation may be greater or less (*i.e.*, of different degrees), two cases being excepted. A subject partaking the form derives its species according to the same form, because essences are indivisible. For

this reason, if a subject possesses whatever constitutes a certain species, it must belong to that species;
if it does not possess the complete essence, obviously
it does not belong to that species. Thus, for instance, from the fact that man derives its species
from humanity, one man cannot be more or less of
a man than another. Secondly, indivisibility is an essential characteristic of a form. If a subject partakes of a form, he must necessarily partake of it
completely. Hence, the species of numbers does not
per se admit of degrees, for one number four is not
greater than another number four, because every
number is a certain special collection. The same
may be said of the species of continuous quality and
of relations among quantities.

From the above principles we may easily draw
the conclusion concerning the intensity and diminution of qualities. It is certain that habits and dispositions admit of varying degrees of intensity *in
se*. For a habit is a living thing; it grows and must
be fed; it grows on acts. Such an increment is called
extensive. However, not all habits admit of degrees
of intensity. Although science and art may be more
or less extended about their proper object, not so
virtue. "Because, whoever has a virtue, *e.g.*, temperance, has it in respect of whatever temperance extends to. But this does not apply to science and
art; for every grammarian does not know everything
relating to grammar. And in this sense the Stoics
said rightly, as Simplicius states in his *Commentary
on the Predicaments*, that virtue cannot be more or
less, as science and art can; because the nature of

virtue consists in a maximum." [19]   According to the
participation of the subject, neither habit nor disposition constitutes the species of the subject; the
note of indivisibility is lacking in the concept of such
qualities.   This other kind of increment is called in-
tensive.   It seems that natural powers or faculties
cannot admit of degrees in the same subject, for they
flow immediately from the very essence of substance,
but the essence is always the same.   As a general rule,
these require certain conditions in exercising their
activities, and some even may find obstacles in their
way.   Hence, the actions of the powers which act
of necessity have not always the same degree of intensity.   In a greater measure this is true of the
actions of free faculties.   However, there is no doubt
that the powers of material agents can be intensified
by addition of subject to a subject, as it is the case
of attraction which is in direct proportion to the
mass.   Qualities resulting from various causes may
admit of increase or decrease due to the fact that
they result from many causes; but they do not consist in indivisibility.   It is experimentally certain
that sensible qualities admit of degrees of intensity.

CONCLUSION

The remaining six categories are extrinsic accidents because they refer primarily to something
distinct from the subject spoken of.   Action (*actio*)
is that accident which denotes a change or movement
produced in a being; passion (*passio*) is the re-

---

[19] *Sum. Theol.,* I-II, q. 66, a. 1.

ceiving of an action. The where (*ubi*) is the accident which determines material substances to a place; the when (*quando*) regards succession in time. Posture (*situs*) is the manner in which the parts of a body are disposed with regard to an adjacent body. Habiliment (*habitus*) is the accident by which one bodily substance is furnished with another as its dress, protection, etc. The last two categories are of minor importance, but they are needed by the philosopher in order that there may be no manner of being which cannot find its place under one of the highest genera.

BIBLIOGRAPHY

ARISTOTLE, *De Anima, Categoriæ, Metaphysica;* ST. ALBERTUS
MAGNUS, *Opera Omnia,* ed. Louis Vives (Paris, 1899); ST. AUGUS-
TINE, *Confessiones, Epistolæ, De Qualitate Animæ, De Trinitate;*
ST. BONAVENTURE, *Opera Omnia* (Ad Claras Aquas, 1883); G.
BERKELEY, *Works of George Berkeley,* ed. George Sampson, 3 vols.
(London, Bell and Sons, 1908); J. BOYVINIUS, *Logica* (Venetiis,
1690); F. H. BRADLEY, *Appearance and Reality* (London, 1930);
T. DE VIO CAJETAN, *De Ente et Essentia D. Thomæ Aquinatis,*
ed. M. H. Laurent (Taurini, Marietti, 1934); M. W. CALKINS,
First Book in Psychology (New York City, Macmillan, 1914); DE
MARIA, S.J., *Philosophia Peripatetico-Scholastica* (Rome, 1913); R.
DESCARTES, *Œuvres,* 12 vols. (Paris, Adam et Tannery, 1897-1910);
M. DE WULF, *Mediæval Philosophy* (Cambridge, Harvard Uni-
versity Press, 1922); C. A. DUBRAY, *Introductory Philosophy*
(London, 1921); A. S. EDDINGTON, *Nature of the Physical World*
(New York City, Macmillan, 1928); A. FRANK, *Dictionnaire Phi-
losophique,* tom. V, "Qualité" (Paris, 1851); V. GIOBERTI, *Proto-
logia Saggi* (Torino, 1857); ANT. GOUDIN, *Philosophia Juxta
Inconcussa Tutissimaque d. Thomæ Dogmata* (Coloniæ, 1723);
J. GREDT, O.S.B., *Elementa Philosophiæ Aristotelico-Thomisticæ*
(Rome, 1899); W. HAMILTON, *Lectures on Logic* (London, 1883);
T. HARPER, S.J., *Metaphysics of the School* (London, 1884); J. S.
HICKEY, O. CIST., *Summula Philosophiæ Scholasticæ* (Dublin,
1919); D. HUME, *Treatise of Human Nature* (Oxford, Selby
Bigges, 1896); J. H. JEANS, *The Mysterious Universe* (New York
City, Macmillan, 1930); W. E. JOHNSON, *Logic* (Cambridge, 1922);
G. H. JOYCE, S.J., *Logic* (London, 1920); E. KANT, *Critique of
Pure Reason,* tr. Max Muller (New York City, 1905); I. LA-
CHELIER, *Psychologie et Metaphysique* (Paris, Alcan, 1916); G.
LEIBNIZ, *Opera Omnia* (Genevæ, 1768); M. LIBERATORE, S.J., *On
Universals,* tr. E. H. Dering (London, 1889); J. LOCKE, *Works.*
2 vols. (Clarendon Press, 1894); J. McCOSH, *Agnosticism of Hume
and Huxley.* Philosophic Series, No. 1 (New York City, C. Scrib-
ner's, 1882); W. McDOUGALL, *Outline of Psychology* (New York
City, C. Scribner's Sons, 1923); M. MAHER, S.J., *Psychology* (New
York City, Longmans, Green & Co., 1926); N. MALEBRANCHE,
Works, edited by Jules Simon (Paris, 1871); D. MERCIER, *Manual
of Modern Scholastic Philosophy,* tr. T. L. and S. A. Parker, 2

286 THE ANALYSIS OF OBJECTS

vols. (London, 1919); J. L. PERRIER, *Revival of Scholastic Philosophy* (New York City, Columbia University Press, 1909); T. PESCH, S.J., *Institutiones Logicales secundum Principia S. Thomæ Aquinatis* (Freiburg, Herder, 1888-90); PLATO, Dialogues, tr. Jewett (Oxford, 1871); A. READ, *Aristotelis Commentaria* (Venetiis, 1550); C. RENOUVIER, *Essai de la Critique Générale* (Paris 1854); J. RICKABY, S.J., *General Metaphysics* (London, Longmans, 1909); JOSEPH RICKABY, S.J., *Moral Philosophy* (London, Longmans, 1918); A. ROSMINI, *Systems of Rosmini*, ed. Thomas Davidson (London, 1882); B. RUSSELL, *Principles of Mathematics* (Cambridge, 1903); G. SANSEVERINO, *Philosophia Christiana cum Antiqua et Nova Comparata* (Neapoli, 1862); G. SAINT-HILAIRE, *Logique d'Aristote* (Paris, 1844); JOANNES DUNS SCOTUS, *Opera Omnia*. Editio novissima (Paris, Vives, 1891); SEXTUS EMPIRICUS, *Adversus Logicos* (Lipsiæ, 1841); F. P. SIEGFRIED, *Catholic Encyclopedia*, *s.v.* "Accident" (New York City, 1913); C. SPEARMAN, *Nature of "Intelligence"* (London, Macmillan, 1923); B. SPINOZA, *Ethics*, tr. White and Sterling (London, 1849); F. SUAREZ, S.J., *Opera*, 26 vols. (Besançon and Paris, 1856-62); A. E. TAYLOR, *Elements of Metaphysics* (London, Methven, 1903); ST. THOMAS AQUINAS, *Opera Omnia* (Rome, Typographica Polyglotta, 1903), from which are taken *Commentaria in Metaphysicam Aristotelis, Contra Gentiles, De Ente et Essentia, In Libros IV Sententiarum, Quæstiones Disputatæ, Quodlibeta;* IDEM, *The Summa Theologica*, tr. Fathers of the Dominican Province (London, 1912); A. F. TRENDELENBURG, *History of the Categories* (translation); W. TURNER, *History of Philosophy* (Boston, Atheneum Press, 1903); *University of California Publications in Philosophy*, vol. IX (1927); E. B. WILSON, *The Cell*, 3rd ed. (1925); C. WOLFF, *Ontologia* (Lipsiæ, 1730); E. ZELLER, *Aristotle* (London, 1897).

GLOSSARY OF TECHNICAL TERMS

Abaleity, dependence of a being on another both for its existence and for its activity; a caused being.

Absolute, a being above all relations, the Unconditioned, the Infinite Substance, God.

Abstract Idea, see **Concept.**

Abstraction, strictly, is the operation of the intellect by which it attends only to the features that are essential to the object of thought, leaving out all unessential and particular features.

Accident, categorical or metaphysical, is that which has no autonomous existence, or that to whose nature it belongs to exist in another. Logical accident (one of the predicables) is a note that may be absent or present in individuals without affecting their essence.

Act, a perfection or determination; the intrinsic principle in virtue of which a thing possesses a certain degree of perfection (*e.g.,* the developed oak, the act of reasoning are actualities).

Action, the actual exercise of an active power. Immanent action is an action terminating within the agent; transitive action, an action terminating outside the agent.

Actual Whole, a complete something consisting of parts either really or mentally distinct. See **Logical Whole.**

Æsthetic, that part of Kant's *Critique of Pure Reason* which treats of the conditions of sense experience.

Agnosticism, the theory that the mind cannot penetrate to what lies behind phenomena, and that the ultimate problems of philosophy are insoluble.

Alteration, a change in quality, and hence an accidental change. See also **Change.**

Analogy, partial identity and partial difference between two things.

Analysis, the intellectual activity of segregating parts or aspects of a whole from the totality first attended to.

Analytic Judgment, one in which the predicate is contained in the nature or essential relations and properties of the subject; or one in which the identity or non-identity of subject and predicate is known from their analysis and comparison.

Antinomy, contradiction, which may be real or apparent.

A posteriori, (1) reasoning from observed facts to a general conclusion; (2) knowledge such as is derived from experience of particular phenomena.

Appetite, a tendency, craving or desire which can be sensory and intellectual.

A priori, (1) reasoning from general laws or principles to particular applications; (2) knowledge independent of the senses.

Aseity, an attribute of God as an absolutely self-existing being.

Atomism, theories which seek an ultimate explanation of phenomena by considering them as mere aggregates of simple elements, which alone are taken to be real.

Atoms, chemical units which, by their regrouping in different manners, give rise to the various compound substances and are indivisible by chemical processes.

Attribute, anything which qualifies a thing. A quality or circumstance which may be affirmed (or denied) of a thing.

Augmentation, an increase in quantity or mass.

Axiom, a rule or first principle serving as a basis for other judgments.

Becoming, passage from non-being to being; or transformation.

Being, (1) in relation to existence, whatever exists or is capable of existing, as opposed to mere nothingness; (2) in relation to our mind, whatever can be an object of thought.

Categories, or predicaments, the most extensive classes into which things can be distributed.

Cause, that by which being begins to be; anything which has a positive influence of any sort on the being or happenings of something else. See also **Efficient Cause.**

Certitude, firm assent of the mind to a truth because of motives which remove all reasonable fear of error.

Change, passing of a thing from one state to another; gain or loss of some perfection. See also **Alteration.**

Comprehension, see **Connotation.**

Concept, abstract and general idea; the result of an act of simple apprehension.

Conceptualism, doctrine that universals or class-ideas (*e.g.,* man) exist in the mind, being intellectual constructions but having no counterpart in things outside the mind.

Condition, that which is required for the efficient cause to act, without exercising a direct and positive influence in the production of an effect (*e.g.,* light for reading).

Connotation, the sum of notes which constitute an idea.

Contiguous Quantity, property of bodies in virtue of which their parts are so joined that the boundary of one is not the boundary of the next.

Contingency, attribute of a being whose essence does not imply actual existence; a caused being.

Continuous Quantity, one which consists of potential parts in an actual unity.

Copula, a logical nexus, synthesis or bond between the subject and predicate in a judgment.

Corruption, the disappearance of a substantial form in the process of a substantial change.

Cosmology, the philosophical study of the origin and nature of the material world.

Cytology, the study of the cell.

Deduction, reasoning from principles or general laws to their special applications.

Demonstration, a reasoning process in which a conclusion is inferred from premises known to be certain.

Denotation, the object or number of objects to which an idea applies.

Differentia, the quality or sum of qualities which mark out one part of a genus from the other part or parts. Thus, if *building* be the genus, and we add the difference *used for a dwelling,* we obtain the species *house.*

Discrete Quantity, made up of discontinuous parts, which coëxist as a plurality (*e.g.,* numbers, words).

Distinction, absence of identity. *Real distinction* exists when things are distinct apart from mental considerations (*e.g.,* several trees, stones, etc.). *Virtual or logical distinction* is the absence of identity between several concepts of the same thing, as the distinction between animality and rationality in man.

Dualism, a theory which explains the world as the manifestation of two principles. See also **Hylomorphism.**

Dynamism, a philosophical system which teaches that the constituents of bodies are simple or unextended units or forces.

Effect, that which exists by virtue of another being.

Efficient Cause, a principle which by its positive influence produces the existence of something (*e.g.,* the sculptor is the efficient cause of the statue.)

Ego, see **Self.**

Empiricism, a theory which advocates that experience, internal and external, is the exclusive source and test of truth.

Energetism, a theory according to which matter is ultimately reduced to force-centers which have no real extension.

Entelechy, the inner nature of anything, determining its development (*e.g.,* the soul is the entelechy of the body).

Epistemology, the study of the origin, nature and validity of knowledge and the conditions of that validity.

Essence, (1) that which makes the thing to be what it is, and distinguishes it from other things; (2) the ground from which the various properties emanate, and to which they are necessarily referred.

Existence, the act by which a being is; that by which the *no*-thing of mere possibility ceases, and *some*-thing begins to be.

Faculty, an operative power which is an immediate principle of action.

Falsity, any positive disagreement between thought and thing.

Form, (1) *substantial* form is that which determines the specific nature of a substance, causing the substance to be what it is (*e.g.,* the sensitive soul in animals); *accidental* forms are accidents which modify the complete substance (*e.g.,* color, figure, activity, etc.).

Generation, the appearance of a new substantial form in the process of a substantial change.

Genus, an idea conceived as common to several classes of individuals and partially constituting their essence (*e.g., animal* is a genus as regards the species *man, horse, fly,* etc.).

Habit, a quality difficult to change which furthers or hinders the movements of a being towards ends.

Hylomorphism, or *physical dualism,* a theory of matter according to which matter and form are the ultimate metaphysical constituents of corporeal substantial being.

Hypostasis, see **Supposit.**

Hypothesis, a proposition which is *assumed* as true in order to explain a fact or a number of facts; a tentative explanation to be verified.

Idea, a simple intellectual representation of the nature or essence of a thing. See also **Concept.**

Idealism, (1) the system which holds that reality is of the nature of mind; (2) as a metaphysical theory, the doctrine that ideas, or thought, are the fundamental reality; (3) as a theory of knowledge, the doctrine that all we can know is our mental states.

Identity (absolute or real), the agreement of a thing with itself. In a broad sense, *identity* denotes the agreement of several things, either in essence (*e.g.,* two men have the same human nature) or in quantity or quality.

Ignoratio Elenchi, consists in arguing to the wrong point; proving a conclusion which was not in question.

Individual, that which is undivided in itself and divided from others. See also **Substance; Supposit.**

Induction, reasoning from observed facts to a general law. The inverse process is deduction.

Infinite, that which actually excludes all limits; a being possessing all conceivable perfections in the most perfect conceivable manner.

Intellect, the faculty by which man knows the essences of things, and the relations between things, such as the relation of effect to cause, of means to an end.

Intention, the referential quality of concepts or universal. (1) A *first intention* is the apprehension of a thing as it is in itself universal. (2) A *second intention* is the reflection of the mind on its universals and activities.

Judgment, an intellectual process affirming the relation of agreement or disagreement between concept and thing or between two concepts.

Law, a guide or rule by which a being is moved to action or restrained.

Logic, science of the laws of thought.

Logical Whole, a whole of extension.

Matter, Second, the complete material substance modified by properties, (*e.g.*, any chemical substance). *Prime matter* is a metaphysical constituent principle of spatio-temporal beings. See Hylomorphism; Form.

Mechanism, the doctrine that all events and thoughts follow the laws of mechanics.

Metaphysics, the inquiry into the ultimate and fundamental nature of being.

Molecule, a physical unit which contains one or more chemical atoms.

Monad, a self-contained being which develops according to the law of its own nature, independently of external influence.

Monism, the doctrine that reality is one, an absolute unity; that all things are the accidental modifications of one ultimate reality.

Nature, denotes the essence of a thing as the principle of activity, or as the ground from which the various properties of a being emanate.

Nominalism, in logic, the doctrine that universals or class-ideas (*e.g.*, man) have no objective reality corresponding to them, but are merely names.

Noumenon (thing-in-itself), something beyond experience, of which we know only *that* it is, and not *what* it is.

Number, an aggregate or totality of units.

Objective, existing outside the perceiving mind.

Occasionalism, the doctrine that secondary causes have no activity of their own, God being the only efficient cause, and that creatures give God occasion for acting.

Ontology, the philosophical study of the substance of individual things.

Ontologism, a theory which holds that what is first in the order of existence is also first in the order of knowledge. Our first idea is the idea of God. We see in God all created things.

Pantheism, the doctrine that God is all things.

Paralogism, an open violation of any of the laws of correct reasoning; when a syllogism becomes invalid unintentionally.

Passion, in metaphysics denotes (a) the effect produced by an agent upon a patient; (b) a quality which modifies a subject by some change.

Perseity, or *Aseity*, attribute of a being existing in itself and by itself, God.

Person, an incommunicable substance complete in itself, endowed with intellect and will.

Petitio Principii, a begging of the question at issue, the fallacy which consists in taking the conclusion itself as one of the premises of an argument.

Phenomenon, that which appears to the senses.

Phenomenalism, the theory that reduces the objects of knowledge to phenomena or appearances, and denies their substantial reality.

Philosophy, the general science of the totality of things through their ultimate reasons and causes as discovered by the unaided light of human reason.

Positivism, the restriction of philosophy to problems open to scientific and empirical investigation.

Potency, that which can be or has the capacity for being.

Power, see Faculty.

Predicables, terms meaning the kinds of attributes which may be predicated of any subject. They are: genus, species, difference, property, and accident.

Predicaments, what can be predicated. See Categories.

Predication, interpretation. See Judgment.

Principle, that from which anything proceeds in any way whatsoever, either through logical or ontological connection.

Proposition, an act of judgment reduced to the form of language.

Property, any attribute which is necessarily connected with and flowing from the essence, although not constituting it (*e.g.,* in man the power of expressing ideas by speech or writing).

Psychology, the philosophical investigation of the ultimate causes of the activities and the nature of man.

Quality, the sort of accident which completes the substance in its existence and activity.

Quantity, that which is divisible into parts which are included in it, so that any and each part can exist separately. See also **Contiguous Quantity; Continuous Quantity; Discrete Quantity.**

Realism, (1) the doctrine that the external world exists independently of perception; (2) the doctrine that universal or class ideas (*e.g.,* man) have objective realities corresponding to them.

Reasoning, that act of the mind by means of which a judgment unknown or less known before is reached.

Reductio ad absurdum, an indirect demonstration founded upon the impossibility of a contrary supposition.

Scepticism, the philosophical tendency to doubt the trustworthiness of our knowledge.

Science, (1) a certain and evident knowledge of things in and through their causes; (2) an organized and systematized body of knowledge.

Scholasticism, the philosophy prevalent during the Middle Ages, from the ninth to the sixteenth centuries, flourishing chiefly in the thirteenth century.

Self, the Ego, a composite substance consisting of body and rational soul.

Sophism, a false or deceptive argument.

Species, the sum-total of notes which constitute the complete essence and only the essence of a class of individuals (*e.g.,* the idea of man as applied to Plato, Aristotle, etc.).

Subjective, existing only in the perceiving mind.

Subsistence, denotes that a thing is self-sufficient, both for existence and action.

Substance, that which has existence in itself and not in something else.

Substantial Form, see **Form.**

Supposit, a substance that is complete in itself and incommunicable.

Syllogism, the act of thought by which from two given propositions we infer a third proposition, which necessarily follows from them.

Synthesis, the mental activity of uniting different aspects of an object, or of uniting similar aspects of various objects into a mental or logical whole.

Terminism, the doctrine that universals are only names or sounds by which we express our knowledge.

Transcendental, an attribute which belongs to being as such, and hence is coëxtensive with being. In Kantian philosophy the term *transcendental* is applied to the *a priori* and necessary factors in knowledge.

Truth, in Logic, adequation or conformity of intellect and reality.

Ultra-Realism, the doctrine that the universal exists in things just as it is in the mind.

Unity, the negation of division in being.

Universal, the concept as applicable in the same sense to any one of an indefinite number of objects of a class.

Univocal Term, one which connotes no more than one single definite meaning.

Whole, see **Actual Whole; Logical Whole.**

INDEX

Absolute: not included in any category, 23 sqq.

Accident: nature of, 35 sqq.; distinct from substance, 36; accidents in general, 75 sqq.; logical accident, 75; categorical accident, 76; intrinsic and extrinsic, 77 sq.; objectivity of, 79 sq.; quantity, first of the nine *genera* of accidents, 176 sq.

Albertus, Magnus, St.: on category of quantity, 177; on continuous quantity, 199 sq.; defines category of quantity, 267.

Alexander, S. S.: regards God as a quality, v; on universality of the cognitive relation, 11.

Anaxagoras: predecessor of modern atomists, 68.

A priori Forms: 7 sqq.

Aquinas: see **Thomas Aquinas, St.**

Archytas of Tarentum: suppositious originator of categories, 3.

Aristotle: originator of the categories, 3 sq.; critics of the categories, 4 sqq.; being as the supposed genus of the categories, 14; category as a mode of predication, 22; proof that being cannot be genus, 27; on division of being, 34; on primary substance, 47 sqq.; substance has no contrary, 56; substance is capable of admitting contrary qualities, 57; recognized kinetic element in natural phenomena, 80; on priority of quantity to quality, 177; ontological definition of quantity, 185; mistaken criticism of this definition by Trendelenberg, 186; regarded quantity as measure of substance, 192; distinction of kinds of quantity, 203; placed relation ahead of quality, 208; introduced distinction of relations into logical and real, 218 sq.; discussed quality in both abstract and concrete, 263 sq.; definition of contraries, 278.

Aseity: 31.

Atomism: doctrine, 58; fails to solve metaphysical problem, 68 sq.

Augustine, St.: exemplification of the categories, 1 sqq.; on substance and accident, 33; substance or person cannot be predicated, 53; on matter and form, 58; retracts former error in having applied categories to God, 111 sq.; on continuous quantity, 196 sqq.; on the relation between the parts of quantity, 203; on types of relation, 213-228 *passim*; inculcated distinction between transcendental and predicamental relations, 238-239; relation is reciprocal, 241; on the two distinct accidental modes of quality, 265.

Balmes: on concept of substance, xi.

Being: several meanings of, 15 sqq.; division of, 30, 32 sq.

297

Locke: theory of knowledge, 118 sqq.; doctrine of substance, 120; denies the objective value of idea of substance, 130; holds that the intrinsic nature of substance is unknown, 144.

Loewenberg, J.: on meaning of *subject* and *substance*, 140 sq.; metaphysical substance, 143 sq.; notion of substance, 153; admits reality of substance, 165.

McCosh, J.: approaches Scholastic doctrine, 45.

McDougall, W.: approaches Scholastic doctrine, 45.

Maher, Michael, S.J.: on nominalism, 11; on substance, essence, nature, 123.

Malebranche, N.: immaterialism of, 94; origin of ideas, 126 sq.; occasionalism, 127.

Mass: definition, 115.

Mercier, D.: application of electronic theory to cosmology, 67.

Metaphysics: objectivity of, ix, 154 sq.; defined, 153 sq.

Monad: definition, 114.

Muirhead: on substance, 139 sq.; the self and substance, 150 sqq.; defends objectivity and knowability of substance, 171; notion of substance ingrained in man, 172.

Müller, Max: on Vaisheshika philosophy, 4.

Murphy, A. S.: metaphysical substance, 146; skeptical attitude towards metaphysics, 153; denies objectivity of substance, 168; refutation of his contentions, 169.

Nature: concept of, 73; as distinguished from substance and essence, 123.

Newton: modern atomist, 68.

Nicholas of Autrecourt: on the notions of causality and substance, 89 sqq.

Nihilism: definition, 44.

Nominalism: treatment of categories, 11 sq.

Noumenon: in Kantian philosophy, 17; Loewenberg on, 142.

Nys, M.: on electronic theory, 67 sq.

Occam, W.: his view on substance, 87 sq.

Padarthas: quasi-categories in Indian philosophy, 4.

Pepper, S. C.: on the textures of qualities, 147; skeptical attitude towards metaphysics, 153; denies objectivity of substance, 168; refutation of his contention, 169.

Peripatetics: on substance and accidents, 78.

Perrier, J. L.: on substance and attributes, 84.

Person: ontological connotation, 73.

Plato: classification of Ideas incomplete, 3; on principles of extension and form, 58; on relation, 220.

Pluralistic World: Scholastic view, 158.

Power: or faculty, definition, 271; active and passive, 272.

Prall, D. W.: analysis and function of logical substance, 144 sq.; on metaphysics, 153; adopts Spinozan concept of substance, 169.

Primary Matter: definition and characteristics, 58 sq.

Principle of Individuation: 70 sqq.; according to Suarez, 94 sq.

Pythagoras: on twenty ultimate groups of things, 3.

Quality: category of, 262 sqq.; definition of, 267; characteristics of, 278 sq.

DATE DUE